The Effects of World War I
The Uprooted:
Hungarian Refugees and Their Impact on Hungary's Domestic Politics, 1918–1921

István I. Mócsy

Social Science Monographs—Brooklyn College Press
Distributed by Columbia University Press, New York

1983

EAST EUROPEAN MONOGRAPHS NO. CXLVII

DB
955
·M63
1983

Copyright © 1983 by Atlantic Research and Publications
Library of Congress Catalog Card Number 83-60781
ISBN 0-88033-039-2

Printed in the United States of America

ATLANTIC STUDIES

Brooklyn College Studies on Society in Change No. 31
Editor-in-Chief Béla K. Király

War and Society in East Central Europe
Vol. XII

Contents

Maps

Acknowledgments

Brooklyn College Program on Society in Change conducts research, organizes conferences, and publishes scholarly books. The Program has been encouraged and supported by Dr. Robert L. Hess, the President of Brooklyn College. The National Endowment for the Humanities awarded the Program a research grant for the years 1978–1981, which was renewed for another three year term (1981–1984). The International Research and Exchanges Board, the Joint Committee on Eastern Europe of the American Council of Learned Societies, and the Social Science Research Council have given additional support. Without these substantial and much appreciated supports, the Program could not realize its goals, indeed, could not exist. The University of Santa Clara provided added help in completing the research, holding conferences, and covering the costs of preparation of the manuscript for publication.

The copy editing was done by Mr. Roberto Cambria; the preparation of the manuscript for publication by Mrs. Dorothy Meyerson, Assistant Director, and Mr. Jonathan A. Chanis, Assistant Editor, both on the staff of Brooklyn College Program on Society in Change. The maps were prepared by Mrs. Ida E. Romann.

To all these institutions and persons, I wish to express my most sincere appreciation and thanks.

Highland Lakes, New Jersey   Béla K. Király
March 15, 1983   Professor Emeritus
                                               Editor-in-Chief

Preface

The present volume is the twelfth in a series which, when completed, hopes to present a comprehensive survey of the many aspects of War and Society in East Central Europe during the past two centuries. These volumes deal with the peoples whose homelands lie between the Germans to the west, the Russians to east and north, and the Mediterranean and Adriatic seas to the south. They constitute a particular civilization, an integral part of Europe, yet substantially different from the West. Within the area, there are intriguing variations in language, religion, and government; so, too, are there differences in concepts of national defense, of the characters of the armed forces, and of the ways of waging war. Study of this complex subject demands a multidisciplinary approach.

The present volume is a pioneering experiment in the history of refugees, who were forced to leave their homeland as a consequence of war. The particular significance of this kind of study is that masses escaping the scenes of ravages of war is a paramount East Central European experience. Within the land of the Crown of St. Stephen, mass exodus of people in all directions was quite a constant phenomenon. Probably the first massive refugee movement into Hungary was that of the Serbs as early as the reign of Matthias Corvinus. The Renaissance Monarch of Hungary opened the southern borders of the kingdom to give refuge to Serbs fleeing Ottoman rule. That movement climaxed with the entry into Hungary of 200,000 Serbs under the leadership of Arzen Černović, the Patriarch of Ipek, in 1690. Major Romanian influx occurred during the reign of the Phanariot Hospodars in the Danubian Principalities between the early eighteenth and early nineteenth centuries: the Phanariots' exploitative rule caused masses of Romanians to seek haven in Hungary.

Hungarians themselves moved in great numbers from the Great Hungarian Plain to the north to escape Ottoman rule. The first time, when Hungarians had to escape from their land of birth and converge in inner Hungary from all directions at the same time, was the half decade immediately following World War I. Their experience, tragic for Hungarians though it was, nonetheless has been but one example of the multitude of similar agonies of East Central Europe.

Professor Mócsy's research fits comfortably into the general line of this series, for we are studying military history, not in a "militaristic" way, but in its relationship to other aspects of history. Our investigation focuses on a comparative survey of military behavior and organization of the various East Central European nations to see what is peculiar to them, what has been socially and culturally determined, and what in their conduct of war was due to circumstance. Besides conducting a historical survey, we try to define different patterns of military behavior, including the decision-making processes, the attitudes and actions of diverse social classes, and the restraints or lack of them shown in war.

We endeavor to present considerable material on the effects of social, economic, political, and technological changes, and of changes in the sciences and in international relations on the development of doctrines of national defense and practices in military organization, command, strategy, and tactics. We present data on the social origins and mobility of the officer corps and the rank and file, on the differences between the officer corps of the various services, and above all, on the civil-military relationship and the origins of the East Central European brand of militarism. This volume certainly casts a glance on all these aspects as well as on the origins of the Horthy Army and its effects on Hungarian society between the two world wars.

Our methodology takes into account that, in the last three decades, the study of war and national defense systems has moved away from narrow concern with battles, campaigns, and leaders and has come to concern itself with the evolution of society as a whole. In fact, the interdependence of changes in society and changes in warfare, and the proposition that military institutions closely reflect the character of the society of which they are a part, have come to be accepted by historians, political scientists, sociologists, philosophers, and other students of war and national defense. Recognition of this fact constitutes one of the keystones of our approach to the subject. This volume, an experiment in the history of refugees, the victims of war, properly indicates the diversification of our interest in the various effects of war on East Central European societies. The particular significance of this volume is the careful examination of the painful birth of a new army built on the ashes of a great empire, after two frustrated revolutions and a successful counterrevolution.

Works in Eastern languages adequately cover the diplomatic, political, intellectual, social, and economic histories of these peoples and this area. In contrast, few substantial studies of their national defense systems have yet appeared in Western languages. Similarly, though some substantial, comprehensive accounts of the nonmilitary aspects of the history of the whole region have been published in the West, nothing has yet appeared in any Western language about the national defense systems of the whole area. Nor is there any study of the mutual effects of the concepts and practices of national defense in East Central Europe. Thus, this comprehensive study on War and Society in East Central Europe is a pioneering work, the present volume being no exception.

The volume investigates one of the effects of World War I on East Central European society. In this respect, this is not the only item in the series; there are four volumes either already published or being published simultaneously with this book which should be considered companion volumes of the present work. Together they offer quite a broad view on what World War I, the first total war, did to East Central Europe. These companion volumes in the *War and Society in East Central Europe* subseries are:

Vol. V. *Essays on World War I: Origins and Prisoners of War.* Edited by Samuel R. Williamson, Jr. and Peter Pastor, 1982.

Vol. VI. *Essays on World War I: Total War and Peacemaking, A Case Study on Trianon.* Edited by Béla K. Király, Peter Pastor, and Ivan Sanders, 1983.

Vol. IX. Kálmán Janics. *Czechoslovak Policy and Hungarian Minority, 1945–1948.* 1982.

Vol. XIII. *Effects of World War I: The Class War After the Great War: The Rise of Communist Parties in East Central Europe, 1918–1921.* Edited by Ivo Banac. 1983.

Introduction

Modern wars and revolutions are frequently accompanied by massive displacement of civilians. Scholars often note the role of political refugees in radical politics, but rarely investigate the causes of their radicalism. This study examines the radicalization of one group of political refugees: the displaced Hungarian nationals, who, after 1918, fled or were expelled from territories seized by the Successor States of Czechoslovakia, Romania, and Yugoslavia. Some fled their native lands in fear for their lives; others left for political or economic reasons. The new regimes of the Successor States actively encouraged their departure and, at times, resorted to outright expulsion.

The study has three basic objectives: first, to establish the causes of the refugee problem and to identify the social background of refugees; then, to analyze the process of the refugees' psychological and political radicalization and their role in the counterrevolutionary movement; and, finally, to examine the social and political assimilation of the refugees and its cost to Hungarian society.

I take the view that radicalization of the refugees was not a psychological, or at least not a purely psychological, phenomenon, but primarily a historical one. Even before the war those who later became refugees were subjected to stress; after the war they experienced extreme psychological trauma. As members of the dominant middle and upper classes of prewar Hungarian society they lived amidst a growing sense of crisis. The end of the war brought physical violence against them in occupied areas, and loss of landed estates, government posts, and prewar social status. The fall from privilege traumatized and psychologically primed the refugees for radical action. But, to understand the process of their radicalization, the tools of psychology, though useful, are inadequate in themselves. It was a complex historical process: the result of a constant interaction between the social backgrounds and personal experiences of the refugees and the general historical developments both within Hungary and in the whole of East Central Europe. Hence, it is necessary to place their story within the context of the dramatic and revolutionary events of the period. From the point of view of their radicalization the day-to-day changes in the official refugee policies of the successive Hungarian governments were of lesser import-

ance. In its stead, therefore, I stress those broader economic and
political trends which had an effect on the lives and mentality of the
refugees.

Although postwar events were catalytic, we must seek the origins of
right-wing radicalization of the refugees in the prewar crisis of the
Hungarian middle class, the class best represented among the refugees.

The key to an understanding of that growing sense of crisis is the
character and history of the Hungarian middle class. Unlike the middle
classes of Western Europe, the Hungarian middle class was not exclusively bourgeois, but rather gentry in origin, and the thin stratum of
non-nobles was, in great part, not Hungarian but German and Jewish.
Classical middle-class or bourgeois ideologies and interests, therefore,
were easily subordinated to those of the gentry. In spite of temporary
successes during the dualist era, it was a declining class. Each step
toward a modern and democratic Hungary strengthened the non-noble
classes and threatened the political power and social status of the
gentry. More than anything else, the fear of loss of status and control of
society forced the gentry-dominated middle class to block the country's
natural political evolution by opposing necessary social and political
reforms.

In a microcosm the refugees represented a cross section of the prewar
political elite: landed and propertyless nobles, gentry officers, state and
local officials, magnates and large-estate owners. Their attitudes and
world views were identical with those of their peers in all parts of the
kingdom. But even before the war those who lived in the minority
areas — where social conflict was always aggravated by national tensions — were more acutely aware of the contradictions and crisis of
society and felt more endangered as a class. Not surprisingly, they were
more prepared to seek and embrace radical solutions. Thus, the experiences of the refugees show more clearly the continuity between the
prewar crisis and the postwar radicalization of the gentry middle class.

The war and subsequent events polarized society, traumatizing every
class, especially the refugees. Count István Bethlen, the conservative
prime minister of Hungary (1921–31) and a leader of the refugees, may
not have been far from the mark when, in 1923, he declared: "The
dismemberment of the country, its defeat during the World War, the
repeated revolutions and foreign occupation — all created a trauma of a
magnitude unmatched in the history of this nation and unparalleled in
other nations, even during the World War."[1] The counterrevolutionary
movement arose in opposition to all these factors. The counterrevolutionaries rejected not only the reforms of the democratic and communist
regimes but also wished to reverse the consequences of the lost war. The

refugees, as the most traumatized group in the country, eagerly participated in the movement. They discovered in it the only chance for
Hungary to recover lost territories and, thus, to assure their own
economic and social restoration.

During the immediate postwar period, however, the future looked
bleak for the refugees and for the traditional ruling elite. Even a few
months before the victory of the counterrevolution, a takeover of
Hungary by the radical right seemed fantastic. After the October 1918
revolution, the right was both defeated and discredited. The reins of
government were solidly in the hands of the democratic left. Political
issues favored by the refugees, such as defense of the interests of the
traditional ruling classes and military resistance to Hungary's partition,
were opposed by the population at large. Public sentiment turned away,
in revulsion, from a resumption of military hostilities and, instead,
focused on long-delayed social and economic reforms. Yet, in August
1919, with Western aid the former ruling classes of Hungary were
restored. But even at the moment of its triumph Admiral Miklós
Horthy's counterrevolutionary army was puny; its active domestic supporters represented only a fraction of the population. Indeed, Horthy's
seizure of power seemed opportunistic and made possible only by the
momentary chaos and in the political vacuum that was left in the wake
of the Hungarian Soviet Republic's defeat. Yet, for a quarter-century
the Horthy regime remained firmly entrenched and met defeat only
during the closing month of World War II.

The reasons for the regime's successes and for those of the refugees
are far too complex to be examined here in detail. We can briefly focus
our attention only on the two most significant developments which had
the most fundamental and lasting impact upon the region and which
placed the political program of the refugees at the center stage of
Hungary's political life. One, the Russian Revolution forced an adjustment in previous political and ideological equations; it changed the
priorities of the Western democracies. Two, the breakup of the Austro-
Hungarian Monarchy and the partition of Hungary reduced the political
weight of domestic social and economic issues and increased those of
territorial, national, and military considerations.

Until 1918 the West was shielded from the impact of events in Russia
by the armies of the Central Powers. But in November 1918 that shield
was removed, and the revolutions which swept through Germany and
Austria-Hungary brought the threat of Bolshevism to the doorsteps of
France. With the success of the Russian Revolution liberal democracy
ceased to be the only alternative to conservatism. To some the new
soviet political system appeared to be an exciting new experiment which

was preferable not only to conservatism, but also to liberalism. Unlike the Social Democratic parties of the West, Russian socialism presented an imminent threat to the fundamentals of the Western economic and political system. Most of the Western Social Democratic parties were already tamed and were, in fact, absorbed into parliamentary democratic systems. They lacked the strength to destroy the capitalist economic order, had, in fact, no intentions of doing so, and were unwilling to abandon the parliamentary democratic political tradition. Russian socialism, however, threatened to abolish both. Fear of the Russian revolutionary tide put the Western Powers on the defensive and containment of Bolshevism became their prime preoccupation. Liberalization of Central and East Central Europe became secondary to the establishment of a buffer zone made up of strong, viable, and anticommunist states. Hence, governments or competing political factions in East Central Europe were increasingly judged less according to their commitments to democratic principles and more by their willingness to participate in an anti-Bolshevik crusade. The neighbors of Hungary took full advantage of this. By exaggerating the danger presented by the Hungarian left, they were able to expand at the expense of the Hungarian state. Hungarian counterrevolutionaries also played upon those fears and with their proven record of anticommunism they became more acceptable and safer to the West than either the radical or the liberal democratic left.

Yet, successful exploitation of Western fears did not in itself assure either the victory or the long-range survival of the regime. The counterrevolutionary movement triumphed and the new regime survived amidst a broadly based shift to the right in most states of the region. That shift was a general phenomenon which cannot be wholly attributed to fears of Bolshevism. The new state structure which emerged after the breakup of the Austro-Hungarian Monarchy was equally or perhaps more responsible. Bethlen may have been correct when he placed the partition of Hungary on the top of his list of cataclysmic events. War brought the country to the point of economic ruin, and massive loss of human life, combined with the prolonged suffering among civilians, left the population exhausted. But economic and psychological recovery would have been more rapid within the prewar territorial framework.

The new territorial arrangement, however, brought revolutionary changes for East Central Europe and the prewar path could no longer be traversed. Before the war the influence of international developments upon domestic politics was limited. The character of the system as well as the major political issues were defined largely by the long-range historical and more recent economic and social developments. That relative immunity of domestic politics to international affairs ended with World War I and subsequent territorial changes. International developments assumed that dominant position in the shaping of internal politics once occupied by domestic issues. The new state structure altered economic realities, cut lines of communications, separated raw materials from industries, broke up a large free market area, erected economic, political, cultural, and military barriers, increased the isolation of each state, and created new priorities and perspectives. The breakup of the monarchy and the partition of Hungary led to the establishment of a group of insecure and antagonistic small states which necessarily increased the importance of such issues as military security and national unity and, conversely, stifled internal debate and reduced the political importance of domestic and social problems. These new priorities in every East Central European state aided the resurgence of the right.

If we recognize the radical character of these changes we gain a new perspective on the failures and successes of the three postwar Hungarian regimes: the democratic government of Mihály Károlyi, the Hungarian Soviet Republic, and the counterrevolutionary government of Admiral Miklós Horthy. The failure of the democratic revolution of October 1918 and the establishment of the Hungarian Soviet Republic were directly related to the partition of the country. The two major issues in the political life of the prewar monarchy were reform of the state's nationality policies and economic and political democratization of society. The defeat of the old empire opened the door to a solution to both problems by sufficiently weakening the traditional conservative opponents of wide-ranging reforms. Károlyi's program enjoyed an initial broad support precisely because it was designed to cure the country's domestic ills by tackling both major issues simultaneously. Democratization of society was to be the key to both problems, which, it was believed, would have led to social, economic, and land reforms as well as to a satisfactory solution to the problems of the national minorities. We cannot but sympathize with Károlyi and admire the wisdom and moderation of his program. But we are also forced to admit that, with the disappearance of the prewar polity, his program designed to reform it, ceased to be opportune or even relevant.

The steady encroachment of the Successor States upon Hungary's territory made a peaceful reconciliation between the former nationalities of the monarchy an illusion; it pushed domestic issues into the background, created a national crisis in Hungary, helped to eclipse Károlyi, and opened the way for the establishment of the Hungarian Soviet state. The four-month tenure of the Hungarian Soviet Republic was a last desperate attempt to force through a radical restructuring of society and, at the same time, to deal with the national crisis by a forceful opposition to the country's partitioning. It is important to note that no popular demand for radical reforms led to the establishment of the Hungarian Soviet Republic, but broadly based disillusionment with a pro-Western orientation of the new democratic state and a perception that the national crisis provoked by the appetites of the Successor States could best be cured by a radical government willing to stand up to the Western Powers and their East Central European allies.

The Hungarian Soviet Republic was quickly defeated, but the sense of national crisis remained which aided the counterrevolutionary cause. Deep-rooted popular support for the policies of the counterrevolutionary government was lacking; yet, the incorporation by the Successor States of nearly three-fourths of the Hungarian kingdom's ancient territories and appendages and three-fifths of its former population, including millions of ethnic Hungarians, created a permanent national grievance that touched every Hungarian. By capitalizing on this issue the counterrevolutionary regime gained a degree of popular support and legitimacy. In the name of national unity it was able to silence demands of significant economic and social reforms. Indeed, the staying power of the regime was in no small part due to its successful mobilization of the emotional energies of the nation behind this genuine grievance. Moreover, the regime could rely on the unconditional support of a sizable army of refugees. From that group and from the other radicalized elements of the middle and upper classes the regime wove an interlocking network of political and social, public and secret, military and civilian associations, which, throughout the interwar period, dominated the political life of the country and assured the survival of the radical right.

Among the refugees the counterrevolutionary movement found a group of righteous, radicalized men, willing to serve as its shock troops. The refugees, especially those from Transylvania, played a prominent and often decisive role in virtually every counterrevolutionary political and military group during 1919 and 1920. They were strongly represented in counterrevolutionary groups organized in Vienna and Szeged, in Admiral Horthy's army and in its officers' detachments that were most responsible for the White Terror, and in the counterrevolutionary governments and National Assemblies of the 1919–22 period. With the victory of the right the refugees became a major political factor in Hungary's political life. Through their firm commitment to the cause of the political right a majority of the refugees were able to gain compensation for their losses and secured positions within Hungary that were similar though not identical to the posts they had left behind in their places of birth now incorporated into the Successor States.

Assimilation of the refugees, however, proved very costly to Hungary. Refugees displaced thousands of liberal officials and educators. To make room for their children the higher educational system was expanded beyond the needs of the country; which added only to the already large stratum of permanently unemployed or underemployed intelligentsia. The size of the state bureaucracy was also greatly increased, posing a crushing burden to taxpayers. Finally, the refugees exerted a powerful influence on foreign policy. Their insistence upon the restoration of lost territories was one of the causes which helped to prevent a reconciliation with the Successor States.

Chapter 1
Origins and Scope of the Refugee Problem

The military collapse of the Habsburg monarchy opened the way to a revolutionary transformation of East Central Europe. Released energies found expression in two forms: in national or social revolutions. The Horthy regime emerged as a negation of both.

Attempts to create new states and carve out nation-states from the body of the destroyed empire, were revolutions of the first type. States whose principal aim was the establishment of a new economic and political order represented the second. Both types of revolution implied a radical revision of assumptions about the state and public authority and a basic restructuring of state institutions. But in regions where the first type prevailed, the main concern of the new leaders was to gain physical control of the sought territories and to establish a new type of public authority based on purely national principles. Where revolution was essentially social, public attention was centered on the ideological foundation of the new society. National revolution was characteristic of territories populated mostly by the national minorities of the old empire. The newly formed states of Czechoslovakia and Yugoslavia, as well as the resurrected Poland and the vastly enlarged Romania fall into this category. Hungary belongs to the second type.

The Hungarian national revolution took place in the nineteenth century. By the twentieth century Hungarian national identity was well defined and the nation's right to an independent existence, to form a nation-state, was universally recognized. But, the social structure was in need of revision.

With the dissolution of the Austro-Hungarian Monarchy, social reformers rose to power in Hungary. In the secessionist states, on the other hand, the nation and state builders came to the fore. The main concern of the revolutionary government of Mihály Károlyi was to create a new concept of loyalty to the state. Loyalty was no longer to be derived from blind nationalism but earned by the state through its commitment to democracy and justice. Hungary's new leaders believed that an alliance of progressive and radical intelligentsia, the urban socialist working class, and the rural proletariat — whose land hunger had to be satisfied — would have the strength to preserve a truly democratic regime. Elimination of social inequalities and restraint of Hungarian nationalism would, they hoped, bring about a reconciliation between all the peoples of the Carpathian basin.

In the Successor States, by contrast, while rhetoric about social justice was not missing, loyalty to the new states had to be based on nationalism. A successful consolidation within the newly formed states depended upon a rapid formation of new loyalties: identification of the population with the territorial extent of the new states. This required a formation of, say, a new Czechoslovak national identity, to correspond with the proposed territory of the Czechoslovak nation-state. It had to replace old separate Czech, Slovak, or Ruthenian regional identities, identification with Austria, or, in the case of Slovaks and Carpatho-Ukrainians, with Hungary. Similar reorientation was required of the new citizens of Yugoslavia and Romania. Croatians and Slovenes had to learn to identify with Yugoslavia,* to become accustomed to look to the former King of Serbia and his government as the natural source of public authority. Romanians of Transylvania had to adjust their visions to look toward Bucharest for political and cultural leadership and to identify with Greater Romania. This new orientation was especially difficult for Croatians, who were always conscious of the independent existence of a Croatian nation, who were separated from Serbians by their Catholicism, and who were proud of their Western as opposed to Serbia's Eastern orientation.

Where national cohesion was absent direct physical force had to compensate. Concepts of Czechoslovak, Yugoslav, and Greater Romanian national identities within the newly acquired territories were introduced by the Czech Legion, the Serbian, and to a lesser degree, Romanian armies. The military forces of these states severed the flow of authority from Budapest, began the process of consolidation and integration of these areas into the new states, and passed judgment upon the potential loyalty or disloyalty of the population to the new regimes. These crude determinations were based not on ideology but on nationality. Only the handful of Communists came under immediate persecution without regard for nationality.

The old Hungarian ruling and official classes of the separated territories were caught between the social revolutionaries in power in Hungary and the nationalism of the Successor States. They were considered *personae non gratae* in both areas. Still, they had to choose between

---

* The Kingdom of the Serbs, Croats, and Slovenes was formally proclaimed on December 4, 1918. For the sake of brevity the term "Yugoslav" will be applied when referring to this Kingdom.

revolutionary Hungary and remaining under foreign rule as a subject minority exposed to economic ruin and political persecution. The great majority of the agrarian Hungarian population of the lost territories decided to remain. But most of those who belonged to the old Hungarian elite opted for, or were compelled to depart and become refugees in Hungary.

Between 1918 and 1924 an estimated 426,000 Hungarians left the territories ceded to Czechoslovakia, Romania, Yugoslavia, and Austria. Precise figures on the number of refugees are not available. Our primary source of information on this subject is the final report of the National Refugee Office (OMH), published at the time of its termination in 1924. According to this report 350,000 refugees were registered by the OMH. Of these, 197,035 came from Romania, 106,841 from Czechoslovakia, 44,903 from Yugoslavia, and 1,221 from the new Austrian province of Burgenland.[1]

A closer examination of the report, however, reveals that these may be considered only minimum figures. Systematic data collection about the refugees did not begin until April 1920, when the OMH was established.[2] Before that date the various refugee aid organizations kept some records on the number of refugees, but these were haphazard and incomplete. The best records were kept by the Transylvanian refugee aid groups.[3] The other refugee organizations, such as the Upland League (*Felvidéki Liga*) and the Szepes Alliance (*Szepesi Szövetség*), servicing the refugees from Czechoslovakia, and the Southland Alliance (*Délvidéki Szövetség*), those from Yugoslavia, covered only a fragment of the total number of refugees; thus their records have little statistical value.

Responsibilities of the National Refugee Office were threefold. First, to unify and centralize aid to all refugees and assure a fair distribution of available funds. Second, to assure the collection of accurate data on the magnitude of the refugee problem. This information was to be used by the Office for Peace Preparations for presenting Hungary's case at the Paris Peace Conference. Lastly, the OMH had to organize the refugees into regional cultural and political associations to preserve group cohesion and to cultivate loyalty to their lost homelands.

The OMH made strenuous efforts to rectify earlier omissions in data collecting. Through press and other channels it officially called upon all refugees in the country to register with the Office. But, according to the *OMH Report*, "the results were not satisfactory. Generally only those registered who were in need of aid."[4] Another attempt was made to arrive at some accurate figures at the time of the 1920 census taking. Even this proved to be a failure because many of those who had already settled were not recorded as refugees. The figures provided in the *OMH Report,* therefore, fall far short of the actual number of refugees.

Several other sources, however, may be used to approximate the number of those individuals who fled to Hungary between 1918 and 1920, but whose presence for various reasons eluded the official regis-trars. The 1920 census figures are useful. At the beginning of 1921, according to these, 265,145 individuals lived within Trianon Hungary who were born in territories ceded to Czechoslovakia, 197,181 such individuals were born in Romania, 97,643 in Yugoslavia (74,412 exclud-ing Croatia-Slavonia), 21,416 in Austria, and 2,206 in Fiume.[5] Without Fiume and Croatia-Slavonia this adds up to 558,154 individuals born in the lost territories. According to the *OMH Report* by the end of 1920 291,287 refugees were present in Hungary.[6] This implies that 266,867 individuals migrated to inner Hungary from the periphery prior to the dismemberment of the country. This would be true, however, only if we accept these figures at their face value. It is possible to estimate the number of those individuals who arrived in Trianon Hungary before and after the war by using two other statistical sources. One, the statistics on internal migration before the war; second, the postwar censuses of the Successor States, which in all cases recorded a much higher decline of the Hungarian population within their territories than would have been justified if the OMH refugee figures were correct. Neither of these two sources is totally reliable. Yet, they serve as a gauge to establish the upper limit of refugee strength.

The main line of internal migration in prewar Hungary was from all parts of the country toward the center, especially from the north toward the south, and from the west in an easterly direction. Upper Hungary lost most heavily through internal migration, second was the southern region, while Transylvania gained in population. Based on migration statistics our estimate for the number of refugees who went unrecorded are as follows:[7]

Migration to Trianon Hungary from the Lost Areas

From:	Slovakia	Romania	Yugoslavia	Total
Number of people in 1920 born in	265,000	197,000	98,000	560,000
Number of recorded refugees in 1920	102,000	154,000	35,000	291,000
Difference	163,000	43,000	63,000	269,000
Estimated migration prior to 1918 from	120,000	20,000	55,000	195,000
Estimated number of unrecorded refugees	43,000	23,000	8,000	74,000

By using the second method of approximation, i.e., by comparing the postwar censuses of the Successor States, the results are:[8]

Estimated Number of Refugees Based on the Postwar Censuses
of the Successor States[9]

Census year	Slovakia 1921	Romania 1927	Yugoslavia 1921
Hungarian population in 1910	1,071,000	1,660,000	578,000
Remaining Hungarian nationals in the postwar censuses	755,000	1,247,000	472,000
Registered decline of Hungarian population	316,000	413,000	106,000
Recorded number of refugees at time of these censuses	102,000	197,000	35,000
Difference	214,000	216,000	71,000
Changed nationality, plus other adjustments[10]	174,000	183,000	55,000
Unaccounted individuals	40,000	33,000	16,000

The combined results of the two tables indicate that we may conservatively estimate that during the 1918–20 period an additional 76,000 unrecorded individuals entered Hungary from the Successor States. Thus, our final estimate on the number of refugees as compared to the OMH figures is as follows:

From	Estimated number	OMH figures
Czechoslovakia	147,000	106,841
Romania	222,000	197,035
Yugoslavia	55,000	44,903
Austria	2,000	1,221
Total	426,000	350,000

As a result of this massive flight of the Hungarian population the total number of Hungarians remaining as minorities in the Successor States sharply declined; in Czechoslovakia (as compared with the 1910 census figures) the size of the Hungarian population decreased by 13.7 percent, in Romania by 13.4 percent, and in Yugoslavia, by 9.5 percent. At the same time the population of Trianon Hungary increased by about 5.3 percent.

The precise time of the arrival of these refugees in Hungary is more difficult to establish. Our only source is the incomplete report of the Refugee Office. According to this document the recorded 350,000 refugees arrived in the following order:[11]

Year From	Slovakia	Romania	Yugoslavia	Austria	Total
1918	12,373	40,952	5,459	—	58,784
1919	57,783	33,551	19,239	—	110,573
1920	31,606	79,773	10,551	—	121,930
1921	1,722	19,879	4,023	499	26,123
1922	2,310	13,651	4,705	576	21,242
1923	852	7,536	541	112	9,041
1924	195	1,693	385	34	2,307
Total	106,841	197,035	44,903	1,221	350,000

It is most likely that the additional 76,000 refugees fled to Hungary during the last two months of 1918 and during the early part of 1919. Generally the rate of refugee flow corresponded to the political changes in Hungary. A correlation can also be established between the number of refugees arriving in each year and the various anti-Hungarian social and economic measures introduced in the Successor States. Romania was the slowest in carrying out those measures which partly accounts for the high rate of refugee flow from that country even in 1921.

The motivation for departure from the Successor States came from several sources. The governments of Czechoslovakia, Romania, and Yugoslavia, stimulated by both excessive nationalism and by anxieties about lack of internal cohesion within their states, introduced policies either to eliminate or at least neutralize the dangers presented by the incorporation of a large number of Hungarians. These governments were determined to wrest political and economic powers from the previous Hungarian ruling classes. Even if their objectives had been merely to establish equality between Hungarians and ex-minorities a large segment of the Hungarian population would have been negatively affected. Transfer of power to the new governments, therefore, threatened the existence of most of the middle and upper class Hungarians in the lost areas. In the final analysis, however, the decision to leave still had to be made individually by most Hungarians. Each person had to decide at one point that his/her existence was no longer assured under one of the new regimes. But what was the breaking point? What were those compelling reasons that forced tens of thousands to leave property, abandon homes, towns, or villages, and accept the uncertain and harsh life of refugees?

We may distinguish four motivating factors which may, at one time or another, have influenced an individual to depart: fear of actual physical danger; nationalism and unwillingness to live under foreign domination; loss of economic security; and finally, inability of many to accept loss of social status. Aristocrats and landed nobles, army officers and soldiers who fought the advancing Romanian or Czech armies were the first to leave. Many state and county officials of the minority regions had reason to fear revenge. Thus county officials, judges, public prosecutors, members of the gendarmerie often fled before the arrival of the invading armies. Most ultranationalists also left before or soon after the physical occupation of these areas. They refused to accept dismemberment of Hungary; most believed that it was possible to continue the struggle against the new states from Hungary. All fervently believed that the new boundaries would be only temporary and that return to their homelands, at the head of a victorious army, was only a matter of time. Also, there were many individuals among the refugees who, motivated by patriotism, refused to take an oath of loyalty to the new governments with the almost inevitable consequence of dismissal from their state or county offices.

For some of the Hungarian middle classes the decisive moment arrived only after the purge of Hungarians from the state administration and educational system began in earnest. Dismissed officials, railroad employees, and teachers faced an immediate economic crisis which forced their departure. Subsequent purges in commercial, financial, and industrial establishments compelled many professionals and members of the managerial strata to make similar decisions. Finally, land reforms destroyed the economic power of Hungarian landowners. Those reforms affected not only the noble owners of estates. A much larger number of estate employees, managers, agronomers, and even servants, whose existence was tied to large-scale agriculture and to the aristocratic style of life found their economic existence undermined. They, too, had to choose between remaining or leaving their homelands. The alternative to a flight to Hungary was to work in less prestigious positions, perhaps, even as manual workers. Most of the officials and state employees were incapable of accepting the loss of social status that would have resulted from their change of occupation.

Chapter 2
Military Occupation of Hungary's Minority Areas and Its Impact on the Local Hungarian Population, November 1918–August 1919

In November 1918, the Western Allies were still without a coherent plan for the future of East Central Europe. Although from the very beginning of the war discussions on the subject were wide ranging, none of the proposed solutions was entirely satisfactory, and each promised to raise problems of enormous complexity.[1]

Concerns about the future were most acute in Hungary. Its population, long cut off from West European news sources, had no realistic view of the degree of hostile attitudes artificially built up against Hungary in Western capitals. During the war the only source of information from the West was the often contradictory public pronouncements of the Western Powers, as filtered through a censored press. But it was difficult to discern which were wartime propaganda and which were expressions of actual policy. Fears of massive territorial losses were mixed with the not entirely unfounded hope that once military considerations ceased to influence political decisions, perspectives on the region might undergo a radical change and old biased assumptions about Hungary and, along with it, plans based upon them, might yet be revised. The rapid changes in East Central Europe, the dissolution of the Habsburg monarchy and the social revolution in Hungary, encouraged such a view. Moreover, the new government of Mihály Károlyi was genuinely friendly toward national minorities. During the previous decades many of the new leaders had fought for complete social and political equality of all peoples in the Dual Monarchy. Oszkár Jászi, the new minister of national minorities, was a long-time advocate of an imperial federation. In 1918 Jászi was prepared to grant extensive cultural autonomy, complete political equality, and extensive local administrative autonomy to all national minorities within Hungary.[2] The Károlyi government hoped that at least some of their former allies among the national minorities with whom they fought the long and bitter struggle against the prewar political and social order, would appreciate the fundamentally new spirit of the regime. Unlike the Successor States, which subsequently signed treaties guaranteeing minimum protection to the national minorities only under Western duress, the Károlyi regime offered to protect fully the rights of the minorities out of conviction. In addition, the planned extensive social and economic reforms would have equally benefited the lower classes among the nationalities. Then, too, the false hope was entertained that some of the minorities might after all realize that separation from Hungary did not mean independence and self-rule, but incorporation into a larger state where the former minorities of Hungary would once again be the ruled minority. Indeed, that is what happened. Slovaks and Ruthenians came to live under Czech tutelage, Croatians and Slovenes under Serbian domination, and the Romanians of Transylvania under that of the conservative leaders of the Regat. Thus, the Károlyi government believed that with its democratic and progressive social program as the basis, a freely negotiated settlement between the Hungarians and the minorities was still possible. Even Károlyi's most persistent opponents had to acknowledge that he was perhaps the only man who could preserve the country's territorial integrity or at least negotiate a fair settlement.

The Károlyi government's foreign policy options, however, were extremely limited. The hoped-for negotiations with the minorities failed to materialize. The only remaining choice, if the territorial integrity of the country was to be preserved, lay between resumption of hostilities against the Great Powers and their East Central European allies and a trust in the good will of the West. The first option was never considered as a realistic possibility. The Károlyi cabinet took its principles seriously and opposed a resolution of differences through a test of strength. Then, too, the Hungarian Army ceased to be an effective fighting force within a few days after the armistice. Soldiers deserted their units by the thousands and flocked home from the fronts in total disarray. Peasant soldiers, excited by the news of the imminent land reform, hurried home to their villages. Others plunged into the revolution in the major cities. Even if an army could have been raised, Hungary would have had to face enemies on three sides.

It was of paramount importance to Károlyi to gain recognition for his government and to dissociate the new regime from the defunct Austro-Hungarian Monarchy. As one of its last acts the Austro-Hungarian army's Supreme Command signed the Padua Armistice Agreement (November 3, 1918). As far as the Allies were concerned Hungary was still bound by this agreement, even though it was signed after Hungary's declaration of independence. The terms of the Armistice specified a reduction of the Austro-Hungarian army to twenty divisions and established a zone of occupation.[3] The most important consideration at that time for the Allied Supreme War Council was a possible attack on Germany across Austrian territory. The Armistice Agreement, therefore, was specific on the military questions and did not provide for a military occupation of Hungary preliminary to peace negotiations. This omission seemed advantageous to Hungary, but was without practical consequences. The Allied Balkan Army and military units of the Successor States continued their advance and crossed the Hungarian borders. On November 7, therefore, Károlyi and Jászi, heading a Hungarian delegation traveled to Belgrade to negotiate a halt to the occupation of the country with the commander of the *Armée de l'Orient,* General Franchet d'Esperey. Such negotiations would have also gained, at least, a *de facto* recognition for the Károlyi government. On November 13, the representatives of the Hungarian government finally signed the Belgrade Military Conventions Agreement.[4] Hungary agreed to reduce its army to eight divisions and recognized the right of the Allies to occupy all places of strategic importance in the country. The Hungarian government also undertook to evacuate its troops behind a line of demarcation, roughly fixed at a line starting at the upper Szamos Valley in the east, running south to the Maros River, then along this river to its junction with the Tisza, and from there in a westerly direction just south of Szeged, and north of Baja and Pécs to the Dráva River, and along this line to the western border of Hungary.[5] The establishment of the zone opened the way to a legal occupation of some of the territories claimed by the Romanian and Serbian governments. No provisions were made for the establishment of a similar zone of occupation in the north, thus raising hopes that at least the Slovak territories might still be retained by Hungary. The military demarcation line, however, was not to be considered the new boundaries of the country. In theory, at least, even those areas that came under foreign occupation were to be considered Hungarian territories until the signing of the peace treaty. On this issue the terms of the Armistice were explicit:

> Civil administration will remain in the hands of the Government. In actual fact only the police and *gendarmerie* will be retained in the evacuated zone, being indispensable to the maintenance of order, and also such men as are required to insure the safety of the railways. . . . The Allies shall not interfere with the internal administration of affairs in Hungary.[6]

That is, Budapest still remained the legal authority for all parts of the country, and the Hungarian officials were to remain at their posts until the signing of the peace treaty. The Hungarian government understood that the demarcation lines established at Belgrade would remain in force until a treaty could be negotiated. But the Successor States were anxious to extend their physical control to all those territories that they wished to incorporate into their respective states even if this necessitated crossing the line of demarcation and incurring the displeasure of the Western Powers. The small powers soon realized that the lack of unity among the Great Powers worked in their favor, and that it was possible to force the hands of their western allies by simply confronting them with *faits accomplis*. Only the French had any military force in East Central Europe. In the absence of a sufficient counterforce the small powers could act boldly with impunity. They also realized that any delay in occupying the claimed territories might jeopardize their chances at the final settlement. They had to act before Hungary could recover from the collapse of the monarchy and mend her diplomatic fences with the Great Powers. They had to act while the situation was fluid and before East Central Europe solidified into a system less favorable to their goals.

Serbian Occupation of the Southern Counties

Events coalesced most rapidly in the South Slav districts of the former monarchy. The idea of a Yugoslav state either within or independent of the Habsburg empire had an almost universal appeal among the Croats and Slovenes. As early as May 1917 the South Slav delegation to the Austrian *Reichsrat* declared that they fully intended to form a separate South Slav state, but still under Habsburg sovereignty. This plan was endorsed even by Emperor Karl.[7] By October 1918, however, popular sentiment favored secession from Austria-Hungary, and remaining independent of Serbia. On October 5–6, the National Council of Slovenes, Croats, and Serbs was established in Zagreb. It soon transformed itself into a *de facto* government of the South Slav population of the empire. On October 19, that is, well before the termination of hostilities, the council issued a provisional constitution for the projected state, and on October 29 declared its independence.

The Serbian government of Nikola Pašić viewed these activities with extreme suspicion, since these plans ran counter to Serbia's declared war aims. Serbia intended to seize the leadership of the South Slav population and she pursued this goal with single-minded determination.

Serbia's expansionist postwar designs became clear in December 1914, when she announced that her goal was not only the liberation of the conquered Serbian territories, but also of all South Slav areas of the Austro-Hungarian Monarchy. The Corfu Declaration (1917), signed jointly by Pašić and the émigré Yugoslav Committee of London, reaffirmed this goal and left no doubt that the new state would be led by the Serbian Karageorgevich dynasty.

Confrontation between the Serbian government and the Zagreb National Council, however, was avoided. Although the Serbian government recognized the legitimacy of the Zagreb authorities on November 8, the inability of the latter to raise troops in her defense and to maintain order in the countryside forced abandonment of dreams about an independent Croatian and Slovenian state. Only with the aid of regular Serbian army units could the revolutionary momentum in the country be checked. The peasantry, taking matters into their own hands, were seizing the large estates, frightening all propertied people, while soldiers returning from the front created a general atmosphere of terror. Faced with anarchy internally and, perhaps more importantly, with an external danger in the West, where Italian troops commenced the occupation of Dalmatia, the Zagreb National Council requested, on November 4, the dispatch of Serbian troops. The presence of those troops sealed the fate of an independent Croatian and Slovenian state. On November 24, the Council decided to recognize the inevitable by voting for union with Serbia, which led to formation of the Kingdom of Serbs, Croats, and Slovenes on December 1.[8]

In the first days of November the most urgent problem of the Serbian government, however, was not the future of Slovenes and Croats, but that of the Voivodina. The Voivodina as a separate entity had no historical antecedent; the name itself came into use only after the war. It was to designate the territories ceded to Yugoslavia by Hungary, including the Bánát, the Bácska, and parts of Baranya county. With its highly mixed population it was doubtful that Serbia's claims to all of the Voivodina could be substantiated on the basis of nationality. If the Great Powers ordered a plebiscite in the area a vote favorable to Hungary was most likely, since the Hungarian and German minorities together formed an absolute majority of the population.[9] But even the attitude of the local Slavic population was ambiguous. With the outbreak of the revolution in Budapest, however, the old Hungarian administration lost control of the population. Power passed to the newly formed nationality councils. Their debates clearly indicated that the population was thoroughly divided about the future of this territory. Many, and not only the Hungarians, argued in favor of remaining within Hungary, while others were divided between the supporters of Belgrade and of the Zagreb authorities.

In view of this situation the haste with which the Serbian government acted is understandable. It was particularly anxious to occupy the Voivodina. On November 3, therefore, the Serbian Regent, Aleksander, announced Serbia's intention to occupy southern Hungary and on November 7, the day Károlyi arrived in Belgrade, the first units of the Serbian army crossed the Danube. Serbia sought to exploit the situation that was created by the negotiations between Károlyi and d'Esperey. The pretense could be maintained that until the signing of a new armistice Hungary was still technically in a state of war. Those territories that came under Serbian control before the date of armistice could be held without restrictions simply by the right of conquest. On the other hand, areas occupied after that date would have had to remain Hungarian territories, under Hungarian civilian administration until the signing of a peace treaty.[10] Available Serbian forces were insufficient to secure the extensive area of the Voivodina. The First and Second Serbian Armies, composed of seven divisions, reached the Save-Danube line on November 1, but only three of these divisions could be used for occupation of Hungarian territories. The Serbian officers drove their troops with utmost haste toward the proposed demarcation line and by avoiding conflicts with the retreating Hungarian and German units and through bypassing major population centers, Serbian forces reached the line before November 13. On the day of the signing of the Belgrade military conventions, Zombor, Szabadka, and Baja were occupied; on the 14th Pécs; on the 20th Temesvár.[11]

Retreat of the Hungarian population began even before the Serbian troops crossed the frontiers. As in so many other parts of the country, with the collapse of Hungarian authority, the area sank into anarchy, and the threat of violence reached everyone. Returning soldiers of the Austro-Hungarian army, Germans, Slavs, or Hungarians, regardless of their nationality, were often forced to fend for themselves through plunder. Fully armed roving bands of soldiers, the "Green Companies," formed from some of the 200,000 South Slav deserters, suddenly emerged from their forest hiding places.[12] In a mood of triumphant self-assertion, seeking revenge for alleged past wrongs, they struck terror in the hearts of the Hungarian population. Landless peasants also added to the general sense of insecurity by seizing land and burning down manor houses. Wild and exaggerated rumors fueled fears generated by actual acts of terror and had a considerable psychological impact upon the Hungarian population. The most intimidated groups, the upper and middle classes, first withdrew to their homes, seeking to remain as inconspicuous as possible. Estate owners, wealthier individuals, and higher officials, the most likely targets of terror, fled with their valuables toward the safety of inner Hungary. In many villages only the peasants remained. County officials, notaries, *gendarmes,* teachers, and even priests fled. Where they were caught they were rudely treated and at times even murdered. Similarly, estate overseers and managers also found it advisable to flee. According to Oszkár Jászi, in the first few days of November alone, about one-third of the notaries were put to flight.[13] The number of fleeing notaries was much higher in the minority areas. Tibor Hajdu estimated that in all about a third of all notaries were chased away in the Hungarian areas, a half from Slovak villages, and nine-tenths from the Romanian regions.[14]

After the arrival of Serbian troops the new local commanders, ignoring the terms of the Belgrade Military Convention, subordinated public administration to the Serb-Croat-Slovene state. In most places this led to the dismissal of most Hungarian civilian and police officials. Only in the predominantly Hungarian cities, such as Pécs, Baja, and Temesvár, did the old officials refuse to leave their posts and were allowed to remain temporarily, but these were exceptions. Ultimately none of these cities remained within the territory of Yugoslavia.[15]

Physical resistance to the Serbian occupation was almost nonexistent in the Voivodina. In one area, however, the Muraköz, or Mura District, the Hungarian government forcefully opposed separation of the region from the country. It had to be taken by force. This triangular-shaped territory in western Hungary, between the Mura and Dráva Rivers and the Austrian border, had always formed a part of the Kingdom of Hungary. In early November the authority of the Zagreb National Council was not extended to this area, although the Council maintained its claims to the district by virtue of the nationality of its population. The Belgrade Military Convention also left the Muraköz under Hungarian control. Serbia was reluctant to violate openly the terms of the Armistice, but she approved of sending irregular units into Muraköz. After an unsuccessful invasion in the latter part of November, a larger, 4000-man "volunteer" army crossed the Dráva during the last days of 1918 and accomplished the occupation of the Muraköz without much resistance.[16]

The primary motivating force for departure of the Hungarian population from the Bánát, Bácska, Baranya, and Muraköz during 1918 and the early part of 1919 was fear for safety of life. Most of those who decided to leave left in a moment of panic, with little thought given to their economic or social losses. During the last two months of 1918 at least 5,000 persons left, while during the first three months of 1919 perhaps three times as many. The number of those who left immediately after the occupation of the southern regions, however, might be substantially higher.

Occupation of Northern Hungary

Gaining physical control of Slovakia by the new Czechoslovak government proved to be a far more difficult undertaking. Unlike Serbia, Czechoslovakia did not possess a seasoned army ready to exploit the chaos created by the military collapse of the monarchy. The Prague government had only a few hastily gathered, ill-equipped and poorly led units of volunteers at its disposal. Its best troops, the Czech legionnaires, were still in Siberia.[17] Until their return, or until a regular army could be formed and trained, it was not possible to think seriously about a military campaign even against the limited resistance of a weak foe.

Nevertheless, on November 11, a small army of approximately 4000 men began to probe the Hungarian defenses in the northwestern corner of the country. The Károlyi government considered these military moves totally illegal and, therefore, ordered a counterattack by its own troops and sent strong reinforcements to Pozsony and Nyitra county.[18] With these moves, as well as with a note of protest to the Prague government, Károlyi intended to signal his conviction that, although Hungary abided by the terms of the Belgrade Convention, it was not willing to permit an unauthorized occupation of territories beyond the demarcation line. The promise of military resistance by Hungary forced Czechoslovakia to halt temporarily any further advance of its troops, while an alternate method was worked out.

The Slovaks themselves offered only limited help toward achievement of Czech objectives. Separatism among Slovaks in Hungary had only a brief history and was limited mostly to a small circle. The idea of uniting Czechs and Slovaks was recent in origin and gained a limited popularity only toward the end of the war. It was much more readily accepted by Czech and Slovak émigrés than by Slovaks living in Hungary.[19] For this reason, the Czech leadership received with relief the October 30 declaration of union between Czechs and Slovaks made by the hastily convened Slovak National Council at Turóczszentmárton. The Council was not genuinely representative; nonetheless, the declaration strengthened Czech legal claims to Upper Hungary and was of great propaganda value. But it did not bring about an immediate change of administration; Hungarian control of the area remained unaffected by it. Moreover, it did not accurately reflect Slovak ambivalence about union with the Czechs. The declaration was made, on the whole, by a random collection of politicians representing the western parts of future Slovakia and the conservative to moderate political factions. Most Slovak politicians, however, even those who were leaning toward union, still hesitated.

In view of Czech military weakness the inability to compel Hungary to evacuate Upper Hungary at the time of the Belgrade negotiations was doubly damaging. The Czech government feared that any significant delay in the occupation of the area might permanently impair the cause of the Czechoslovak state. It was well known that Jászi, the Hungarian minister of nationalities, promised complete autonomy to the Slovaks, which indeed was more than the Czechs themselves were thinking of granting. Any delay in occupation might have provided the necessary time for the anti-Hungarian sentiment of early November to subside and for the negotiation of a satisfactory agreement between Hungarian and Slovak leaders.

The revolutionary mood of the Slovak peasantry only added to the sense of Czech urgency. The danger was real, for the more democratic and socially more progressive Hungarian government was in a good position to convince the lower classes that their economic future was brighter in Hungary than in a Czechoslovak state dominated by propertied bourgeois classes.

The burden of forcing an immediate evacuation of northern Hungary fell to Czech diplomacy. Its principal objectives were to keep the Károlyi government in complete diplomatic isolation, and, simultaneously, to gain the support of the Western Powers for the creation of a northern zone of military occupation. In both of these efforts Edvard Beneš was ultimately successful. A key weapon in the arsenal of Czech diplomacy was its easy access to Western leaders and public opinion. Unlike Hungarian leaders, Beneš was keenly aware of the subtle changes in the Western political climate and recognized the rapid ascendance of conservative opinion. In his diplomatic and press campaign to discredit the Károlyi government, therefore, he stressed the radical character of the democratic revolution in Hungary, which, in his view, was only a prelude to a Bolshevik revolution. Conversely, Czechoslovakia was painted as the only safe bastion of capitalism. To prevent the spread of Bolshevism to the West an immediate Czech occupation of Upper Hungary was necessary.[20] Anti-Hungarian feelings were also fanned by growing Western anti-Semitism, which was closely linked to a fear of Bolshevism. Western reaction to Károlyi's appointment of Róza Bédy-Schwimmer as minister to Switzerland clearly illustrated this. The French and other Western diplomats were outraged by what they called "this perfidious" and "ultra-democratic" act of Károlyi of sending as his country's representative not only a radical Jew but a feminist woman.[21] Thus, in a way, Hungary was to lose much of its territory because of the conservative, undemocratic spirit of its past governments and was isolated because of its democratic and progressive new regime.

Not surprisingly, given the strongly anti-Hungarian mood in Paris, the revolutionary government of Hungary was not recognized by the Allies. Already in mid-1918, the British adopted the policy of not treating with Károlyi because "of a grave danger . . . of our alienating the only straightforward enemies of Germany within the Monarchy,"[22] meaning the nationalities and especially the Czechs. The policy evidently remained in force even after the end of the war.

Károlyi, who wished to establish personal contacts with leaders of the Great Powers, more particularly to plead the case of the young Hungarian democracy with President Woodrow Wilson, was refused even an entry permit to France. The French government simply declared that it "could not under any circumstances recognize the Károlyi Government, which represented a tenth part of the population of Hungary. . . ."[23] The French also cooperated with Prague in forcing Hungary to evacuate Upper Hungary. Beneš and Marshal Ferdinand Foch, the Supreme Commander of the Allies, bypassing the other Western Powers, drew up an agreement which extended the terms of the Belgrade Convention to include Upper Hungary in the area that was to be occupied by the Western Powers or their eastern allies. The note ordering the evacuation of "Slovak territories" was delivered on December 3 to the Hungarian government by Lieutenant Colonel Fernand Vix, the head of the Allied Military Mission in Budapest. This note, however, failed to define the boundary of Slovakia.[24]

On November 25, the Slovak politician Milan Hodža was sent to Budapest as the representative of Czechoslovakia. Hodža, though not authorized by Prague to negotiate the boundary question, nevertheless did so with the support of the Slovak National Council.[25]

On December 6, an agreement was worked out between Hodža and the Károlyi government on the details of the northern zone of occupation. The area that was to be evacuated included nearly all of the predominantly Slovak-populated territories, except in the eastern tip of Upper Hungary, but excluded some mixed or purely Hungarian areas demanded by Beneš at the Paris Peace Conference.

By the beginning of December, two Czech divisions, commanded by Italian officers, were ready for service in Slovakia. Thus, when the agreement was reached on the demarcation line in Budapest, these troops began to move forward, cautiously following the withdrawing Hungarian Army. By December 12, Nyitra was occupied and nearly everywhere in western Slovakia the Czech troops reached the Hodža demarcation line. Within two weeks central and most of eastern Slovakia were also occupied, with the exception of those towns where the Hungarian population, without the consent of the Budapest government, organized forces to resist the loss of their homeland.

On December 24, Lieutenant Colonel Vix presented Károlyi with a second note containing a new line of demarcation, which was defined as the "historic boundaries" of the Czecho-Slovak state. The new line was to run from the west along the Danube to the Ipoly River, to the town of Rimaszombat, from there toward the east to the Ung, and then along that river to the old frontiers. That is, roughly along the line that ultimately became the border between Czechoslovakia and Hungary. In his reply Károlyi rejected the demand to withdraw, stating that no such geographic or political entity called Slovakia ever existed, that northern Hungary had always formed an integral part of Hungary itself. Moreover, he argued, over 39 percent of the population to be transferred was non-Slovak.[26]

Nevertheless, Károlyi had no other option than to accept. Those army units rushed to reinforce the Hungarian defenses in the north in the first part of November had by the end of December largely melted away. Evacuation of the remaining Hungarian army units was completed peacefully also by the end of December. Only in a few areas was momentary resistance attempted. Thus, on December 26, Eperjes was occupied, on December 29, Kassa, and on New Year's day 1918, after several days of Hungarian military resistance, the future capital of Slovakia, Pozsony.[27]

Publication of the terms of the Belgrade agreement in early November had given a ray of hope to the Hungarian population of the northern districts. The hope ended when military operations commenced and the demands of the Prague government became known. Hope soon turned to bitterness over the realization that the Hungarian government was unable to put up a fight, and then to panic as the Czech occupation forces arrived. Only a few diehards thought of resistance without government help. In town after town politicians of the old regime, county and local officials, or demobilized officers tried to mobilize the Hungarian population for resistance. Without exception, their efforts failed. The war-weary population turned a deaf ear to their appeals; the people could think only of their personal safety. Those who feared the arrival of the Czech troops, though sympathizing with the idea of resistance, were at the moment hastily organizing their own flight to central Hungary.

Typical of the feeble attempts to organize volunteer armies of resistance, were the efforts of a group led by György Szmrecsányi. On October 31, the day of the revolution in Budapest, at Érsekújvár in the Nyitra Valley, the mayor of the town began to organize a small security force. Most of the three hundred volunteers came from the ranks of the local police and demobilized army officers. At first they concentrated on arresting Czech and Slovak agitators and on subduing the restless population of the surrounding villages.[28] This group soon merged into a larger organization called the National Defense Movement. It was commanded by György Szmrecsányi, a member of the prewar Hungarian parliament, representing Árva county and a former high-sheriff (*Főispán*) of Pozsony county. Optimistically, Szmrecsányi had envisaged the establishment of an army of 50,000 men, to be drawn from the Hungarian population of the most exposed western regions of northern Hungary. His aims were, first, expulsion of the invading forces from northern Hungary and, second, overthrow of the liberal government of Károlyi.[29] Without authorization he declared martial law, ordered to arms all men between the ages of twenty and forty, and sent his representatives to the villages to aid recruitment. Even more ambitiously, he sought to create an umbrella organization for the entire Hungarian population of northern Hungary that, in effect, would have functioned as an independent government. Such an organization was deemed necessary to synchronize the national resistance in the endangered Nyitra, Pozsony, Komárom, Bars, and Hont counties. It also would have rallied all the counterrevolutionaries to his side.

On December 21, representatives of these counties met at Érsekújvár and, to the cheering of some 20,000 people, elected a Defense Committee to organize military resistance. Leading figures in the committee were György Szmrecsányi, Ödön Beniczky, high-sheriff of Bars and Esztergom counties, Béla Perczel and János Bartos from Komárom and Bars counties. Leaders, however, were more readily available and plentiful than followers. In spite of all the patriotic appeals and grandiose designs recruitment failed: when the Czechs finally mounted a major offensive to occupy all of Slovakia, Szmrecsányi had no more than eighty men at his disposal. On January 8, 1919, Érsekújvár fell without a struggle. Deeply embittered and bewildered by the nearly total lack of mass support Szmrecsányi and his small army abandoned all hopes of saving northern Hungary and, along with his political supporters, he retired to Budapest.[30] They blamed their failure on socialist agitators, on the personal cowardice of some politicians, and, above all, on the criminal sabotage of their efforts by the pacifists in the Károlyi government.

In other parts of northern Hungary state or county officials made similar attempts at organizing the population for a national resistance, but in every town and county the result was the same. Only some of the county or state officials, members of the police or *gendarmerie,* and demobilized officers responded to the call to arms. In Selmecbánya, for example, a high state official, László Pethes, led the resistance. His group, consisting mostly of officers and noncommissioned officers, was too small to be effective. They could only delay the occupation of towns.[31] After all resistance became hopeless, Pethes, with some other resistants, was forced to flee to Budapest. Later, during the Hungarian Soviet regime several members of this group fled to Szeged, where they became active in organizing the National Army. A similar officer's detachment was formed in Gömör country by the deputy high-sheriff (*Alispán*) Gyula Fornet. It was able to retain control of the county only until the Czech troops arrived in force during January 1919. Then this small army, too, retired to Hungary. Another group of police and army officers made a desperate attempt to prevent, by force, Czech occupation at Balassagyarmat. At Losonc a few hundred insurgents abandoned the idea of a struggle when they were so ordered by the government at Budapest.[32]

In Ruthenia, Miklós Kutkafalvy, editor of a pro-Hungarian newspaper and head of Bereg county during the Károlyi regime, was the leader of resistance and commander of an extra-legal military force. His group fought several skirmishes with invading bands of Ukrainian nationalists and forced them to retire behind the Carpathians. Small clashes also took place with some advanced guards of Romanians. Kutkafalvy was equally active in the organization of the pro-Hungarian Ruthenian People's Council; it went on record as opposing the forceful separation of Ruthenia from Hungary. Just as everywhere else occupation was inevitable, and those who attempted to resist it were forced to flee to inner Hungary.[33]

Others merely sent repeated urgent messages or delegations to Budapest, protesting the absence of military protection against foreign invaders. All, regardless of their roles in the resistance, even if they were nothing but passive supporters, believed, nevertheless, that they had compromised themselves in the eyes of the occupying powers. However reluctantly they came to the conclusion that their lives, as well as those of their families were endangered, and they felt compelled to withdraw into the unoccupied interior of Hungary.

The leaders of these and similar groups remained politically active as refugees. For their activities some were rewarded in 1920 with seats in parliament or high government posts.[34]

Thousands of people from all walks of life fled before the approaching army. The mere thought of a hostile foreign army, fueled by rumors about the treatment the Hungarian population could expect, was sufficient for many to seek safety on the southern side of the demarcation line. Most Hungarian peasants remained in their villages, except in the border areas, where, at times, nearly all young people fled; and in some instances, entire villages were suddenly depopulated. Many who remained were arrested immediately after the arrival of Czech troops; some were tortured; after their release they either voluntarily crossed the demarcation line or were forcefully expelled.

The hopes of the Hungarian minority in Czechoslovakia were raised once more during the summer of 1919; for a part of Slovakia was briefly restored to Hungary as a consequence of the highly successful invasion by the army of the Hungarian Soviet Republic. The incident was provoked by additional territorial demands by the Czechs, who discovered that they had failed to claim some important railroad junctions on the main east-west Hungarian railway axis. Prague also raised the question of Ruthenia, which still remained in Hungary, on grounds that its possession by the Czechoslovak Republic was necessary to assure a direct frontier between Czechoslovakia and Romania and, thus, to separate the Poles and Hungarians, both hostile to Czechoslovakia. These demands were made soon after another ultimatum was delivered to Hungary ordering the evacuation of additional territories to permit the advance of the Romanian forces. Under these pressures the Károlyi government could no longer function, and power in Hungary passed into the hands of the Communists. The Hungarian Soviet leadership was determined to end the gradual encroachment of neighboring states on Hungarian territory. Therefore, it replaced the policy of cooperation with the Allies with one of resistance. Béla Kun was convinced that an international coalition would soon attack the Hungarian Soviet Republic from three sides to exterminate Communism from East Central Europe.[35] His belief proved correct. Like many faithful Communists of his time, he believed that if the Hungarian Soviet state survived, its example would be followed in the other nations of East Central Europe and soon the world would be engulfed in a great revolution. Thus his primary objective was to prolong the life of the Communist regime until that day.

In view of this it was logical to attempt to fight Hungary's opponents separately, and on the terms set by the Red Army. On April 16, Romania opened full-scale attack from the east. Five days later the Czech army crossed the line of demarcation, apparently without the full knowledge or approval of the Allies, and occupied Miskolc and the important coal mining district of Salgótarján. The Soviet Republic took advantage of these violations of Hungary's demarcation lines and, after stabilizing the eastern front, went on the offensive in the north. The Hungarian Red Army launched a full-scale invasion of Czech-occupied northern Hungary (May 20, 1919) and caught the Czech legions by surprise. Within a few weeks most of the eastern regions of Upper Hungary and nearly all of the Hungarian-populated areas were again in Hungarian hands. The Western Powers, however, intervened and ordered an immediate withdrawal, though promising at the same time to compel the Romanians to withdraw behind the designated demarcation line in the east. Béla Kun yielded and Slovakia was evacuated, but the Romanians remained at their advanced position on the left bank of the Tisza River.

From Kassa to Eperjes, to Losonc and Érsekújvár, the Hungarian population welcomed the Hungarian Red Army as liberators. Hundreds joined the army and thousands aided it in one form or another. Once the area returned to Czech control those individuals were doubly punished: as Hungarian nationalists and as suspected Communists. Anyone suspected of complicity with the Red Army was hunted down, beaten, imprisoned, or expelled. Thousands of others left with the retreating Red Army.

Occupation of Transylvania and Eastern Hungary

In 1918 most Hungarians of eastern Hungary viewed the future of their homeland with grave apprehension. Romanian designs on Transylvania were well known. Romanian nationalists viewed Transylvania as the birthplace of the Romanian nation and culture and pressed for the annexation of eastern Hungary into a Greater Romania. But the cultural and historical bonds between Transylvania and Hungary were even stronger. For a millenium Transylvania formed an integral part of the Kingdom of Hungary. Although for centuries Transylvania was ruled under its own laws by its own Hungarian princes, virtually independent of the Hungarian king, the constitutional subordination of the Transylvanian principality to the Hungarian crown was always recognized, at least in principle.

Already at the beginning of the World War the explosive nature of the Romanian problem was recognized by most politicians, but a sharp disagreement prevailed over the question of how to deal with it. Most people in the position of power and influence had believed that granting concessions to the Romanians would be interpreted as a sign of weakness that would lead to disintegration of the Hungarian state. During the first year of the war Prime Minister István Tisza, to keep the Kingdom of Romania neutral and under strong German and Austrian pressure, held out the possibility of concessions to the Romanian minority. But even the promise of minor concessions aroused the ire of such men as Counts Albert Apponyi, Gyula Andrássy, Jr., and of the most radical champion of Hungarian supremacy, István Bethlen.[36]

Once Romania abandoned its neutrality and invaded Transylvania, restraints were removed. The Hungarian population fled in massive numbers before the approaching Romanian army. The remaining Hungarians were subjected to violent treatment, and atrocities against them were not infrequent. When the Central Powers counterattacked, the retreating Romanian forces carried off hundreds of prominent Hungarians as hostages. Although the Romanian population generally adopted a noncommittal attitude toward the invading forces, some welcomed them; some cooperated with them. Along with the Romanian army, therefore, thousands of Romanians fearing Hungarian retaliation also fled to Romania. The restoration of Hungarian authority indeed brought repressive measures against those suspected of collaboration with the enemy.[37]

Mutual repressions only made postwar reconciliation between Romanians and Hungarians more difficult. The anti-Hungarian bias of the Romanian population was clearly understood by the Károlyi government as well as by the Székely and Hungarian population of Transylvania.[38] Although Károlyi and Jászi were more or less resigned to the loss of at least part of Transylvania, Hungarians like the Székelys still believed that resistance was possible. In northern Hungary as well as in territories ceded to Yugoslavia, organized resistance was at best sporadic, but Hungarians, including the Székelys, of eastern Hungary and Transylvania lost no time in establishing resistance organizations, both in Budapest and in Transylvania. The reason for this difference is that unlike Hungarians of northern and southern Hungary, Transylvanians always possessed their own strong separate corporate identity. To them, Transylvania with its proud history represented the best and the purest qualities of the Hungarian nation. This view was shared by many even outside Transylvania. Transylvania had retained much of its independence during the long Turkish presence in central Hungary. It was a reservoir for the struggle against Habsburg domination during the sixteeenth and seventeenth centuries. Transylvania had stood in the forefront of the fight for religious toleration, for freedom of conscience in face of the religious bigotry of the Catholic Habsburgs. The Transylvanians also liked to think of their province as an eastern replica of Switzerland, where people of various nationalities and religions could live in harmony. They pointed to the equality and peaceful coexistence among the three "nations" of Transylvania: the Hungarians, the Székelys, and the Saxons. These claims might have been justified had the

Romanians been admitted as the fourth "nation," but they were not recognized as such.

The Transylvanians also liked to point to some of the democratic traditions and practices within each of the recognized "nations," especially among the Székelys. The historic privileges of the urban Saxons and the Székelys helped them to evolve a kind of protodemocracy that was based, however, not on a modern theory of equality, but on the remnants of medieval privileges.

The Székely National Council was formed in Budapest during November 1918, under the guidance of Counts István Bethlen and Pál Teleki, members of illustrious Transylvanian families, and under the active leadership of Benedek Jancsó, Dénes Sebess, Gábor Ugron, and Nándor Urmánczy. The purpose of this organization was to save in Transylvania what still could be saved and to organize and supply a military force willing to defend the territorial integrity of Transylvania. The so-called *Székely akció* managed to collect a considerable amount of arms, accumulate a sizable war chest, and recruit a number of Székely soldiers, mostly from the ranks of demobilized army units returning from the Italian front.[39]

Soon after the establishment of the Székely National Council a general meeting was held in Marosvásárhely, in the heart of Transylvania, to debate the fate of the province. Many at the meeting felt that the Hungarian government could not be entrusted with the defense of their homeland and proposed some kind of independent action. The idea of secession from Hungary and the establishment of an independent Transylvania, or the formation of a Székely Republic from the purely Székely or Hungarian counties, was especially popular with the younger men and junior officers. This suggestion appeared even more tempting since it was believed that General August von Mackensen, the commander of the German army in Romania, facing an uncertain line of withdrawal to Germany, offered the military assistance of his considerable army against the Romanians if he received authorization from an independent Székely Republic.[40] The idea of an independent Székely Republic as an alternative to union of Transylvania with Romania received some support within the government itself. But Károlyi could not endorse an adventure which would have engulfed the area in a general war. Hungary was economically and emotionally exhausted; no amount of patriotic agitation could have brought the vast majority of the population to take upon its shoulders the burden of a new war. Only a revolutionary army, fighting for revolutionary ideas, could have generated sufficient energy to meet the challenge from the neighboring countries. The Károlyi revolution did not arouse such revolutionary enthusiasm. The proposal of secession was voted down by the assembly at Marosvásárhely, and the policies decreed by Budapest remained applicable to Transylvania.

In the Belgrade agreement (November 13, 1918) the Károlyi government agreed to the evacuation of its military forces from the area south of the Maros line.[41] This evacuation was accomplished very rapidly since at that time no regular Hungarian units were guarding the Romanian borders; in all of Transylvania only a few administrative military units were present. Nevertheless, the Romanian authorities could not take control of the area until much later. For, Romania at the time of the armistice was still under German and Austro-Hungarian military control, and while the Austro-Hungarian divisions were returning in great disarray, the German army began its withdrawal toward Transylvania in an orderly and leisurely fashion. Thus the occupation of Transylvania did not commence until December 1918. It had to be delayed for another reason. Romania herself was extremely weak militarily, and even months later it could commit to Transylvania only three of its eight divisions. In December the number of Romanian troops in Transylvania was still only between 8–10,000. In these early months, the Romanian authorities relied much on irregular native Transylvanian Romanian units, the Romanian National Guards, and on legions formed from Transylvanian refugees in Romania, who hurriedly returned to their homeland. The National Guards sprang to life spontaneously from the discharged or deserting Romanian soldiers of the Austro-Hungarian army and from the local Romanian population who either brought their weapons home from the front or armed themselves by seizing unguarded ammunition stores.

These units operated on both sides of the demarcation line. They took it upon themselves, especially in the predominantly Romanian counties, to oust Hungarian officials and generally did much to instill terror in the hearts of the Hungarian population. In many areas these undisciplined National Guards were totally indistinguishable from the rebellious peasantry. Pent-up nationalist and class hatred was suddenly released against everything Hungarian: institutions, property, and even people.

The peasant revolt that swept every corner of Hungary the month of November was slower in spreading among the Romanian peasantry. Once it got under way it was much more difficult to extinguish. It started in the Bánát and neighboring counties, from there the revolt spread to south Transylvania, and finally, though with lesser force, it hit central and northern Transylvania. The rebellious peasants together with the National Guards seized lands, looted the storehouses of the great estates, hunted in the forbidden game preserves of the magnates, and forced the effected Hungarians to flee in panic. The path of these men over the countryside was often lit by the burning castles and manor houses of the once powerful Hungarian landowners. But the greatest hatred of the peasantry, as everywhere in the country, was reserved for the notaries and *gendarmes,* regardless of nationality. Romanian notaries suffered as cruelly as the Hungarians. As a result, ninety percent of the notaries fled from the Romanian-populated areas; *gendarmes* either shed uniforms and tried to melt into the population, or fled along with the other refugees.[42]

During the last days of October, Romanian minority political organizations sprang up on both the local and national levels. The Károlyi government, wishing to open negotiations with the representatives of every national minority, supported these activities. The Central Romanian National Council was formed on October 30, in Budapest and moved to Arad on November 3–4. Initially its members were drawn in equal numbers from the liberal Romanian National Party and from the ranks of the Romanian Social Democrats.[43] In the local national councils leadership was in the hands of well-to-do Romanians: lawyers, teachers, intellectuals, Orthodox priests, wealthier businessmen, landowners, and prosperous peasants. These leaders were both anxious to halt peasant attacks on property and, at the same time, to harness the revolutionary energies of the peasantry behind a separatist, national movement. To some, and especially to the conservatives, the safest course was immediate union with the conservative Old Kingdom of Romania. Bypassing the Romanian National Council, some appealed directly to the Romanian government, requesting a quick military occupation of Transylvania. The Romanian government in Iaşi, anxious to force an immediate decision on the fate of Transylvania, welcomed these appeals. In their responses the various Romanian politicians urged the Transylvanian leaders to act at the earliest possible date and declare Transylvania's unconditional union with Romania. The Romanian government intended to view such a declaration as the equivalent of a plebiscite and, therefore, to demand an immediate evacuation of the Hungarian forces from Transylvania.

Most Romanian leaders in Transylvania favored secession from Hungary. But their attitude on unconditional union was ambiguous. The liberals and the socialists wished to receive guarantees of political autonomy for Transylvania before the declaration for union was made. They believed that only within an autonomous Transylvania would it be possible to carry out a radical land reform and to establish liberal democratic institutions. What they feared most was that once union was achieved without a guaranteed autonomy, Transylvania would be swallowed up by the more backward and conservative Old Kingdom. Especially the socialists had difficulty reconciling their ideology with joining a monarchy which was dominated by reactionary boyars.[44] In the light of the region's subsequent history, such misgivings were not entirely unjustified.

The Károlyi government hoped that its cooperation with the Romanian National Council and its promise of far-reaching reforms would discourage secession and pave the way to a negotiated settlement. On November 16, as a last minute effort to open dialogue between the Hungarian government and the Romanian minority, a delegation headed by Jászi was sent to Arad. But the mission had the opposite effect.[45] The time for a peaceful accord had passed. At its meeting on November 18, the Romanian National Council, after cataloguing the Romanian population's grievances, decided to proclaim the separation of Transylvania from Hungary as soon as the military protection of the Romanian population could be secured. The National Council also sent a delegation to the city of Iaşi to communicate these intentions of Transylvanian Romanians to the Romanian government.[46] Union with Romania was declared just a few days later (December 1, 1918) at the meeting of some 700 Romanian delegates from all parts of Transylvania at Gyulafehérvár (Alba Iulia). According to a Romanian account, these delegates in

> the old capital of the principality of Transylvania . . . proclaimed unanimously, amid indescribable enthusiasm, the definitive and unconditional union of these provinces with Romania.
>
> One hundred thousand inhabitants, from all parts of the country, gathered around the place of meeting, awaited the result of the deliberations. When the result was made known to the throng, it was received with delirious joy. The Romanian people knew such happiness as never before.[47]

On December 11, the Romanian government issued a royal proclamation which, disregarding all plans of the Western Powers to reach a settlement regarding the issue of Transylvania only at the Paris Peace Conference, declared unilaterally the unification with Romania of Transylvania, the Bánát, and other eastern parts of Hungary, adjacent to Transylvania. Neither the Western Powers, nor the Hungarian government recognized the validity of this proclamation.[48] Nevertheless, Romania treated those territories already under her control as an integral part of Romania, and those territories that she claimed but still did not hold as territories under foreign occupation. From the time of the proclamation, Romania made repeated representations to the Western

Powers demanding the evacuation of the Hungarian forces from those areas that she believed were rightfully hers.

The Hungarian population of Transylvania interpreted the actions of the Romanians at Gyulafehérvár as treason and open rebellion; consequently it demanded from Budapest some forceful action to repel the invaders and to secure Hungarian sovereignty in Transylvania. The Károlyi government, however, lacking the military means, was powerless to do so. The demobilization of the Hungarian army was so rapid that the government, in November, was forced to appeal to the population for volunteers, or to send out new draft notices. The response to these calls was extremely poor. To defend Transylvania and to guard the Maros demarcation line the Ministry of Defense established a new division, with headquarters at Kolozsvár and commanded by an able officer, Colonel Károly Kratochwill. This was the 38th, or as it later came to be known, the Székely Division. Colonel Kratochwill increasingly filled the ranks of the division with volunteers from among Székely refugees.[49]

Simultaneously, in many parts of Transylvania irregular military formations were also created, mostly from junior grade and noncommissioned officers, local landowners, and *gendarmes*. In Zilah, for example, a 600-man detachment was formed calling itself the "Hungarian Liberation Army of Transylvania." Many of these irregular units were soon merged into the Székely Division. The size of Kratochwill's little army had also increased by recruits sent to the east by the Székely National Council in Budapest. But aside from the most patriotic elements and the refugees, only the population most immediately affected by the advancing Romanian army offered aid to the Székely Division. The Saxons of Transylvania passively accepted the sudden turn of events and the Declaration of Gyulafehérvár and quietly awaited the arrival of Romanian troops.

Gathered on the eastern front, the Székely Division was woefully inadequate to meet the serious military challenge by the Romanian army, in the coming months. On December 2, the Romanian troops began crossing the demarcation line. The Hungarian government vainly protested the illegality of these moves in view of the recently signed Belgrade agreement. The Allies chose to give credence to the Romanian charges of atrocities in Hungarian-administered areas, and on December 16, Lieutenant Colonel Vix announced the extension of the demarcation line. Hungarians were ordered to withdraw behind a line west of Kolozsvár; the area was to be temporarily occupied by the Romanian army. Károlyi again protested, but to avoid senseless shedding of blood he ordered the evacuation of the city. On December 24, the Romanian army occupied the city.[50] Kolozsvár was filled with refugees from all parts of Transylvania. These along with many residents of the city, in all according to one source some 17,000 families, withdrew with the retiring Hungarian army.[51]

On January 6, 1919, an agreement was worked out between István Apáthy, the representative of the Károlyi government, General Henri Berthelot of the French army, and General Neculcea representing Romania, establishing a fifteen-kilometer wide neutral zone between Hungarian and Romanian troops so that further clashes might be avoided.[52] This new line of demarcation was to run from Nagybánya to Kolozsvár and from there to Déva, and then along the course of the Maros to the Tisza River. The two allied generals gave specific assurances to the Hungarian population that the Romanian troops would not interfere in local civilian administration; this was to remain in the hands of Hungarian officials. Further guarantees were given concerning the safety of Hungarian lives and property, and, in general, to the effect that the terms of the Belgrade Convention were to be scrupulously observed. Within a few days, however, the Romanians began to demand a further withdrawal of Hungarian troops behind a new line, roughly corresponding to the western boundaries of historic Transylvania. Romanian troops began to cross the neutral zone during the second half of January and occupied several towns.[53] After some sharp clashes with the Székely Division, the Károlyi government was once again forced to acquiesce in the loss of additional territory, and order its troops not to resist.

With each new retreat the despair of the Székely troops increased and their bitterness about government inaction was almost as great as their hatred of the Romanians.

In mid-January 1919, the commanders of the Székely Division resolved to make a stand regardless of orders from Budapest; consequently, between January and April, the front remained stationary. Both sides, in fact, limited their actions to minor probes across the latest demarcation line, but the position of the Székely Division became increasingly precarious. As the line it was forced to defend stretched to 150 kilometers, and as conditions in the hinterland became more chaotic, making resupplying and communications even more difficult, the division increasingly became divided into smaller units. Each local commander operated his sector independently, planned and executed raids into Romanian-held areas on his own authority.

Many of these raids were executed with great daring and courage, but while they caused some anxiety to the Romanian commanders, their military value was slight. Often Székely units crossed the lines on missions of mercy, responding to news or rumors of an impending Romanian atrocity or executions. They wished to protect, save, or rescue the Hungarian population and, indeed, at times, they were successful in these efforts. A case in point was an incident toward the end of January at Egeres, where a raiding party rescued from a group of Romanian soldiers a number of Hungarians who were found bound in the snow. The Romanian troops' real intent will never be known, but the terrified Hungarians were certain that they faced imminent execution.[54] In many instances these raiders sought out isolated Hungarian settlements and brought those families back to the safety of unoccupied Hungary. A large number of railroad employees and state officials were rescued in such fashion from their remote posts, where often they were the only Hungarians in the area; natural targets of attack by Romanian troops or population.

These raids had the effect of a double-edged sword for Hungarians, especially for those who originally wished to remain in Transylvania. The raid on Zilah serves as a good example. A company of soldiers, recruited mostly from that town, embittered by the news of persecution of their families, under cover of night stormed into the town and forced a hasty withdrawal of the Romanians. The Romanians soon recovered from the surprise attack and the Hungarian soldiers had to evacuate the city without achieving anything; the local Hungarian population in fear of a Romanian retaliation was forced to leave the city in large numbers. Within a few days these people reached Debrecen, adding to the already considerable number of homeless and penniless refugees.[55]

Fear of retaliation was not without foundation. In mid-April at the village of Köröstarkány, for example, eighty-one villagers and seventeen from the neighboring Négerfalu were massacred for aiding a Székely unit. Twenty-eight persons were killed in Apátfalva for similar reasons.[56]

The Hungarian population was continually bombarded with news of such events: some true, some exaggerated, and others passed on imagined fears as true. Each new atrocity, each new persecution added to fears for their own safety and to their intimidation. For many these fears served as a sufficient reason to depart from areas to be incorporated into Romania.

The results generally corresponded with the aims of the Romanian government. To be sure, massacres were not a part of official government policy. But a vocal and defiant Hungarian population could have presented a grave danger to the militarily weak Romania. As long as the state was uncertain of its ability to control all organs of state power and the population, local Romanian officials were free to elect harsh methods and intimidation to force Hungarians to play a passive role. They used various means: taking of hostages, random and nuisance arrests for brief periods of time, public flogging, internment of the officers of the old Austro-Hungarian army, mass arrests of striking Hungarian workers; all served to create a climate in which organized resistance would be unthinkable.

Another frequently used method was expulsion of entire families, mostly those of more prosperous or prominent citizens who were likely leaders of any organized opposition or resistance. This method was regularly employed also by the other Successor States, Yugoslavia and Czechoslovakia. The head of the family would merely receive a form letter informing him that:

> by virtue of decree 8272/919 of the Department of Interior . . . you are herewith invited to leave the town of . . . [name of the town] with your family by the . . . [date]. In case of refusal you will be deported by the *gendarmerie*, and you will not be allowed to take your movables with you. The Police supplies the permit of travel on condition that you will leave the country definitely [*sic*].[57]

The massive scale of expulsion and voluntary flight of the Hungarian population sharply reduced the number of Hungarians who were to remain in Romania. For this reason the Romanian government, as well as the other two Successor States, encouraged or at least did not hinder the departure of Hungarian families.

With the establishment of the Hungarian Soviet Republic the Székely Division found itself in an increasingly impossible situation. The division recognized the new government and in turn it was recognized by the regime as a semi-independent unit of the Hungarian army, but the division often found itself in conflict with two opponents, one in the front, and the other in the rear. It continued to oppose the Romanian army for patriotic reasons, but it also felt that its prime loyalty lay with the cause of counterrevolution. A recruiting campaign was successful only among the refugees from Transylvania and in the villages next to the demarcation line.[58] Soon after the declaration of the Soviet Republic hostilities between the Székely and Red troops reached the point of imminent open conflict. Confronted with this impossible situation the commander of the division, Colonel Kratochwill, through General Gondrecourt, opened negotiations with the Romanians. In exchange for their surrender the Székely Division was offered safe return to Transylvania, and there the free enjoyment of their property. On April 25, the division commander informed his troops of this offer and left the decision up to the individual soldiers. About 5000 men accepted and laid

down their arms. Officers were interned in Brassó; soldiers, in Fogaras. Upon their release they all were required to agree to remain within
their towns or villages, and to report regularly to the local authorities.
Within a year most soldiers fled to Hungary.[59]

Many who refused the surrender terms found their way to Szeged,
where they joined Admiral Horthy's counterrevolutionary army. Yet
another group remained in the field as an organized unit, as the
Székely Brigade, under the nominal command of the Red Army. They
participated in the June offensive against Czech-occupied northern
Hungary, but were back on the Tisza line when the ill-fated Communist
attack began against the Romanians in July. During August 6–7, when
the Romanians marched into Budapest, some of the officers and men
were captured; thirty-two officers were executed and the rest were
interned at Brassó until 1920.

The majority of the brigade, some 3500 men, bypassed Budapest and
crossed over to Transdanubia. There they joined the fledgling counterrevolutionary movement and helped to put down the last desperate
revolt of the workers, the strike of some 40,000 miners of Tata. On
August 19, Horthy took official command of the brigade, which became
an integral part of the new National Army. With the addition of these
refugee soldiers, over half of the counterrevolutionary army in Transdanubia — which, on August 9, consisted of only 10,700 men — was
composed of refugees, mostly from Transylvania and in lesser number
from Yugoslavia and Slovakia. As we shall see, as this army expanded,
the unemployed, homeless, and radicalized refugees continued to be
major sources of recruits. From the prisoners of war camp at Csót
alone, where the returning prisoners from Italy were processed, during
the fall of 1919, about 1300 Székelys joined the National Army.[60]

It is difficult to estimate the total number of refugees who were forced
to leave as a direct consequence of the military operations in their native
lands and as a result of the physical maltreatment of the population in
the early months of occupation by troops of the Successor States.
Perhaps 200,000 individuals would fall into this category. But the end to
military hostilities did not mean an end to the suffering of Hungarians in
the lost territories. More subtle administrative or economic changes
were just as effective in ultimately forcing, perhaps, an equal number of
other individuals to follow the well-worn path of earlier refugees. We
shall now turn our attention to these changes and the men they affected.

Chapter 3
Uprooting of the Hungarian Administration and Educational System in the Successor States

The Belgrade Military Convention stipulated that within the occupied territories civil administration was to remain in the hands of the Hungarian government.[1] Nevertheless, the purge of the administration and educational institutions of Hungarian influence commenced as soon as the Successor States established their military control over the sought areas. In the predominantly Romanian-populated counties of Transylvania, this process began even before the arrival of the regular Romanian army, by the population and by the Romanian National Council.[2]

Summary dismissal of Hungarian officials was a clear violation of the Belgrade Convention, but all three of the Successor States were determined to take this action. The principle of national self-rule served as a justification. Replacement of Hungarian officials in the predominantly Hungarian areas, however, was contradictory to that principle. In those areas, therefore, officials were replaced in the name of security. It is perhaps paradoxical that in Paris several of the territorial claims against Hungary were advanced by the Successor States in the name of security even though these claims were not justified on the basis of nationality. Such was the Czech demand for the incorporation of the purely Hungarian district of Csallóköz in spite of the fact that it involved the risk of adding to Czechoslovakia a large number of hostile Hungarians.[3] In other words, when confronted with the choice of a larger territory and an enlarged *irredenta* on the one hand, and smaller territory and greater internal cohesion on the other, all of the Successor States chose the former.

In the West, as well as in some of the capitals of the Successor States, hopes were entertained about eventual reconciliation of the various national groups under democratic regimes. These hopes, however, never materialized. First, the Hungarian minority in all three states remained steadfastly opposed to separation from their country and never accepted the new boundaries as anything but temporary. Too, the embers of hostility between the ruling nations and the Hungarian minorities, were constantly fanned by a virtual psychosis for security.

Here again, it was in Czechoslovakia, the most heterogeneous of the Successor States, where this security consciousness was most accentuated. In the minds of the Czechs, there existed a constant, if only partially admitted, fear that the creation of their state was a mere historical accident, that under some unfavorable turn of events the state could vanish just as rapidly as it had come into being. Without doubt, the Hungarians were totally committed, as a minimum demand, to a restoration of the predominantly Hungarian border areas, and if possible, all of Slovakia. If Hungary was successful in separating Slovakia from Czechoslovakia, Bohemia would cease to be a viable state and soon would be submerged in the surrounding sea of Germans.

This was the nightmare of all Czech nationalists. At times, therefore, they felt compelled to take strong measures for the preservation of the Czechoslovak state, especially against the most ardent *irredenta* group, the Hungarians. Every Hungarian was looked on as a potential member of a fifth column bent on the destruction of Czechoslovakia. Not surprisingly, Czechoslovakia was flooded with a constant stream of spy scares, arrests, and political trials. Rumors about an imminent Hungarian invasion, or about infiltration of Slovakia by Hungarian freebooters and saboteurs, were regularly circulated. The credibility of these rumors was reinforced by the violently nationalistic Hungarian press. Actually plans for an invasion of Slovakia were entertained even in the highest Hungarian circles, but a realistic evaluation of Hungary's military strength should have dissolved all doubts about the capacity of Hungary to realize these ambitions.[4] To the Czechs, it, nevertheless, appeared a reasonable security measure to remove the Hungarian officials from their positions of power even in predominantly Hungarian areas.

The issues were less complicated to the Hungarian population. Clearly, to them, at the core of every policy of the Successor States was an unbending determination to destroy the Hungarian character of the conquered lands, to erase all the cultural and political marks that a thousand years of association of these areas with Hungary had inevitably left upon them. In the dismissals the Hungarian population discovered a perhaps even more sinister design: a clearly discernible policy, aimed at nothing less than the destruction of the Hungarian middle class. By eliminating this politically most conscious and articulate and, therefore, most dangerous class, the new states seriously impaired the remaining predominantly agricultural Hungarian minority's ability to resist.

Dismissal from state employment served this policy effectively. Unlike the industrialized Western countries, where the commercial and industrial classes formed the backbone of the bourgeoisie, in mostly agrarian Hungary the "intelligentsia," composed of professionals and gentry bureaucrats, formed the middle class. In 1910, out of roughly 300,000 individuals classified as intellectuals, 182,000, or about sixty percent, belonged to these groups, and most found employment in the bureaucracy or the public sector of the economy.[5] This excessive dependence of the middle class on the state made it especially vulnerable in the Successor States.

A loss of a minor bureaucratic post or a teaching position often meant a loss of ability to survive. Armed with their Hungarian law degrees, teaching credentials or with even less, the Hungarian officials and teachers had no other qualifications for employment than that required in the Hungarian classrooms or bureaucracy.

These men had only two options: either to accept the most menial jobs or to cross the border into unoccupied Hungary. For a shorter or longer period of time, many of the dismissed state employees attempted to maintain themselves through physical labor in the vain hope of a sudden reversal of their country's fortunes. As the Hungarian Peace Delegation to Paris bitterly complained: "The discharged and ruined Hungarian teachers are not allowed to live by their work and thus to maintain their families. Professors, officials, magistrates, having a secondary and . . . [university] education, undertake street paving or work as stable servants, as porters . . ." and in similar occupations.[6] As we shall see most, sooner or later, decided to abandon their homes and become refugees in Hungary.

Uprooting of Hungarian administrative personnel was carried out with the greatest thoroughness and dispatch in the Voivodina. In places the hastily formed South Slav Councils took it upon themselves to seize the town halls and to appoint new officials from their own ranks, without awaiting the arrival of Serbian troops. The Serbian occupation of the area sealed the fate of some of the Hungarian officials. One of the first acts of many Serbian military commanders was to dismiss nearly all Hungarian administrators from their posts. Only those officials who suddenly discovered their minority ancestors and renounced Hungarian nationality managed to salvage their jobs. In fact, this rapid change of nationality was a practice not uncommon in the other occupied areas — a considerable number of ex-Hungarian officials saved their careers in this fashion in Slovakia and in Romania as well.

Most of the Hungarian officials, especially those in higher posts, did not await removal by the new Serbian authorities; they fled with their families to inner Hungary even before completion of the military occupation of the southern counties. During 1918 and 1919, 525 state functionaries, 255 county officials, and 210 judges and public prosecutors were registered officially as refugees from Yugoslavia,[7] as well as much larger number of junior officials, clerks, and other state, county, municipal and village office personnel. Those who were not immediately replaced were subjected to a more drawn out war of attrition. Failure to take the oath of loyalty led to suspension and loss of all benefits by many officials. Others were harassed, arrested, flogged, or, simply, expelled from the country. Finally, strict enforcement of the official Serbian language in all state affairs even in the purely Hungarian or German districts, made the replacement of Hungarian officials with Serbians, drawn mostly from the Old Kingdom, inevitable.[8]

These refugees accepted their displacement from their offices and homes with greater passivity than did the officials of Transylvania and Slovakia. The explanation for this difference is to be found in the composition and evolution of the middle class in the southern regions of Hungary. The Voivodina was one of Hungary's least diversified areas, with an extremely thin stratum of middle class and an overwhelming peasant majority. Unlike Upper Hungary and the eastern regions, the gentry in the Bánát and Bácska could never fully reestablish itself after the Turkish wars. Thus the intelligentsia, the local bureaucracy, did not grow out of a native nobility, but was mostly either non-noble in origin or transplanted from other regions. Their roots were shallow; their historical attachments and identification with the area slight; and, therefore, their uprooting less traumatic.

In Czechoslovakia the first law concerning Hungarian state employees was issued on December 10, 1918. It stated: "All municipal and communal assemblies are dissolved, and their jurisdiction is transferred to a Commission to be formed by the plenipotentiary of the Government."[9] Control of the entire administrative structure passed to the 'Government Office,' a branch of the Ministry for Slovakia, whose first director, Vavro Šrobár, was granted extraordinary powers to reorganize Slovakia. Immediately under him were thirteen referents, acting more or less in the capacity of cabinet ministers, while seventeen *Župan*s were appointed, one to head each of the seventeen counties of Slovakia.

Responsibility for screening out "untrustworthy" Hungarians from the state administration fell on the shoulders of these last-named officials. Guidelines were set down in the same law that dissolved the old administrative system. They specified that some of the Hungarian officials would be retained if they met three requirements: if they were willing to take an oath of allegiance to the Czechoslovak constitution; if they learned to speak, within one year, the new official langage of the state; and, finally, if they met certain unspecified qualifications required for holding a particular office.[10]

During the first months of occupation these regulations were generally enforced against only the higher officials, judges, and the most vociferous opponents of the Czechoslovak state. The demand for an oath of loyalty, however, confronted every Hungarian state employee with a thorny problem. According to the terms of the Belgrade Military Convention such a requirement was illegal. Legally, until the signing of the peace treaty, all occupied territories still formed a part of Hungary and the population remained Hungarian citizens.[11] Therefore, officials in those areas were still bound by their previous oaths to the Hungarian state. As Hungarian patriots they were also opposed to taking such an oath; more important, most feared the stigma of collaboration should any part of the occupied areas ultimately be returned to Hungary. To refuse, however, threatened them with an immediate loss of livelihood.

Loyalty oaths were required not only in Czechoslovakia, but also in Yugoslavia and Romania. Thus, from every part of the occupied areas Budapest was besieged with letters from officials caught in this dilemma asking for guidance or instructions. At first these requests were handled on the lower level by officials of various ministries. This resulted in a series of contradictory instructions being sent across the demarcation lines, compounding the confusion among the hapless Hungarian officials. After stormy debates the issue was resolved at the cabinet level. Hungarian officials were given permission to take these oaths under compulsion. Count Tivadar Battyány, the Hungarian Minister of Interior, sent the following telegram to all government employees under his jurisdiction: "The government calls upon all public employees to remain at their posts, to try to cooperate with the Czecho-Slovak and Romanian National Councils, but to take a loyalty oath only as a last restort, under duress. The government will not consider a forced oath a violation of citizen loyalty and official obligation. . . ."[12]

At the same time the Károlyi government assured those who refused the oath for whatever reason that Hungary would continue to pay their salaries.

Wholesale and summary dismissal of the Hungarian state employees in Slovakia did not prove practicable if any degree of continuity was to be retained. In fact, without the temporary services of the Hungarian officials the entire state administration was in danger of collapsing. The principal reason for this was the appallingly low number of qualified Slovaks to take their places. The entire Hungarian state bureaucracy had only thirty-six state functionaries, twelve clerks, thirty-eight county and twenty-one city officials and clerks, 119 village notaries, and one judge of Slovak nationality.[13] Shortage of educated Slovaks allegedly forced Prague to seek an alternate solution to the administrative problem.[14]

In Bohemia and Moravia local administration was largely in the hands of the Czechs — even under Austrian rule. An inordinately large number of Czechs also served in other parts of the monarchy in the Austrian bureaucracy. As these officials returned from the far-flung corners of the Austrian half of the monarchy or from military service, they created a surplus of office seekers in Bohemia. It was natural for the Prague government to send these officials to areas where the need was greatest. Transfer of Czech officials in large numbers could not take place until 1919. Only then were most of those Hungarians who were retained earlier and who met all the requirements for holding office dismissed under pretenses such as "intransigence" or "actions against the state."

In spite of careful planning the loss of the Hungarian official class created temporary chaos. This was especially true in the case of the judiciary. Law 1 of 1918 declared that all existing legal codes were to remain in force until they were superseded by new laws passed by the Prague parliament. That is, in Bohemia the old Austrian, and in Slovakia the old Hungarian, laws prevailed. Nevertheless, the old judicial system was one of the first targets for a thorough purge. In eastern Slovakia, for example, out of the 718 judges and prosecutors, after those who refused to take the oath of loyalty were dismissed, only five judges remained on the bench.[15] Even the best trained Czech judges could not interpret laws which they were unable to read.

Many dismissed state employees continued to cling to hopes of a reversal of the political situation or a change of heart by the Czechoslovak government. They sent petitions and protested their mistreatment but without result. Encouraged by the promise of continued payment of salaries and pensions in Hungary, in increasing numbers they came to the bitter decision that they had to leave Czechoslovakia. By early 1920 at least 926 state officials, 915 county officials, and 493 judges and prosecutors and their dependents arrived in Hungary, from Czechoslovakia.[16]

The uprooting of the Hungarian state administration and the destruction of the Hungarian middle class in Transylvania followed a pattern similar to that established in Slovakia. Legal authority to carry out wholesale changes in Transylvania issued from the Declaration of the Romanian National Council at Gyulafehérvár (December 2, 1918) and from the Royal Proclamation of Union of Transylvania with the Old Kingdom. Though the union was not recognized by the West until the Treaty of Trianon came into force in 1920, the Romanian government considered these matters strictly internal and, therefore, ignored all communications and protests on the subject.

The Romanian authorities used various methods to bring about reductions in the number of Hungarian officials and to force the departure of members of the Hungarian intelligentsia. In January 1919, the government announced the dissolution of the old Hungarian administration. Elected officials of villages, towns, and counties were replaced by prefects appointed by the central government. Lower officials in these administrative units were simultaneously informed that they would be retained at their posts if they were willing to take an oath of loyalty to the new Romanian authorities, whereby they would automatically acquire Romanian citizenship.[17]

Motivated by Hungarian patriotism most Hungarian officials were reluctant to sign such an oath despite the threat of dismissal, internment, or immediate expulsion. In characteristic fashion, however, dismissal did not always follow such refusal. In some areas the Hungarian officials were called upon, repeatedly, to comply with the order, without ever losing their jobs; while in other parts of Transylvania even those who did agree to sign were dismissed without any justification. In a rather arbitrary fashion some of the dismissed officials were declared *personae non gratae,* and given a short period of time to depart from the country.

Expulsion orders were issued in great numbers, without any discernible pattern except that they were almost inevitably directed against the Hungarian middle class — officials, nobles, lawyers, journalists, clergymen, teachers, and other civic leaders or more prosperous individuals. Often the reason was not more complicated than that the home of one or another Hungarian was coveted by a newly appointed Romanian official. For example, while some 17,000 families left Kolozsvár, the arrival of some 20,000 new Romanian officials and teachers created a grave housing shortage. As a result, in Kolozsvár alone, the lodgings of some 2000 teachers, professors, and officials were seized.[18] These individuals simply received notification that their apartments or houses had been reassigned by the housing authorities. They were ordered to vacate the premises within a few days and depart from the city. As it was impossible to acquire resident permits in other towns of Transylvania, loss of one's lodging was tantamount to expulsion from the country.

In late August 1919, another wave of expulsion orders struck shorttime residents of Transylvania, who were classified as strangers. According to these orders:

All strangers who had come to [in this case] Cluj [Kolozsvár] since the

30th of June 1914, are obliged to leave the city together with their families by the 15th of September 1919. Prior to their departure they have to report to the Commissioner of the Government in order to receive their gratuitous passports. . . .[19]

In addition, all those individuals who were born outside the new Kingdom of Romania had to reconfirm their residence papers, which, if denied, forced the departure of the individual concerned.

During the summer of 1920, after Hungary signed the Treaty of Trianon, the question of loyalty oath came up once more. The government again called upon all those Hungarian state officials still at their posts as well as those who in the past had lost their positions or pensions as a result of their refusal to sign the oath to do so within one month. This demand was coupled with a vague promise of restitution of rights and employment.[20] Some who complied were, indeed, given state employment though normally at a lower level than held in Hungary. Even those officials who were restored and were willing to cooperate with the Romanian authorities, frequently found their position increasingly precarious. Often they had to accept repeated demotions and reductions in pay. More important, in 1920, they were ordered to learn Romanian within one year or face dismissal once again.[21] This requirement was enforced also in the most arbitrary fashion. Since standards of proficiency were set by the local prefect, the Hungarian officials, fate depended upon the whims and fancies, the good will or venality of the prefect. Faced with these constant uncertainties, humiliations, deterioration of living standards, many Hungarian officials, even if they were not dismissed in 1920, decided to exercise the right granted in the Treaty of Trianon to leave Romania within one year of the ratification of that document.

In general the administrative change-over in Transylvania was executed at a slower rate and with far less efficiency than in Slovakia. It was carried out in a piecemeal, arbitrary fashion, without coordination or sufficient supervision by the central government. This gave rise to a considerable amount of corruption and abuse at the lower levels — often a blessing in disguise for the Hungarian population. Many of the easy-going Romanian officials closed their eyes to government orders whenever it seemed convenient to do so. These extremely poorly paid bureaucrats were often willing to make exceptions in exchange for small bribes. At the same time, however, some of them were also prone to respond to provocation with arbitrary acts and even brutality. This unpredictable behavior many Hungarians feared and found intolerable.

Replacement of Hungarian officials never reached the proportions achieved in Slovakia and the Voivodina. In the eastern Székely counties, for example, where the Hungarian population of Maros-Torda county comprised 57 percent of the total population, in Háromszék 83 percent, in Csík 86 percent, and in Udvarhely county 95 percent, a purely Romanian bureaucracy would have been totally ineffective. Transylvania, just like Slovakia, suffered from a shortage of qualified Romanian officials. Although in the old Hungarian state administration there were about six times as many Romanians as Slovak officials, their number was still minuscule. In 1910 out of 64,797 state employees 1889 were of Romanian origin. That is, although the Romanian minority had comprised approximately 16.1 percent of the total population of Hungary, less than one percent of the state employees and less than one half of one percent of the county and city officials had been Romanians. Only in the lowest positions and on the village level had their presence been numerically significant.[22]

In historic Transylvania 5.4 percent of the state officials, 7.4 percent of the county and city officials and 20.8 percent of the village notaries were Romanian. Unlike Slovakia, where qualified Czechs could be rushed in to fill the vacuum created by the removal of Hungarian officials, in Transylvania only the most poorly trained office seekers were available as replacements.

The official stratum was only one group of state employees that was affected by the anti-Hungarian policies of the Successor States. Officials and workers of the state enterprises, state monopolies, such as the salt and tobacco monopolies, and particularly the employees of state railways and postal service, were hit with almost the same severity. These enterprises, especially the white collar jobs, were also staffed predominantly by Hungarians. For example, 95.5 percent of the officers and 83 percent of the lesser personnel in the Hungarian Postal Service were Hungarians.[23] None of the Successor States was willing to leave these services in the hands of the Hungarians. In the Voivodina, and in Transylvania these officials and workers were eliminated as replacements for them were found. Again the largest numbers of Hungarians were retained in Transylvania, even after the purges. In Slovakia, on the other other, by a single dramatic action all Hungarian postal and railway employees were swept aside. This came about as the direct result of a patriotic strike by all Hungarian postal and railroad workers in the spring of 1919. The strike failed when thousands of Czech railway employees were rushed in to fill the gap. After this incident none of the striking workers were allowed to return to their job. Many of the Hungarian railroad workers and postal employees thereupon left Czechoslovakia. They, together with other groups of railroad workers expelled from Yugoslavia and Romania, were to form the only sizable group of refugees with a working-class background.[24]

Educational Reforms in the Successor States

Next to the state administration, the effects of uprooting Hungarians were most severely felt in the field of education. The leaders of the Successor States considered themselves duty bound to destroy the old Hungarian educational system and to provide the Slovaks, South Slavs, and Romanians with an adequate education in their native tongues. To achieve this goal it was necessary to remove most of the Hungarian school administrators, elementary and secondary teachers in the non-Hungarian areas, and to transform the universities to serve the new ruling nations.

Teachers in Hungarian state schools were the hardest hit, but the lay teachers of the denominational schools and subsequently even members of the teaching orders found it increasingly difficult to continue their educational functions. With their dismissal the careers of these teachers in the lost territories came to a sudden end. At best, neglected by the new authorities who failed to make any provisions for their employment, they had only one hope left. They could try to pick up pieces of their shattered lives across the Hungarian frontiers. With the closing of many Hungarian secondary schools and especially the Hungarian universities many of the Hungarian students also saw all opportunities for the future closed to them in the Successor States and joined their teachers in Hungary.

The Successor States inherited an educationally backward, often illiterate population. According to the 1910 census figures the lowest literacy rate existed in Ruthenia, where only 27.7 percent of the Ruthenian population was able to read and write. In some of the other minority areas the rate was almost as low. Only 36 percent of the Romanians, 48.5 percent of the Serbians, and 65 percent of the Slovaks were literate. At the same time this figure was 79 percent for the Hungarians and 82.3 percent for the German population of the country. It should be noted, however, that the rate of literacy in the Old Kingdom of Romania was no better than among the Romanians of Hungary (36 percent) and in Serbia it was worse (20.3 percent in 1900).[25]

State-owned and operated Hungarian schools, which comprised about a quarter of the transferred schools and had about a third of the teaching staff, were the first to fall victim to educational reforms in the Successor States.

Elementary Schools in the Transferred Territories
According to Language of Instruction[26]

| Language of Instruction | Transferred to | | | | | | | |
| | Czechoslovakia | | Romania | | Yugoslavia | | Bánát | |
	Schools	Teachers	Schools	Teachers	Schools	Teachers	Schools	Teachers
Hungarian	4,069	6,851	2,339	5,172	477	1,286	444	1,363
German	20	27	254	620	11	29	2	13
Slovak	287	425	1	9	12	38	3	12
Romanian	5	5	2,385	2,899			178	276
Serbian			6	6	99	248	117	352
Ruthenian	45	50			2	5		
Other					1	3	1	1
Total	4,426	7,358	5,045	8,706	602	1,609	745	2,017
Of these State Schools	1,070	2,294	1,319	3,269	176	424	218	722

It was simple enough to take over the physical facilities and to dismiss the Hungarian staff, but to find qualified replacements for the departing Hungarian teachers presented, at times, insoluble problems.

In Slovakia the solution to this problem was found through transfer of a large number of Czech teachers. This solution, however, soon created great tensions between Slovaks and Czechs. By 1926/27 the old situation was virtually reversed. The number of state-run Hungarian schools were reduced to 695 with 1235 teachers, while Slovak schools increased in number to 2652, with a teaching staff of 4354 Slovaks and Czechs.[27] In addition many of smaller, less-efficient communal or denominational schools were closed; in others the language of instruction was changed. The churches themselves were compelled to reduce the number of schools they maintained partly because of loss of revenue from their confiscated estates. In all, the number of Hungarian teachers was cut in about half. Over two-thirds of the dismissed Hungarian teachers left Slovakia; some found employment in the Hungarian schools, replacing those teachers who were purged because of their political views.[28]

The transfer of territories had the greatest impact on institutions of higher learning. The state-run School of Law of Kassa ceased to be Hungarian. Already, in 1918, the faculty and student body of the school was reestablished in Sopron. Similarly, the Protestant School of Law of Eperjes was transplanted to Miskolc. In the spring of 1920 the history and language departments of the Queen Elizabeth University of Pozsony was moved to Budapest, followed by the medical school in the fall and by the law and political science divisions at the end of the 1920–21 academic year. Ultimately, in 1923, the university was relocated to Pécs.[29]

In 1914 the number of Hungarian elementary schools in the Voivodina was 645. These schools employed 1832 teachers, nearly all Hungarians.[30] In 1919 the Serbian government with a single blow abolished the old Hungarian school system and dismissed over two-thirds of the Hungarian teachers. Thereafter, the educational facilities available to the Hungarian minority was limited to some 450 parallel or mixed Serbian-Hungarian schools, a number equivalent, in capacity, to about a sixth of what had been used by the Hungarian population before the war. Consequently, nearly half of the Hungarian parents had to send their children to Serbian schools, or as it often happened they kept their children away from school altogether. Those who still insisted on a Hungarian education had only one available option: to send their children to Hungary. This often resulted in the moving of the entire family to Hungary.

The number of Hungarian elementary schools in Transylvania was above 2600. Out of these the Hungarian state maintained about 1600; the rest were community, Catholic, Unitarian, and Calvinist schools.[31] Destroying the Hungarian character of the educational system began in 1919, with the takeover of the state-run schools. In roughly two-thirds of these the language of instruction was changed to Romanian; by 1922 only 562 did remain Hungarian.[32] But even in Hungarian schools part of the teaching staff was replaced with Romanian teachers who were to instruct the pupils in the Romanian language and history. Loss of schools, for Hungarians, sharply increased pressure on the private, denominational educational system. As a result of the rapid increase of pupils between 1919–20 the number of church-operated schools doubled. Most new schools were poorly financed, substandard, makeshift operations, in unsuitable buildings with all-too-few teachers.

In 1921 the Romanian government decided to reduce the number of private schools. By 1925 about 250 denominational schools had had to close their doors, with the dismissal of a corresponding proportion of teachers.[33] The attack upon the private school system was many sided but uncoordinated. Almost from the first month of occupation most church schools found themselves in great financial difficulties. They lost the substantial state support they enjoyed in the past; contributions from the church membership fell off sharply; and the land reform cut deeply into the wealth of the churches and into school endowments.[34] Even more important, most private schools lost accreditation. After

1924 they could no longer issue valid diplomas, only certificates of attendance. Private *gymnasiums* were not allowed to administer their own baccalaureate examinations and the state examining boards refused to pass most of the Hungarian students. In 1925, for example, 77 percent of the Calvinist, 79 percent of the Unitarian, and 70 percent of the Catholic students failed. Even more severely hit were the Jewish students of Moldavia, where only 4 percent were allowed to pass. This policy served as a *de facto numerus clausus,* limiting the number of Hungarian students who became eligible to continue their education at the universities.

In 1919 the University of Kolozsvár was closed after its Hungarian faculty refused to take the required oath of loyalty to King Ferdinand. This was a major blow to the entire Hungarian minority. The university was reopened with a new Romanian faculty, but the majority of the Hungarian students, suspected of irredentist sentiments, were not readmitted.[35] As a result almost the entire faculty and a majority of the Hungarian students crossed over to Hungary, where, in the spring of 1920, the university was reestablished at Budapest. Subsequently the university found a permanent home in the city of Szeged. The Law School of Nagyvárad also lost its Hungarian character and that of Máramarossziget was first relocated in Hódmezővásárhely and then merged with the School of Law of Kecskemét.[36]

The attacks on the powers of the churches had a deeper political significance. In the past the churches had formed the basic communities that embraced the various nationalities. Since membership in a church generally coincided with a particular nationality, the attack on Hungarian influence in Transylvania had to be coupled with destruction of the power and influence of Hungarian churches. As the Hungarian political organizations, newspapers, clubs, and cultural institutions were suppressed, and as the Hungarian bureaucracy was destroyed as an organized group, these Hungarian churches, Catholic, Calvinist and Unitarian, assumed a greater role in the lives of the Hungarians; they became the focal point of national loyalties. Only these churches remained purely Hungarian minority institutions, hence they increasingly became politicized, becoming the most vocal defenders of the rights of Hungarians. It was not possible to destroy these institutions completely. But it was within the power of the Romanian government to silence the most ardent and outspoken church leaders through intimidation or expulsion, to reduce their economic power, and through secularization of education to remove at least in part the masses of Hungarian children from the influence of these churches.

Thus through often negative and arbitrary measures the Hungarian minority was largely deprived of their schools without, however, achieving a corresponding improvement for the Romanian population. The Romanian government's most important political objective, however, was achieved, which in the early postwar years seemed far more important than long-range benefits of a carefully thought-out restructuring of the educational system. By reducing the number of Hungarian schools and limiting the number of Hungarians with secondary and university education, a long-range emasculation of the Hungarian middle class was assured. Without proper degrees the children of the middle class could not maintain the status of their parents. The prospect of loss of social status in the extremely hierarchical and status conscious Hungarian society was looked upon as perhaps even a greater tragedy than the loss of political power. Understandably, Hungarians of Transylvania bitterly opposed these measures and considered the educational and cultural policies of the Romanian government as nothing short of attempted cultural and class genocide. To them, the Romanians, it seemed, were bent on a total eradication of everything that was Hungarian — culture, education, administration, system of law, theaters, universities, language, and, ultimately, even the Hungarian minority.

Both the educational reforms and the reorganization of the administrative structures in the Successor States displaced thousands of Hungarian officials and educators. A vast majority could not again fit into the economy of the new states; consequently, they were forced to flee to Hungary. In 1924, according to the somewhat incomplete figures of the National Refugee Office, 15,835 state functionaries from the Successor States were living in Hungary. Additionally, there were 5772 municipal and village officials, 19,092 railway employees, and 3554 other state employees. The number of refugee students was 86,323.[37] László Buday provided the most detailed breakdown of the various categories. He accounts for 18,707 refugee state employees, distributed among the various categories as follows:[38]

Distribution of Refugee State Employees in 1920

Occupation	Slovakia	Romania	From Yugoslavia	Other	Total
State officials	1,926	2,843	525	260	5,554
County officials	915	1,406	255	98	2,674
Judges and public prosecutors	493	854	210	52	1,609
Elementary school teachers	2,121	2,795	795	136	5,847
Commercial high school teachers	360	418	156	63	997
Gymnasium teachers	276	391	95	76	838
Vocational school teachers	65	14	27	20	126
Kindergarten teachers	345	408	98	29	880
Teacher schools	76	87	19	—	182
Total	6,577	9,216	2,180	734	18,707

Chapter 4
Effects of the Land Reforms in
The Successor States

The effect of land, administrative, and educational reforms caused the Hungarian minority to lose its former leading social position and political power. Through the loss of much of its upper and middle classes, it became a sociologically less differentiated group. This was part of the intended goal of the governments in all the Successor States. Dominated by fear of a Hungarian irredenta within their borders, they decided on taking drastic measures against the potentially most volatile and economically most affluent strata of Hungarian minorities. Administrative and education reforms destroyed the power of the middle classes; agrarian reforms eliminated the economic strength and political influence of the landed nobility.

Without doubt the archaic landownership system of Hungary needed reform. But poverty among the national minorities was not due to the nationality policies of Hungary as, at times, it was asserted. It had many causes: poor agricultural soil in the mountainous regions where some of the minorities were concentrated, rapid increase of rural population, and the survival of a feudal aristocracy, in itself an amalgam of various nationalities. In fact, the ratio of landless peasants was the highest among the Hungarians. The proportion of landless peasants among the various nationalities was as follows: Hungarian 49.6 percent; Serbian 41.9 percent; Slovak 33.7 percent; Romanian 32.3 percent; Ruthenian 24.4 percent; and German 29 percent.[1]

During the last two decades before the war, pressures for land reform had greatly intensified. Despite rapid industrialization, the country's economy could not absorb the growing agricultural population. With the passing of each generation the tiny peasant plots dwindled to insignificance as heirs divided meager legacies among themselves. The poverty of the countryside was further aggravated by a series of poor harvests at home, and by depressed grain prices in the West. A growing revolutionary movement among the underemployed and unemployed rural proletariat merely underlined the gravity of the situation.

Some viewed increased overseas emigration as the only solution to the rural overpopulation problem, as a safety valve that promised to relieve the pressures for land reform. The Hungarian government seemed to have shared this view and did little to discourage the nearly one and a half million people who emigrated to the United States between 1900 and 1912.[2] Mass exodus of peasants, which in some areas reached epidemic proportions, however, aroused the concern of Hungarian patriots. Large-scale emigration of Hungarian peasants promised to reduce the proportion of the Hungarian population in the country. To prevent their departure, the Hungarian peasants had to be drawn into the life of the nation by satisfying their ancient hunger for land. Thus, the question of land reform, and, in general, the question of social reform, came to be entwined with the complicated nationality problem. Nonetheless, before World War I no substantial social or land reform was introduced.

Promise of a radical land redistribution by the Károlyi government and, still more important, by the Hungarian Soviet Republic, acted as a sharp spur to all the Successor States to carry out similar programs. It was inconceivable that Slovak, Romanian, or Serbian peasants should be receiving less under their own governments than they were promised by the Hungarians. As Karel Kramář, the prime minister of Czechoslovakia, put it: "It is necessary to take measures concerning the selling of the large estates in Slovakia, that the people may see that we have in this respect as much socialistic sense as the Hungarians who suddenly promise the Slovaks immediate division and distribution of the large estates."[3] The Romanian government had already committed itself to land reform, long before acquisition of any part of Hungary was predictable. This commitment was made by King Ferdinand in a Royal Proclamation to his soldiers on the battlefield of Mareşeşti,[4] and it was reconfirmed, in 1917, by the Romanian parliament. The Successor States were also very conscious of the far-reaching political and social consequences of land expropriation. It was just as important to destroy the economic power of the Hungarian landowners as it was to wrest from the middle class the instruments of political power, that is, if the integration of the newly gained territories into a new nation-state was to succeed.

Despite pressures it was not possible to put into effect the most radical land reform proposals. The Hungarian landowners found some powerful allies, especially in Czechoslovakia, in the native landowners and upper bourgeoisie. In Czechoslovakia not only Czech, but also German landowners, who were treated with greater circumspection than the Hungarians were staunchly opposed to radical land reform. Even the Czech bourgeoisie urged moderation. They believed that outright confiscation of landed property without compensation would establish a dangerous precedent. Thus when the land reform was carried out, the landowners were not completely dispossessed and some of the lesser holdings remained altogether intact. In Romania and Yugoslavia, on the other hand, where legal consistency seemed less important, the native landowning classes were placated by a double standard of reform that allowed a more severe treatment of Hungarian landowners.

The first land expropriation law in Czechoslovakia was passed in December 1918, primarily directed against Habsburg estates. In the following year the complete Land Expropriation Act was passed. Under this law all arable land holdings above 150 hectares, or above 250 hectares of mixed agricultural and forest lands, were subject to expropriation. The law allowed an individual, under some special circumstances, to retain a larger estate if its retention was in the public interest, but under no circumstances could this estate exceed 500 hectares. Agricultural industries not dependent on the estate for raw materials were exempt from expropriation, as were the properties of local communities. The law guaranteed compensation for the expropriated land, except to the Habsburgs and to "citizens of an enemy state." This latter stipulation had ominous implication for Hungarians. Even those who were compensated did not receive a fair price. Land values were assessed at 1913–15 prices. Compensation was paid in Czechoslovak crowns, equating it with the prewar Austrian crown. In 1920, however, the actual value of the Czech crown was not more than one-sixth of the 1914 Austrian crown.[5]

Slightly above four million hectares of land were sequestered for land reform, comprising 28.6 percent of the total territory of Czechoslovakia. Out of this 1,396,135 hectares were in Slovakia, and 238,908 hectares in Ruthenia. From these, however, only 498,693 hectares in Slovakia and 45,379 hectares in Ruthenia were arable land, suitable for distribution among the landless of dwarfholding peasantry.[6]

In all Czechoslovakia 1913 owners of large estates suffered expropriation of some land. Through political maneuvering, however, they were able to retain a far greater share of land than the maximum set by the land reform law. From the roughly 4-million hectares of land subject to expropriation the landowners kept over 2 million; from the 1.3-million hectares of arable land about 426,000. In Slovakia, 873, mostly Hungarian landowners, came under the Land Expropriation Act. Yet, in 1932 they still had in their possession 1,118,417 hectares of land, of which 229,406 were arable.[7]

In territories ceded to Yugoslavia the number of Hungarian landowners who suffered under the land reform was smaller, but their losses were more extensive. The land reform process was put into motion in January 1919 by a Royal Proclamation, followed in February by the Preliminary Order for Land Reform. This order became the governing law for expropriation and redistribution of land, though subsequently it had to be amended to cover unexpected cases and to clarify points which had been left obscure by the initial act. In the three provinces where Hungarians owned land — the Voivodina, Croatia-Slavonia, and Slovenia — 850 large estates were subject to expropriation. Of the 675 private estates, 123 had Hungarian owners.[8] In these provinces the state expropriated 436,000 hectares of arable land and a grand total of 750,000 hectares. From their roughly 180,000 hectares the Hungarian landowners lost about 111,000, comprising about 61.5 percent of the total land they owned.[9] Furthermore, the property that they were allowed to retain was generally of poor quality and of little economic value.

Out of the 123 Hungarian landowners 61 had fled to Hungary before the land reform. Collectively they owned about 126,000 hectares of land in Yugoslavia, or over 2,000 hectares a holding. The losses of these refugee landowners account for about 81 percent, or 90,000 hectares, of the total property that was expropriated from Hungarian landlords. The 62 landowners who remained in Yugoslavia owned much smaller es-

Property Losses of Hungarian Refugee Landlords[10]

Estates in	Number of landlords	Property owned (in hectares)	From this expropriated (in hectares)	percentage
Voivodina	41	74,199	57,356	77.3
Croatia-Slavonia	13	37,267	20,922	56.1
Slovenia	7	14,989	11,784	78.6
Total	61	126,455	90,062	71.2

Property Losses of Hungarian Landlords
Remaining in Yugoslavia

Estates in	Number of landlords	Property owned (in hectares)	From this expropriated (in hectares)	percentage
Voivodina	50	31,045	11,146	35.9
Croatia-Slavonia	11	17,340	6,434	37.1
Slovenia	1	5,011	3,042	60.7
Total	62	53,396	20,622	38.6
Combined total	123	179,851	110,684	61.5

tates, about 860 hectares each. The refugees were allowed to retain only about a third of their property; those who accepted Yugoslav citizenship kept about 61 percent of their smaller estates.[11]

The Romanian agrarian reform was the most extensive in East Central Europe;[12] it was also the most controversial. A poisonous dispute between Hungary and Romania raged for over a decade over Romania's right to expropriate the private property of refugee Hungarians.

The Romanian land reform evoked the greatest emotional response in Hungary, mostly because the loss of Transylvania was considered to be the most unjust part of the Trianon treaty. In reality, the Hungarian peasant population was treated with greater severity during the land reforms in Yugoslavia. Also, and contrary to assertions of some Hungarians, the Romanian land reform was not introduced with the sole intention of taking revenge on the Hungarian population. It was as much a response to the severe agrarian crisis in the Regat itself. As we have noted, the Romanian government made a wartime promise to peasants to distribute, after the war, land holdings of the crown, foreigners, corporations, and absentee landlords, and to expropriate, for purpose of land reform, 2-million hectares of land from the native aristocracy. Several times before World War I, promises of major land reform had been made to the Romanian peasantry. Each time — 1864, 1881, 1889, and 1907 — they were made after peasant uprisings of varying intensity, but each time the boyar class was able to circumvent reform. Thus, in 1918, large estates still contained nearly half of all arable land in the Kingdom of Romania.[13] Postponement of the promised land reform after the war, however, was not possible if an even greater peasant revolt than that of 1907 was to be averted. Naturally, the principle of land reform had to be also extended to the newly acquired territories.

Hungarian critics of the Romanian reform, especially the refugees argued that, although in the Regat land reform was perhaps justifiable, in Transylvania landed property was more evenly distributed. Some even boldly asserted that the existing "distribution of property was ideal."[14] There is an element of truth in this statement. In Transylvania aristocratic estates were generally smaller than in other parts of Hungary, as were the middle and small noble holdings. At the same time the number of landowners was greater. The nobility itself was more numerous, but, more imporant, large privileged groups such as the Székelys owned individual small plots, and held communally substantial amounts of mostly forest and pasture lands. Consequently land was more evenly distributed among holdings of various sizes:[15]

Land Distribution in Historic Transylvania

Size of land holdings		Percentage of land held	
Dwarf Holdings	0–5 yokes*		19.88
	5–10	19.25	
Small Holdings	10–50	33.67	58.60
	50–100	5.68	
	100–200	4.04	
Middle Estates	200–500	6.16	15.18
	500–1,000	4.98	
Great Estates	1,000 and above		6.34

* 1 yoke = 0.75 hectares

The Romanian population, comprising 16.1 percent of the total population of the Kingdom of Hungary, possessed roughly 16 percent of the land in the country, that is, their landholdings were commensurate with their numbers. Hungarian polemists on this issue insist that, starting with the emancipation of the serfs, the Romanian population had made some significant gains in terms of acquiring wealth. During the last decades of the monarchy a rapid stratification of the once homogeneous Romanian population was clearly discernible. A significant number of rich peasants arose, from whose ranks the Romanian intelligentsia and a thin stratum of commercial bourgeois class also emerged.[16] During the 1890s Romanian peasants with the aid of land speculators and various Romanian banks in Transylvania began to purchase estates from the Hungarian landowners at an accelerating rate,[17] and subdivided these into smaller parcels suitable for single family cultivation. This process, however, was merely part of the overall economic transformation of the country. In other parts of Hungary absorption of the small- and medium-sized noble estates into the great estates was well advanced by the 1890s. There the landless nobility was already urbanized and integrated into the state bureaucracy. In more backward Transylvania, where much of the broken mountainous landscape was unsuitable for large-scale cultivation, the pressure of the large estates was felt less intensely. Consequently small- and medium-sized noble estates survived longer. By the 1890s, however, unprofitability of these estates made their possession increasingly less desirable and, to many gentry families, the high prices offered by the land speculators proved to be irresistible. Romanian peasants, to whom most other avenues of advancement remained closed, gladly paid the often exorbitant price for land. Despite these gains the Romanian population was still at a great disadvantage when compared with the other national groups in Transylvania. While about a third of the Romanian peasants were moderately well off, two-thirds of them lived in poverty. And, although they collectively owned 16 percent of the total territory of Hungary, in historic Transylvania, where their numbers made up 55.9 percent of the population, they owned only about 24 percent of the land. Nor was this property evenly distributed among Romanians. In the southern counties peasants were more prosperous than in the north, and the registered property gains left the vast majority of poorer peasants untouched everywhere. According to Zoltán Szász, in historic Transylvania, 61.7 percent of the landless agricultural workers, 68 percent of the agricultural workers on the estates and 71.6 percent of the peasants with less than five yokes of land were Romanian.[18]

The Romanians' steady acquisition of land was viewed by the Hungarians, and especially by the Transylvanian landowners, with increasing alarm.[19] In it, they perceived the beginnings of the Romanization of Transylvania, a process which they felt powerless to halt. The rapid concentration of the Hungarian population in urban areas, and the abandonment of the countryside to the Romanian peasantry signified, to them, the twilight of the Hungarian character of Transylvania. To the Hungarian gentry, this process of destruction of the landed class in the minority areas represented a double danger. First, growth of an independent land-holding peasantry endangered their power base as the dominant economic and social group. Second, departure of Hungarian landlord from the minority village promoted the growth of minority nationalism.

In discussions among landowners about this rapid loss of Hungarian presence in the Transylvanian countryside, one detects a rising anxiety, a sense of doom and desperation. In a highly revealing speech in 1912, Count István Bethlen, who after the war became the leading spokesman of the refugees, commented on developments in Szolnok-Doboka county:

> The village which a Hungarian landlord leaves falls to Romanian leadership on the day of his departure, and in the same hour the assimilation of the remaining Hungarian minority begins.
>
> For this reason . . . it is not possible to overemphasize the nation-sustaining role of the Hungarian landholding class not only in Szolnok-Doboka, but also in the entire Transylvanian basin. . . . Nor can one sufficiently lament the destruction of the middle-sized estates during the last few years. . . .[20]

To Bethlen the issue was simple: if Transylvania was to be saved the Hungarian landed class had to be saved first. He proposed, therefore, extensive financial aid to the Hungarian middle- and large-estate owners, massive repurchasing of Romanian-owned land, entailment of Hungarian properties by enacting a law of primogeniture to prevent proliferation of estates, and an energetic colonization of Transylvania by Hungarian peasants.

To many Hungarians it was a silent but deadly war with the survival of Hungary as a Hungarian nation-state at stake; resistance to the "New Conquest" of Hungary by the Romanians through gradual infiltration and subversion. The Hungarian population was slowly forced back to urban islands and slowly but inevitably Hungarians were engulfed by the surrounding sea of Romanians.[21]

To the Transylvanian Hungarian landowners the Romanian postwar land reform was only the final act in this long struggle for Romanization of Transylvania through deliberate destruction of the Hungarian land-owning stratum.

Actual expropriation and redistribution of Hungarian estates began long before the Romanian government could work out a program for land reform. The Romanian peasantry, after news of the monarchy's collapse reached them, sensing that the old order was also to disappear, spontaneously began seizing castles and lands of the Hungarian landlords. The Romanian government, when it finally established its authority over Transylvania, had no alternative but to sanction what was already in some places a *fait accompli*. In August 1919 the government permitted, as an intermediate measure, the seizure of large estates for the purpose of forced leases. Thus, even before the 1921 land reform law went into effect, 2.38 million yokes of land were expropriated in Transylvania, mostly from Hungarian landlords.[22]

Under the 1921 act the government was empowered to expropriate, in full, estates of foreign citizens and those of public and private institutions. Private landlords in Transylvania were allowed to retain 28.7 hectares of land in the mountainous region; 57.5 hectares in the hills; and 115 hectares in the plains, provided the demand in the area was moderate; and in cases when demands were satisfied, up to 287 hectares of land in all.[23] This upper limit, however, was rarely reached. In contrast the Romanian landowners of the Regat retained a minimum of 100 hectares in the mountains, 150–250 hectares in the hills, and up to 500 hectares in the plains. Furthermore, they were allowed to retain maximum limits from each of the categories separately, whereas in Transylvania the maximum limit applied to the total holdings of a single owner.

In all, about 2.9 million yokes of private and 210,000 yokes of state lands were expropriated. About two-thirds of the expropriated private property was owned by individual proprietors, and the rest by churches, educational institutions, and communes. The exact number of the injured parties is not known, but the number of estates affected by the land reform was estimated to be 8963.[24] Since public institutions and some of the magnates often owned several estates, the number of individuals who suffered some loss must have been under 8000. This number excludes all communes, where every individual member was affected by the loss, but it includes some 1700 of the 8865 Hungarian peasant families who settled in Transylvania after 1869. On the average they owned small farms of 14–16 yokes in extent and lost collectively 58 percent of their land.

Distribution of land among various peasant applicants followed a slightly different pattern in the three Successor States. In Transylvania, from the 3.1 million yokes of expropriated land, only between 800–900,000 yokes were suitable for distribution. From this amount about 633,000 yokes were actually distributed among poor peasants who owned less than 10 yokes of land. 213,000 of the recipients were Romanians, 46,000 Hungarians, 16,000 Germans, and 6000 of other nationalities.[25] Thus, at the expense of less than 9000 private landowners around 300,000 impoverished peasants acquired some land. Although most of the injured parties were Hungarians and although impoverished or landless Romanian peasants were far more likely to have received land than their Hungarian counterparts, the number of Hungarians whose lives improved through the land reform was only a fraction of those who lost. Not surprisingly, no mass exodus of Hungarian peasants took place from Transylvania. Those few who did flee to Hungary left for other reasons; their displacement was not the result of Romanian agrarian policies. Significantly, even the dispossessed Hungarian peasant settlers, whose cause was publicly championed by the Hungarian government, when they finally decided to leave Transylvania, instead of going to Hungary, emigrated to North America. The Hungary of the 1920s, where the old land tenure system remained in force, held but few incentives and few attractions to the Hungarian peasants in the Successor States.

Treatment of Hungarian peasants was less generous in Czechoslovakia; yet, the Hungarian peasant population also made some gains through the land reform. Out of a total of 175,000 small land grants in Slovakia, only an estimated 17,000 recipients were Hungarians. Together they received less than 18,000 hectares of land. True, too, Hungarian peasants were generally better off than their Slovak counterparts. They owned more land and lived in the more fertile plain region.

The principal grievance of the Hungarians, and indeed the Slovaks as well, was that the chief beneficiaries of the land reform were not the landless peasants. First priority in granting the allotments went to the legionnaires and ex-soldiers of the republic, who received 10 hectares each. A blatantly political attempt was also made to change the predominantly Hungarian composition of the population along the Hungarian frontiers through colonization. These colonists were selected from the politically trustworthy, mostly Czech peasants, who on the average received 16 hectares of land each; the average allotment of the Slovak and Hungarian peasants was only 1.4 hectares. The population was equally resentful of the way the "estate remnants" were distributed. These were mostly formed around the old manor houses, agricultural buildings, that could not be utilized as small farms; hence, from these, middle-sized farms were created. In Slovakia 55,000 hectares were distributed, in the form of residual estates, among 455 individuals, mostly as outright political favors. Out of these, 102 recipients were enterprising Hungarians, who collectively received nearly 10,000 hectares of land.[26]

On the whole, just as in Romania, the overall treatment of the Hungarian peasant population was not such as to induce it to leave the country. The Hungarian peasantry, like the entire agrarian population of Czechoslovakia, benefited from agricultural policies that were designed to make Czechoslovakia agriculturally self-sufficient. Hungarian peasants left the country only under special circumstances, when, for example, the new boundaries cut them off from their lands, or when separated families wished to reunite.

Yugoslavia meted out the harshest treatment of the Hungarian peasantry in all of the Successor States. The Serbian government looked on the conquered lands as spoils of war to be divided among its own soldiers. As a result, Hungarian peasants were completely excluded from the benefits of land reform. The Belgrade government, ostensibly for military reasons, prohibited land grants to the minorities within a 50 kilometer zone along the Hungarian frontier. Since most Hungarian peasants resided within this zone, they could not even apply for a grant from the confiscated estates. With a single stroke of the pen, another edict issued in September 1920, excluded all Hungarians by stating that "land may be received only by those families whose family heads are Yugoslav citizens and who at the time are residents of the affected village."[27] Thus, a Hungarian peasant, who was excluded within the border zone, could not apply in another area. Furthermore, at the time of this edict the citizenship of the minorities were still in doubt. This harsh treatment was especially unjustified in Yugoslavia, where most of the Hungarian peasants were, at best, dwarf holders or landless. At the same time, the Serbian population of the Voivodina was more prosperous; yet, they were the chief beneficiaries of the reform. Consequently, in 1930, out of some 120,000 landless agricultural laborers in the area, some 90,000, or about 75 percent were Hungarians.[28] As a result of a proportionally larger percentage of the refugees from Yugoslavia were of peasant origin than either those from Czechoslovakia or Romania. The strongest peasant movement across the frontiers can be detected in the immediate border regions, especially in Bács-Bodrog and Zala counties. The peasant refugees played an insignificant role in the political life of Hungary of the 1920s; largely ignored by the government, they remained passive.

Among the refugees in Hungary there was another substantial group whose displacement was directly related to the agrarian reforms in the Successor States. The destruction of the large estates spelled economic ruin not only for the landlords themselves, but for all those whose employment or livelihood depended on the survival of the great estate system and the aristocratic style of life. Such were large- and medium-sized lease-holders from the great estates, and commercial agents of the aristocrats. Also, most estate employees, managers, overseers, book-keepers, clerks, as well as agricultural and forestry experts, hunters, and game keepers, fell into this category. In addition, many of the lesser employees and servants in the household of the owners were suddenly without employment. Skills of a coachman, hunting dog expert, saddle maker, and of the many craftsmen working on the estates, were useless in an egalitarian society. Some of these men were pensioned off; others received small plots of land. But the fate of the majority was bleak. Even those who benefited from the land reforms found that the few acres they received were insufficient to maintain themselves. The destruction of the estates also meant social disaster for many of those individuals who had risen from the ranks of the peasantry to posts in the estate hierarchy, or, in the case of the poorest members of the gentry, who had sunk to the post of a clerk. Some could not accept the idea of becoming again, or for the first time, a peasant.

Even agricultural experts had difficulty in finding employment. Peasants tilling their few acres could not utilize their expertise. The governments of Czechoslovakia and Romania made some attempts at salvaging their skills by making provisions for carving out larger units from the old estates or using some of the estate remnants to set up model farms. Few Hungarian agriculturalists could qualify for these choice grants. Most, therefore, along with other estate employees, followed their employers to Hungary, where often they found employment on the remaining estates of the latter.

In summary, it was the aristocracy, and to a lesser degree, the gentry that was most negatively affected by the postwar land reforms in the Successor States. The psychological impact of the destruction of the large estate system, however, was felt beyond the landowning class itself; it was registered also by the landless gentry as a blow to their status in society. Disappearance of the Hungarian landowning class symbolized, to them, the passing of a social and value system that was based on the privileged position of the nobility. Though these gentry families had lost their lands, they clung desperately to their noble titles, attitudes, and customs, but these could remain meaningful only as long as the landed nobility survived. With the passing into oblivion of the aristocracy, the lower nobility also had to face the danger of extinction. In postwar Hungary these two classes would join hands, led by the refugees, to restore the old order they had once enjoyed.

Chapter 5
Radicalization of the Refugees:
Crisis in the Hungarian Noble Identity

The suicide note of a young Polish refugee in Balzac's *Cousin Bette* reads:

> I am Count Wenceslas Steinbock, born in Prelia, in Livonia.
> Let no one be blamed for my death; the reasons for my suicide are in these words of Kosciusko's [sic]: *Finis Poloniae!*
> The great-nephew of a brave general of Charles XII could not beg. A delicate constitution made military service impossible for me, and yesterday saw the end of the hundred thalers with which I came to Paris from Dresden. . . .
> I beg my compatriots not to blame the French Government. I did not make myself known as a refugee; I did not ask for aid. . . . I met no other exile; no one in Paris knows that I exist.
> I die in Christian faith. May God forgive the last of the Steinbocks![1]

Many elements of the complex psychological chemistry of the refugees are compressed into this note. The pride of this young Polish aristocrat, his sense of isolation, loneliness, and worthlessness, his inability to function in a new environment, his yearning for death with the death of Poland, all are, in some form, typical responses of political exiles.

In general, the emotional crisis in the life of a refugee issues from sudden uprooting and from an inability to adjust psychologically to the impact of rapid change.

There are various types of responses to the resulting emotional loss. Some are extremes: exaggerated passivity, or violent aggressive behavior. Neither of these reactions seems permanent; the same individual may, upon provocation, pass from one emotional state to the other. This behavior may be interpreted as an indication of intense stress, and of a serious damage to the inner personality core of an individual that he can no longer defend through normal means.

The sudden surge of new experiences tends to inflict precisely such stresses upon the refugees. They are disoriented and overwhelmed by the total change of their environment. To new situations, to a new environment, the refugees react by turning inward and erecting blocks against new stimuli, that is, by a reduced emotional response.[2] Since it is not possible to revenge their loss, the refugees turn the accumulated aggression against themselves, which ultimately may find its overt manifestation in a high rate of neuroses.[3]

But for Hungarian refugees, who were displaced through changes in boundaries, yet who still remained within the confines of their native civilization, the crisis of identity assumed different dimensions. Their response to displacement was also different. The psychological adjustments demanded of them was not so drastic. Their losses were partially shared by some of their fellow countrymen in Hungary. Their disorientation and sense of hopelessness was also less intense. The most significant difference was, however, the absence of pressures to abandon their national identity. Thus is was only part of their identity that was endangered and made nonfunctional. The shared cultural roots with the population of inner Hungary also provided a realistic base for adjustment. The refugees, however, often resisted assimilation; they, instead, made attempts to reshape Hungarian society in their own image.

At the same time, while their national identity was not directly threatened, the sense of guilt for forsaking the lost territories was just as severe as for those who took refuge in foreign countries. That sense of guilt, combined with anxieties emerging from their endangered social identities, created pressures in the refugees to amplify those parts of their identity in which they still felt secure. They felt compelled to take, if necessary, extreme measures to restore or gain compensation for their various losses. They stood ready to join virtually any radical political movement that promised a restoration, or a relief from the emotional stress. Instead of passivity, these refugees directed their accumulated aggression outward, against common enemies. Their political organizations, therefore, tended toward violence, at times toward extreme violence.

Evolution of Noble Identity and Attitudes

Two main pillars of the Hungarian noble's identity were his corporate and national consciousness. For centuries these two levels of consciousness were inseparably intertwined in the minds of the nobility. Consciousness of nationality, in fact, was a derivative of class consciousness. Historically it represented an awareness of the common interest of the privileged population of Hungary to the exclusion of the non-noble or bonded population. That is, Hungarian noble national identity was not a substitute for or alternative to the traditional corporate identity, but merely an elaboration of it. There is scattered evidence that already in the thirteenth century the term *natio* was used in describing the community of the privileged. But not until the early sixteenth century was the noble estate-consciousness welded into a coherent national ideology.[4]

If we are to understand the remarkable survival of this ideology down to the twentieth century, we must appreciate three historical factors: the survival of the Hungarian nobility as a functional elite; the unusual size and distribution of the noble class; and, finally, the adaptability of this class to economic and political changes throughout the centuries.

In the Balkans the Ottoman invasion led to a disappearance of the native nobility. In Hungary, the opposite happened: the Battle of Mohács (1526) signaled the beginning of a revitalization of the Hungarian nobility. This was achieved, first, through the development and monopolization of the county institutions; second, by opening the ranks of the nobility to new recruits. With the disappearance of central authority the burden of defense fell on the shoulders of the nobility, forcing it to resume its original military function. The counties, led by the local magnates and nobility, quickly became centers of military organizations; they exercised power in nearly complete freedom, independently levied taxes, raised armies, maintained fortifications, and even negotiated with foreign powers. Throughout subsequent centuries the counties retained much of their autonomy and remained the power base and focal point of life for the local nobility. Defense of the privileges of the counties — in their minds — became synonymous with the interests of the nobility and the interests of the nation.

The great increase in the size of the nobility also dates back to the sixteenth and seventeenth centuries. Ranks of the old nobility, decimated by constant warfare, had to be replenished. Ennoblement served as an incentive to military recruitment. At times it also was used to disarm dangerous and rebellious groups, as in the case of the *hajdúk*, who, otherwise, might have become instruments of social revolution. Runaway or uprooted serfs, retainers of nobles, upon joining the garrisons of frontier forts gained their freedom from feudal bondage and could hope for a noble title as reward for their services. As a contemporary poem put it, these soldiers "drew their noble crests with swords dipped in red blood. . . ." Militant refugee nobles from the Turkish-occupied territories captained many of these garrisons, and were also prominent among the *hajdúk*. These refugee nobles also led the fight for extention of nobility to their soldiers, and often divided the lands surrounding their forts in forms of *timars,* retaining for themselves a lion's share as compensation for their own losses.[5] The newly elevated individuals joined the 'Hungarian nation' by adopting the ideology and attitudes of the nobility.

The first relatively reliable statistics on the distribution and extraordinary size of the nobility date from the reign of Joseph II. According to the 1788 census figures the total number of nobles in Hungary and Transylvania was about 370,000, comprising about 4.8 percent and 4.4 percent respectively of the total population of these areas. During the nineteenth century the number of nobles increased in absolute figures, but their proportion to the rest of the population remained about the same, around five percent.[6] That is, about one out of every twenty persons was a member of the privileged estate, and 9.7 percent, or one in ten, among the Hungarian population.

The basic patterns of the nobility's geographic distribution were also established during the sixteenth and seventeenth centuries. The proportion of nobles to commoners and serfs was the lowest in those areas which for 150 years formed a part of the Ottoman Empire. The territories which were subsequently transferred to Yugoslavia fall into this category. It was especially low in the Bánát, where, for example, in Torontál county less than one person in a hundred was a nobleman. The proportion of the nobles was well above the national average in the Great Plain region, 8.6 percent. It was highest in eastern Hungary and parts of Transylvania, most of which were acquired by Romania and Czechoslovakia. In Szabolcs county, say, the nobility comprised 13.3 percent of the county's population, in Szatmár, 14.1 percent, and Máramaros, 16.6 percent.[7] High ratios, such as in Máramaros county, where the national minorities made up a great majority of the population, actually meant that a majority of Hungarians claimed noble titles.

In some Western European countries the nobility reacted to the challenge of the bourgeoisie by rigidly closing its ranks and by withdrawing into an untenable defensive position. Soon they became isolated and their views became representative of a mere fraction of one end of the political spectrum. In Hungary, where the bourgeoisie was weak and the nobility far more powerful, the nobility never found it necessary to close ranks, nor would this have been possible because of the nobility's size and diversity. The Hungarian nobility was a highly stratified estate, diverse in its wealth, education, economic interests, religion, attitude toward the Habsburg rulers and toward new ideas coming from the West and challenging the established order. This stratum was held together by its consciousness of being members of a privileged elite, as well as by a shared belief in a common historical mission. Diverse, yet unified, and backed by numbers, enabled the Hungarian nobility to become adaptive to change. Nearly every new idea that reached the country found adherents among the nobility, who by virtue of their social prestige assumed leadership of virtually every new intellectual movement. This intellectual diversity did not cause schisms in their ranks; new movements were quickly reconciled with group interest and were transformed into weapons to defend the nobility.[8]

This pattern was already apparent at the time of the Reformation. Calvinism in Hungary became a weapon of the lesser nobility to mobilize the Protestant population in defense of the "ancient privileges and liberties of the Hungarian nation," that is, for a defense of noble political privileges against Catholic and centralizing policies of the Habsburgs. Religious differences never split the unity of the nobility, and religious freedom was always considered a part of a nobleman's political freedom.

Similarly late eighteenth-century Enlightenment as well as nineteenth-century liberalism and nationalism were easily reconciled with, and incorporated into, the noble national ideology. Faced with the challenge of a new age, the nobility realized that if it wished to remain a functional elite it had to adopt the methods of production of the age, and to modernize its means of control. Although Count István Széchenyi addressed his words primarily to the aristocracy, and, in many ways, his program of reform represented the views of the progressive members of his estate, Lajos Kossuth spoke for the dispossessed lesser nobility, whose group identity and social standing were endangered by its economic decline. According to Andrew János these "common nobles formed a highly cohesive and articulate group . . . who were accustomed to achieve their goals through political action." They were "a radicalized group of potential politicians, for whom progress through economic reforms was slow and cumbersome and the institutional structure of feudal society antiquated and ridden with vested interest."[9]

The lesser nobles were impatient with Széchenyi's evolutionary program; it offered few tangible and immediate benefits. Since the county structure was no longer capable of absorbing surplus nobles, and urban, capitalist development was still in its infancy, they set their eyes on the capture of the state machinery, which if staffed with Hungarian nobles and modernized could restore their lost status. They also championed modernization and promotion of commerce and agriculture. In sum, the lesser nobility adopted some of the aims of the Western bourgeoisie. Thus, the dispossessed nobles became the Hungarian middle class. They differed, however, from their Western counterparts in that they remained faithful to their agrarian origins and continued to defend the privileges of their estate.

The vehicle for attainment of the goals of that middle class was primarily nationalism and liberalism. Their concept of nation —though, in certain specific contexts, it included the entire Hungarian-speaking population — in its essential features was still based on the ancient noble national ideology. The lesser nobles equated the nation with the state, and national interest with that of the state. These interests were defined by the same social group that had founded and historically maintained the state, the Hungarian nobility.

Estate interest in the *Vormärz* period required liquidation of the uneconomical system of serfdom, with proper compensation for the nobility, and establishment of an autonomous Hungarian state administration. The first part of this program of reform triumphed in April 1848 with the abolition of serfdom. The second demand was achieved only in the Compromise of 1867.

The Compromise was a complete victory for the nobility. Paradoxically, this victory also signaled the acceleration of the economic decline, particularly after 1880, of the middle- and small-sized gentry estates. The revolution of 1848 accelerated a capitalistic transformation of Hungarian agriculture, and under the new economic conditions only those estates were able to survive which were capable of adopting capitalistic methods of cultivation.[10] Such was the price that the gentry had to pay for its revitalization, for its preservation as a functional elite.

After the Compromise the gentry took full control of the administrative apparatus and the coercive powers of the state; they reshaped the country's insitutions to guarantee their continued preeminence. The most significant institutional change carried out was the creation of a Hungarian centralized state administration. Before 1867 the county system, and the particularism which it represented, was the prime instrument for the nobility. With the triumph of the nobility in 1867 the *raison d'être* of independence of the county assemblies disappeared. Although the county system was not abolished and did not lose completely its autonomy, it was integrated into, and made partially subservient to, the central government. It became an intermediate level of government where the interests of the state and those of the local population were in some form reconciled. Its key official, the high-sheriff [*Főispán*] was appointed by the central government; nevertheless, the local landowners, and especially the magnates, still retained an often decisive voice in matters affecting their counties. The day-to-day supervision of county affairs remained in the hands of the local lesser nobility, from whose ranks, even in the minority areas, a large majority of the county officials and clerks were recruited.

The new Hungarian state bureaucracy was able to absorb most of the dispossessed lesser nobility by expanding wherever the need arose.[11] Positions where a high degree of expertise was not required generally went to the unemployed gentry. As a result a third to a half of the posts in the state bureaucracy and in the ministries and between two-thirds and three-fourths of those in the county administration were held by the gentry.[12] Expansion of the central bureaucracy, of course, cannot be solely attributed to pressures by gentry office seekers. As the country began its modernization, industrialization, and as the state saw fit to extend its supervision and control over different aspects of life, such expansion was a natural process; but the Hungarian government was forced to enlarge its bureaucracy beyond reasonable limits. Thus the number of state officials rose from 20,000 in 1870, to 111,000 by 1899, and still higher, to 153,000 by 1909.[13]

Like the bureaucracy, the executive and legislative branches of government also came under the domination of the gentry. The Liberal Party of Kálmán Tisza, the governing party for nearly three decades, was an alliance of the landed gentry, state bureaucracy, and the emerging bourgeoisie. Interests of this last stratum were safeguarded by the Tisza party as long as they did not conflict with agrarian interests.

A majority of the aristocrats after the Compromise retreated into a mild opposition to the government party. Nevertheless, through utilizing their considerable social prestige, personal connections, and economic power, the aristocrats were able to assure extensive state protection of the interests of the great estates. The aristocratic opposition, however, did not become significant until the general crisis of the dualist system surfaced after 1900.

Noble Mentality

The three decades following the Compromise became a kind of golden age of the Hungarian gentry. Imbued with a self-confidence born out of the compromise with the Habsburgs and the Austrian bourgeoisie, secure in its powers, without enemies in sight capable of challenging its primacy, the gentry settled down to enjoy the good life offered by the new age. Its political experience seemed to confirm that the noble identity and national ideology remained functional; it merely had to be adjusted, not abandoned. Thus attitudes, hierarchies, and values of an agrarian society, the old self-image of the nobility, and their traditional dicta of social intercourse, all remained firmly entrenched in the minds and character of the gentry. If, at times, these seemed anachronistic and even quixotic, they nevertheless continued to form the basis of a functional and secure noble identity.

Thus in its new capacity as member of a bureaucracy, the Hungarian gentry remained first and foremost gentlemen of noble birth. If there existed a collegiate spirit among the officials, similar to that which prevailed in some Western bureaucracies, it still formed part of a broader noble corporate consciousness. The gentry officials did not adopt the mentality, work ethic, or frugal habits of the Western bureaucrats. They executed the duties of their office with the typical casualness of their group, acting as if the bureaucratic chores were merely incidental to their true function. Their behavior was marked by arrogance toward their social inferiors, tempered at times by paternalism, and by a self-confidence typical of men who believed that it was their birth right to rule over others.

The gentry bureaucrats were free from some of the worst shortcomings of their Western counterparts, but they also lacked some of their virtues. We search in vain for that typical bureaucratic mentality, for petty narrow-mindedness and corruption, for servility, pedantry, and love of routinized work. The Hungarian officials, since they did not derive their sense of importance from the office but from their birth and family connections, did not feel compelled to elaborate on their work or to enlarge the importance of their office through red tape. In them the prime virtues of the Western bureaucrats, their "sense of duty, industry, love of the common welfare, and simple loyalty,"[14] as characterized by Eugene N. Anderson, were also absent.

The Hungarian bureaucracy was not a modern civil service in the sense that it equated public interest with the general welfare. Nor did it serve dynastic interests as in Prussia and Austria. It was a class bureaucracy. It was not an impersonal mechanism, rigidly structured by rules, regulations, and hierarchies. The bureaucracy resembled, instead, a large fraternity of equals, held together by personal relations. Excessive servility, the hallmark of the Austrian bureaucracy, was missing in Hungary.

They were generally well paid, especially in the higher grades, which partly explains the relative honesty of the Hungarian officials. They exploited their office to the fullest, but more to aid friends and relatives than to enrich themselves. Petty corruption and bribery on a small scale were considered unbecoming to a gentleman; acceptance of a small bribe would have indicated a character weakness in that it betrayed acquisitiveness.[15]

Though the gentry moved to urban areas it never severed emotional ties with the countryside. For them land ownership retained a special mystique. A country squire's life remained their ideal. Only if we appreciate the powerful hold land ownership exercised on the minds of the gentry can we understand the exaggerated emotional response to loss of landed estates in the Successor States. Land reforms represented not only a financial loss to some land owners; it was a loss to the entire nobility. It ended the "Hungarian style of life," and the dream of return to the land.

The Hungarian nobility was not attracted to army life. Most nobles, during the Dualist Era, after fulfilling their minimum military obligations, returned to civilian life. The discipline and tedium of army life was far too restrictive for the casual Hungarian gentry. Those who joined the army were concentrated in the cavalry regiments where nobles and aristocrats formed the dominant group. The rest of the Hungarian professional officers corps, in fact, was mostly made up of assimilated Germans and other minorities, or of men from the non-noble classes. In its social origins the corps was decidedly lower middle class: children of lower officials, teachers, noncommissioned officers, craftsmen, or more prosperous peasants. Military schools, however, trained them to identify with the noble national ideology and to adopt the mentality, social habits, virtues, and even vices of the gentry.[16]

Manifestations in civilian life of these characteristics are numerous. The colorful national dress with sword at side, designed to accentuate masculine qualities, were worn on public occasions until 1945. A gentleman was expected to adhere to a chivalric code; its violation, or an insult to name or honor, often resulted in a duel.

Women were generally excluded from such pleasures of men as hunting, horseback riding, and card playing, but this did not mean that they were excluded from society. Unlike Germany, where the authoritarian family structure tended to force women into submissive roles, in Hungary, women were expected to serve as a constant challenge to men. Strong female character, therefore, offered the greatest challenge, greatest triumph, and much admiration.

Crisis and Radicalization of the Nobility

Until the mid-nineteenth century the Hungarian political nation was largely limited to the nobility. Even after 1867, and in spite of rapid industrialization and economic transformation of the country, opposition to the noble ideology and noble domination was slow in emerging. As long as the nobility was able to offer a spectrum of ideas sufficiently broad to satisfy most of the politically conscious population, its identity remained secure.

The new bourgeoisie, in general, seemed incapable of developing a coherent ideology and a stable identity of their own. Its insecurity stemmed mostly from its own origins. For, the Hungarian bourgeoisie around the turn of the century was largely made up of recently assimilated Germans, Jews, and, to a lesser degree, Slovaks and Serbs, who were eager to prove their newly found loyalty to the Hungarian nation. Instead of challenging and offering a realistic alternative to the prevailing agrarian noble political and social ideology, they adopted it unquestioningly. They identified with the nobility, imitated their behavior, sent their children to Hungarian schools, adopted ancient Hungarian noble names, and, at times, became champions of the most virulent forms of Hungarian nationalism.[17] Yet, the identity of the new middle class was not secure. It was artificial, corresponding only outwardly to the trappings of the nobility. It was not legitimate, nor was it rooted in traditional society; its ties with the agrarian community and mentality were superficial. The gentry-imitating, or, as expression sometimes goes, the gentroid class, whose adherence to the noble values was only tenuous, formed an unstable part of Hungarian society.

Around the 1890s, the gentry, itself, began to lose its old confidence. In spite of its successes in capturing the state machinery it remained a declining group. Weak and insecure as the bourgeoisie itself was, its growing cultural and economic influence presented a direct threat to the gentry middle class. Perceiving its decline the gentry responded with a shift in political attitudes. It turned its back on the tradition of 1848 with its liberal nationalism; the nationalism of the gentry ceased to be liberal; its liberalism became only selectively democratic. In an attempt to revitalize itself the gentry reaffirmed its traditional agrarian ideology, became anticapitalist, and succeeded only in becoming further removed from objective reality.[18] Between 1900 and the early 1920s the nobility, and especially those who became refugees after 1918, were further traumatized by a series of events which completely shattered their old identity.

First, a challenge to noble ideology came from the radical intelligentsia and national minorities; second, a powerful blow was dealt by the war and the defeat. This was followed by a political and social revolution in Hungary carried out by the radical intelligentsia and then by the Communists. And, finally, the most crippling blow, the loss of territories, which dispossessed and forced a retreat of the nobility from two-thirds of of Hungary's former territory.

Toward the end of the nineteenth century two new groups came to maturity whose views could be no longer fitted into the noble political spectrum; they could be neither brought under the control of nobility, nor reconciled with the noble ideology. The radical intelligentsia, strongly influenced by Western socialist and radical thought, attempted to counter the gentry's sham parliamentary liberalism with democratic radicalism. Their demands for a genuine democracy, radical social and land reforms, and their conciliatory attitude toward national minorities ran counter to every interest and inclination of the nobility. Similarly, views of another, and more important group, the politically articulate leaders of the national minorities who resisted the forces of assimilation, developed a national consciousness of their own, and challenged directly the Hungarian noble national and social ideology.

The nobility reacted to this dual challenge with predictable aggressiveness, especially toward the minorities. In response to this challenge around this time, the heady dream of an "Empire of thirty million Hungarians" was born. This was popular not only among the members of the new middle class, where this ideas was conceived, but also among the gentry, who spread it in bureaucratic and government chambers. The assertion of Hungarian cultural superiority and national vitality made assimilation a viable solution.[19]

The nobility was not uniform in its response to threats of social revolution and of the national minorities. In inner Hungary, with its predominantly Hungarian population, the danger from the nationalities appeared somewhat remote. It seemed less important than the radical or socialist agitation in urban areas and among the rural proletariat. There the danger from the minority areas was treated legalistically, without much realism, largely as an academic question of the legal rights of the Hungarian nation and Hungarian state; as essentially a problem of statistics. Official census figures, which showed that between 1860 and 1910 the ratio of Hungarians to non-Hungarians was reversed, seemed to encourage optimism about the viability of the assimilation policies. To the casual observer these figures were proof of the greater virility of the Hungarians and of the attraction of the Hungarian culture; but, in fact, they mostly reflected only the assimilation of urban Germans and Jews.[20]

In the minority areas, however, and especially in Transylvania, official optimism and official statistics were meaningless in the face of a much more tangible personal experience. As we have noted earlier, in Transylvania, during the first decade of the twentieth century, a quiet agrarian revolution had begun in the predominantly Romanian counties. With the disappearance of the Hungarian middle- and small-sized estates and the gentry landlords, control of the rural countryside through the traditional methods became increasingly difficult. In Transylvania, therefore, the old sense of self-confidence and security gradually gave way to anxieties, fears, and even panic, to a sense of impotence before the rising tide of Romanians. The nobles' reactions increasingly took extreme forms. They began to oscillate between exaggerated pessimism and fatalistic passivity, and aggressive rage born of panic. Their mood became somber as if they were preparing for certain impending doom; the conflict between the Hungarians and Romanians, to them, was a "life and death struggle" of two nations.[21] If in this battle the Hungarian nation had to perish, its death was to be a noble, heroic death, worthy of a race of warriors.

That syndrome is a relatively common psychological phenomenon. Generalized social danger and status anxiety, brought about by the challenge of the nationalities, and the inability of the nobility to cope with the danger, created a sense of powerlessness. These anxieties were especially accentuated among the younger generations, that is, among those born during and after the 1880s. The older generation was emotionally less affected. Its members grew up in a secure age; their identities were stable, rooted in the values of a traditional society. The younger generation began to reach maturity, define themselves, acquire a conceptual framework, during a period of crisis, when the values and methods to deal with problems of the traditional society were besieged from every side. Though they wished to emulate their elders' attitudes, say, their natural authoritativeness, they were able to do so only superficially. The negative characteristics of the older generation appeared, in them, naked, without the counterbalancing positive features of poise, casualness, paternalism, and self-confidence.

Thus the younger noble generation in its emotional makeup increasingly resembled that of the new middle class, with which after 1919 they indeed formed an alliance. To bridge the gulf between their imperfectly formed identitied and what they wished to be, they were increasingly more receptive to radical ideas and solutions of the problems of society. They were more inclined to counter the revolutionary forces within Hungary with a revolution of their own.

This generation of the 1880s reached maturity and entered the state and county bureaucracies during the first decade of the twentieth century. They were immediately confronted with the growing problem of nationalities and the burning issue of the Hungarian "national resistance," issuing from the constitutional crisis of 1904–1906. Many young men who rose to political prominence during the early 1920s served their apprenticeship in the state administration during this tense decade. Thus, when the war broke out in 1914, it did not shatter a tranquil society, rather it fractured a society that was filled with revolutionary tensions — a society at an impasse, unable to transform itself, unable to abandon old habits.

The gentry accepted and welcomed the challenge of war. War with Serbia was popular. As Leslie Tihany aptly characterized Hungarian attitudes toward Serbs: they "had an ingrained habit of considering Serbs political upstarts and cultural inferiors. Yet, at the same time, contempt was mixed with a certain amount of admiration for the manly virtues, especially military valor. The Serbs were the Hungarians' favorite enemies."[22] The Hungarian nobles expected quick victory, much honor; they lived up to their martial self-image, flocking to the colors by the thousands.

In the first euphoric weeks of the war it was hoped that victory, which seemed certain, would act as a catharsis, as a purification and revitalization of society, and would strengthen Hungarian domination over the country. The war offered avenues of release for tensions built up during the previous two decades. It may sound paradoxical, but in these early hours of war when emotions no longer had to be under strict control, the capacity for love of fellow nationals increased greatly. Earlier differences and resentments vanished, and, at the moment when free aggression became possible again, the people behaved as if suddenly total freedom had been gained.

This sense of freedom, however, was illusory. To maximize the power of the state, far greater restrictions upon life had to be imposed than ever existed before. Thus, to the people of Hungary, the end of war brought a sudden liberation from prolonged tension, and from the strict discipline of the war as well as from the structure and formalities of the old civilization. To the nobility it was a defeat and a confirmation of their powerlessness.

With the collapse of the armies on the front and the outbreak of the revolution at home, the whole fabric of society began to disintegrate. Old spectrums, gradations, those fine subliminal forms and subtle nuances so essential for civilized existence became meaningless. Hierarchies of the old order, social, economic, and moral restrictions, which defined the existence of a social being, abruptly became inoperative.

Life became less civilized; survival more precarious. Revolutions always seem to bring about a simplification of life, a reduction to its most elemental forms, marked by extremes and contradictions. Violence and brutality may exist side by side with compassion and self-sacrifice. Some respond to the atomization of society with introversion and paralysis of will; others with lively aggression.

Atomization of society did not affect the entire population with

uniform severity. Social structures based on immediate personal rela-
tionships seemed to be more enduring than more complex but less
personal systems. Thus less differentiated rural communities were far
more resilient than urban society. In villages preservation of the existing
structures was a precondition of survival; ties with the external world,
identification with the greater social units, incidental. Collapse of the
larger community, therefore, did not necessarily create an immediate
crisis. Thus the peasantry, in spite of its initial assault upon the old rural
elite, was far less radicalized. It merely withdrew into a passive, protective isolation, and restricted its limited revolutionary fervor to local
affairs.

Survival of urban society, on the other hand, depended on a smooth
and coordinated functioning of most social, economic, and political
institutions. With the collapse of the old order, therefore, the urbanized
classes themselves were thrown into confusion.

The most traumatized urban group was the official class, the urbanized gentry and, in general, the old ruling class. That is, the class whose
identification with the old regime and the old civilization was the most
intense. The revolution destroyed their old status, prestige, the threat of
land reform and wholesale personnel changes in the bureaucracy undermined their economic position. With the establishment of the Hungarian Soviet Republic they became the hated class enemy; thereafter even
their personal safety was no longer assured. Some of them left the cities
and went into hiding in more remote parts of the country, but tens of
thousands of others, landowners, magnates, politicians, officials, and
army officers fled to Vienna or to areas under French occupation.

In Vienna and in Szeged these refugees from Soviet Hungary met
with refugees pouring out of the minority areas, where the revolutionary
transformation of the old society and the destruction of the old values
were brought about by the transfer of power to the subject nationalities.
Welded together, these two refugee groups became the driving force
behind the Hungarian counterrevolution.

Both these refugee groups were under extreme emotional stress. Cut
off from their roots they felt isolated, disoriented, and powerless. These
refugees, in fact, were defending themselves against a set of triple-tiered
anxiety: against dangers growing out of their uprooting and the turbu-
lance of the times; against anxieties issuing from the shattered synthesis
and challenge to the functionality of their old identity; and, against
anxieties arising from an unconscious admission that they, as individuals, and as a class, had failed to live up to their self-image. A defense
against these anxieties was found within the framework of a radical
movement. This movement was brought to life as a substitute for the

disintegrating old community, in which the old and now endangered noble identities were rooted. Thus the suddenly intensified ethnocentricism of the refugees, and their embracing of right-wing ideologies and the cause of the counterrevolution, served a vital psychological purpose.

One further source of anxiety among the refugees cannot be ignored. This was the fear of physical ethnic extinction. This fear is virtually unknown among larger nations. It is peculiar to small nations, who either live under the domination of a larger nation or surrounded by larger and hostile nations. The danger is real for many small nations or national minorities especially in modern times. Whether extinction takes place benignly, through a process of slow assimilation, or through violent means, the end result is all the same: the extinction of the nation, its culture, and language. To members of an endangered nation this is far more frightening to contemplate than the death of the individual.

The Hungarians had lived long with this fear. The idea of assimilation of the non-Hungarian population became popular around the turn of the century precisely for this reason. They wished to reverse the assimilation process by the national minorities, which in their eyes threatened them with certain extinction. All measures seemed justified in order to save the small Hungarian nation, which was gradually being engulfed by the Slavic, Germanic, and Romanian sea around it.

With the loss of a third of the Hungarian nation and nearly two-thirds of Hungary's territory, the pessimistic conclusion that the nation once more faced the danger of extermination came easily. The danger was a double one. Reduced in numbers, Hungary could not defend itself against its hostile neighbors. It was also feared that in the lost territories the Hungarian minorities would be subjected to extreme pressures to assimilate. Once a nation, or a national minority begins to decline in numbers, according to the argument of the Hungarian Eugenic Society, it is only a matter of time before the critical point is reached, beyond which there is no possibility of reversing the downward course, and the minority is doomed to oblivion.[23] The minorities in all of the lost territories were already seriously weakened by the flight of the refugees. Especially those elements fled which, in the past, were the strongest protectors of the national consciousness, and which would have been most able to preserve the vitality of the minority culture against the inroad of the majority culture.

To the refugees this presented an extreme dilemma. They, by their actions, were actually dooming their fellow nationals to a more rapid decline. This aroused an enormous feeling of guilt. The contemporary press relentlessly urged all refugees to return to their native lands to strengthen the resistance of the minority and, incidentally, to ease the great economic burden which their presence in the reduced territory of Hungary represented. Their return was also necessary lest Hungary should lose all claims to the lost areas by the disappearance of the Hungarian minorities.

The refugees, therefore, had to justify both to themselves and to fellow countrymen their departures. It would have been insufficient merely to argue that they departed, for example, for personal economic reasons, or that their chances of success or economic status were better assured in reduced Hungary than in the occupied areas. Their departure had to be justified by higher, more moral, or more compelling, reasons. The danger of real physical harm had to be conjured up if it was absent. Or the refugees had to prove that their absence from their native land was only temporary, that, in fact, they were working for the return of these lands. They had to prove that their presence in Hungary was desirable by demonstrating their willingness to sacrifice their lives for the reconquest of these territories. The most effective way to demonstrate this was by joining the counterrevolutionary movement or one of the many militant irredentist groups.

Refugee Participation in the Revolution and Counterrevolution, October 1918–August 1919

The disintegration of the old order stunned and temporarily paralyzed the old ruling classes of Hungary. The revolution, led by Mihály Károlyi, triumphed virtually without bloodshed. One of the few bullets fired in anger, however, felled Count István Tisza. His death was a momentous event. According to Tibor Hajdu: "In Hungary there was no man more hated than Tisza: he grew to become the symbol of the war, of the rule of Vienna, thus his murder was also a symbolic act. His blood saved the other representatives of the old regime, since the thirst of the people for revenge was quenched with the death of Tisza."[1] Tisza was the symbol of the old social order. He personified the strength of the gentry, their obstinate endurance, and their domination of all the political instruments of the state. The announcement of his assassination was greeted by crowds on the streets of Budapest with jubilation. But the gentry and the aristocracy viewed his death not only as the closing of a chapter in the long history of the nobility, but also as a portentous sign of impending disaster.

To the nobility resistance to the forces of revolution seemed both futile and impossible. Public opinion was overwhelmingly in favor of the new regime of Károlyi. Budapest was thoroughly revolutionized and controlled by opponents of the old regime. In rural areas, swept by peasant revolts, power passed, without resistance, to the revolutionary councils. The right was further weakened by an increasingly apparent division within its own ranks. The conservative right, drawn from the landed aristocracy, gentry, members of the upper bureaucracy, and the church, favored an outright restoration of the prewar social system but felt powerless to do so. The radical right, representing the dispossessed lesser nobility, junior officers, the younger generation, members of the new middle class, and the ever present refugees, were willing to contemplate a reshaping of society by force, though their program of change was poorly articulated and the group was still disorganized. The first instinct of both groups, therefore, was to find an accommodation with the new regime and, if possible, to coopt the revolution. Many subse-

quent leaders of the counterrevolutionary movement, in these early
stages of the revolution, suddenly discovered their liberal loyalties and
rushed to take oath to the revolutionary government. Bishops, counts,
princes, bank directors, presidents of commercial and agricultural societies, according to Károlyi, besieged the new government "begging
permission to take the oath of fidelity."[2]

During the first month of the revolution an overwhelming majority of
the population gave its support to the new government. Each group and
each class looked to the government for fulfillment of their economic
and political programs. Workers expected a socialist transformation of
society, peasants a great land reform, and the progressive intelligentsia
hoped for a democratization of society. Supporters of the old order
could not resist the combined strength of the nation. The cause of social
revolution appeared irresistable and the victory of democratic Hungary
complete. The only course remaining open to the members of the old
ruling elite was to try to save their positions individually.

The initial strength of the new regime was largely due to its moral
superiority over the old and to the fact that momentarily it was able to
unite the aspirations of all those who demanded significant social
change. However, this unity of the nation and, therefore, the power of
the Károlyi government was fragile. The chaos, which accompanied
the collapse of the empire and which initially aided the revolution,
hindered efforts of the new regime to gain control of events and to give a
moderate direction to the revolution. By September 1918 some 400,000
soldiers deserted and more during October. Of the 2.1-million Austro-
Hungarian prisoners of war in Russia, about 725,000 returned by the fall
of 1918. Of these an estimated 152,000 were Hungarians.[3] By the end of
November about 700,000 Hungarian soldiers returned from the front
and by the end of December about 1,200,000, or perhaps as many as
1,500,000, were demobilized.[4] Disturbances caused by these soldiers
combined with the peasant uprisings forced the government to concen-
trate on restoration of order and protection of life and property. The
moderate elements in society refused to participate in the restoration of
order, whereas rightist officers often resorted to the use of excessive
force. This was doubly damaging to the regime. It helped the political
right and alienated some of the would-be supporters of the regime.
Preoccupation with restoration of order also postponed immediate
implementation of planned reforms. Yet, to restore order was judged to
be necessary for reasons of foreign policy: the regime wished to demonstrate to the West that it was in full control of the situation and to
counter demands by some of the Successor States for an immediate
occupation of Hungary to prevent the spread of chaos and Bolshevism.[5]

Reflecting upon the difficult choices his government faced in repressing the peasant revolt, Károlyi subsequently wrote: "We feared that 'Jacqueries' would break out and that we might lose control." And he added: "I have often wondered if it would not have been wiser to refrain from keeping down the passions of discontent during the first weeks and let them loose, as victorious generals allow their enemies to run wild for a couple of days. The peasants would then have taken possession of the long coveted land as they did in 1944 and would, thus, have been firmly linked to our new order. This would have avoided the regime of Béla Kun as well as the Counter-Revolution. We chose instead the road of legality and order, discarding that of social justice."[6]

The vulnerability of the Károlyi regime soon became apparent. Its weaknesses were due to an absence of an organized mass base of support; to an imperfect control of political institutions; to a lack of military and police force; and finally, to ineffectiveness of the government in the field of foreign policy.

As the euphoria born out of the sudden victory over the old regime began to dissipate, it became increasingly evident that the rapidly expanding political spectrum was becoming too broad to be bridged by the moderate democratic program of Károlyi. That program fell far short of the expectations of precisely those groups which were most responsible for the victory of the revolution. The working class and the Social Democratic Party were increasingly dissatisfied with the slow pace of social reforms, hence their support for the government was at times no more than lukewarm. The prevailing political anarchy and the disastrous economic conditions, shortage of food, fuel, and all necessities of life, rapidly radicalized a large number of workers and intellectuals. Although these groups were originally supporters of the regime, they were no longer willing to accept a moderate program and further delays; they demanded an immediate realization of all the goals of the revolution. Postponement of land reform and the sporadic violent repressive measures disillusioned the impatient peasantry; radicalization of society and the lackluster leadership of Károlyi lost for the government some of its original middle-class supporters.

Soon it became apparent that the transfer of political power from the hands of the gentry to the new regime was far less complete than it was originally imagined and planned. Although personnel in key military and government posts changed, the entire state and county apparatus remained shot through with men who, in the past, had faithfully served the old regime. It was not possible to expect that these men would carry out with any degree of enthusiasm the radical reforms that were demanded or even those minimal reforms that were necessary to save the regime. Even in those areas where office holders changed, dedication and loyalty of the new men to the principles of Károlyi were often suspect. Adventurers, demobilized officers, refugees, opportunists of incredibly varied political and social backgrounds surfaced and assumed posts often without any qualification or even authorization. They saw in the revolution an opportunity to advance, and they were determined to carve out for themselves a new status and a new role that was equal or superior to their old. To these men ideological consistency meant little; they swam with the tide of events; some of them turned sharply to the left and rose to even more prominent positions during the Hungarian Soviet Republic, while others became sworn enemies of the Károlyi regime and ultimately attached themselves to one or another of the counterrevolutionary groups.

The third weakness of the Károlyi regime, one even more important than the unreliability of the state apparatus, consisted of its inability to develop its coercive forces. The Károlyi government owed its existence to the daring of rebellious solider groups, who in October 1918 took it upon themselves to overthrow the old regime. These groups were never integrated into a revolutionary army, an army committed to the preservation of democracy, but remained semi-autonomous and semi-military units. "In these bands of soldiers," according to Oszkár Jászi, Károlyi's minister of nationalities, "it was not always the serious and responsible elements, but frequently the desperadoes of the front who had taken the lead, and who now hastened to present their accounts to the revolutionary government." These groups at times were, in fact, more dangerous to the government than the enemies of the revolution. Commenting on the extreme vulnerability of the regime to these soldiers, Jászi continued: "Often enough when we retired to rest, we found ourselves wondering which of the dissatisfied condottieri would put the whole government under arrest in the course of the night."[7] It is indicative of the degree of disintegration of the old army that the minister of war, on November 6, 1918, was unable to provide a few dozen reliable soldiers to escort Károlyi and his entourage to Belgrade. Only *gendarmes,* the border guards, a few units of the People's Guard, plus one or two half-demobilized battalions could the government count on to respond in case of a domestic disturbance.[8]

Despite repeated appeals to the population, it proved impossible to find volunteers to increase the size of the army. Many of the demobilized soldiers found it far more attractive to serve on the Soldiers' Councils in the hope of some political gains, or to join some of the semi-military, semi-private groups, or for the workers to join the Social Democratic Party-controlled People's Guards than to endure the discipline, boredom, or, perhaps, dangers of regular army life. The vast majority of the demobilized soldiers were only too happy to shed their uniforms and to return to their homes. Pacifist and antimilitarist sentiment, resulting from the extreme hardships of the war, also made recruitment of a new army in defense of the new democratic government nearly impossible. It was this military weakness that was the Achilles heel of the Károlyi regime. As Jászi has written:

> We knew that our situation would sooner or later become untenable without a reliable, well organized military force in sympathy with democratic aims. There has probably never been a government so entirely dependent on moral force as the Károlyi government, which for months was absolutely without a military arm. It was impossible to prevent the dissolution of the old army; the men streamed away from all military units like wine from a burst cask. The few who remained were not the sort of human material on which the democratic and revolutionary government could have relied.[9]

Thus the Károlyi government was faced with the unattractive choice of dependence for support on the old officers' corps or on the Social Democratic party, the only two groups capable of organizing a military force sufficient for ending the postwar anarchy. It was in fact a choice between either the continuation of the revolution or a counterrevolution. Károlyi never hesitated on this point: an alliance with the officers' corps would have destroyed all his achievements; a socialist partnership, provided that the radical or Communist faction was held in check, should have been able to guarantee the success of both the democratic and social revolutions. That this coalition failed to fulfil Károlyi's hopes was not entirely his fault; responsibility rests equally on the shoulders of the Social Democratic Party.

The impotence of the Károlyi government was nowhere more pronounced than in the field of foreign affairs. Károlyi had no illusions about the the possibility of preserving the territorial integrity of prewar Hungary. But he misjudged the sincerity of the proclaimed war aims of the Western Powers. He anticipated the inflated territorial demands of the Successor States, but he believed that ultimately the cooler counsels of President Wilson would prevail and that the Allies would be as persevering in enforcing the Wilsonian principles as they were prosecuting the war.[10]

Károlyi also assumed that the Western Allies were familiar with the affairs of East Central Europe, if not in detail at least in broad principles, and, therefore, that they understood the origins and complex nature of the national minorities' grievances. To him those were not the result of oppression by one nation of another, but the consequence of an antiquated political and social system in which the nobility had oppressed with equal severity both the Hungarian and non-Hungarian working and peasant masses. In other words, he believed, and correctly, that the nationality question was first and foremost social and political in nature, and only secondarily national. Consequently, he held that the remedy for these problems had to be also social and political, combined with complete guarantees of the cultural rights of the minorities.

Jászi's plan for reorganizing Hungary along the Swiss model seemed to fulfill all these requirements;[11] it was logical and accurate assessment but no longer practical.

Károlyi had also hoped that he would succeed in dissociating his government from responsibility for the war, and that by demonstrating the genuine democratic and pacifist sympathies of his regime, he would be able to gain recognition for his government and negotiate a just peace. According to Jászi:

> We had confidence in the democratic and pacifist quality of public opinion in the Entente states and especially in the policy of President Wilson, a policy which stood higher than any mere nationalism. We did not deceive ourselves for a moment with thoughts of preserving the territorial integrity of Hungary in the geographic sense; but we were convinced that the conquering allies would show the utmost goodwill to her pacifist and anti-militarist government, and especially to Károlyi, who had so often stood with unexampled courage for the policy of the Entente. . . ."[12]

At first these hopes were widely shared by the population. It was generally believed that Károlyi was perhaps the only man who could gain the trust of the Western Powers and save Hungary from total dismemberment. A policy of cooperation with the Allies, therefore, seemed to be the only logical course. It was also in harmony with the prevailing pacifist mood of the country. The energies of the population were exhausted in the war. No amount of propaganda in the first months of the revolution could rekindle the patriotic spirit; not even the extreme danger of territorial dismemberment of Hungary could galvanize the nation into action to fight a new war. Thus at first everyone was willing to pin hopes on the success of the course followed by Károlyi. Hopes of a fair treatment, however, soon faded as it became clear that, though they considered Károlyi the best man to lead Hungary, the Allies refused even to recognize and negotiate with his government about the future of Hungary.[13] Instead the occupation of the country by foreign troops began; the dream of the Danubian Federation and the policy of reconciliation became meaningless.

As the weakness of the Károlyi regime became more and more accentuated, supporters of the old regime regained their nerves and, along with the radical left, began to capitalize on the popular disillusionment. They joined hands with each other to erode the power of the moderate center and propelled the revolution into its radical phase. Though poles apart in ideology and in goals, both the left and the right agreed in rejecting Károlyi's pacifist, democratic, and moderate course. They were further united by their belief that only extreme measures could extricate Hungary from its difficult position.

The failure of Károlyi's foreign policy, combined with his government's inability to carry out the promised social revolution during the first enthusiastic weeks of the October Revolution, brought about a collapse of the regime's credibility and the loss of support of those who wished for a radical transformation of the country through democratic means. Every reform had to be postponed, Károlyi believed, until the election of a new parliament, yet he permitted interminable delays in calling these elections, mostly because of his conscientiousness for absolute fairness and legality. From the time of the assassination of Count Tisza, his archenemy, Károlyi, it seems, suffered from a paralysis of will — the fiery radical, the titan killer, as many viewed Károlyi, was incapable of resolving upon action once he seized the office that Tisza had made so powerful. The Károlyi regime, therefore, stood doomed to failure, among other more forceful causes, by its own inability to bring about a social revolution through revolutionary means.

Károlyi was ripe for replacement by a more radical leadership that was willing to act and use every method to achieve its goals. The five months during which Károlyi held power may seem to be a relatively short period of time. The country that had been waiting for decades for democratization and land reform perhaps should have granted to a well-meaning government more time to organize these reforms. Revolutionary times, however, defy the passage of time measured by the clock. Change crowds upon change and its accelerating pace becomes the rule of society. Károlyi proved to be a failure as the helmsman of this change, and the revolution passed him by. A great humanitarian, a man with a keen sense of justice, endowed with a high moral purpose, passed from the scene of history without notice. Few heeded his last-minute appeal to the public to show their support for his regime by joining the military forces of his government. This should be contrasted with the greatly successful recruiting efforts of the Hungarian Soviet Republic a short time later. Not only the Communist workers but old officers and soldiers, intellectuals and even some of the peasantry responded to the call of the Soviet posters crying: "To Arms! To Arms!" Hungary had chosen a more radical course.

Waning popular support for Károlyi paralyzed his regime. He never had a mass party of his own. The success of his regime always depended upon the preservation of a coalition embracing the progressive bourgeoisie, the intelligentsia, and the Social Democratic Party. His position became totally untenable after the "Vix note" was delivered on March 20, 1919. That note spelled out for the first time the terms of the severe territorial settlement contemplated for Hungary.[14] At this point, desertion of the Social Democrats was crucial. Without their support Károlyi no longer felt able to carry on his work and resigned from office, leaving the door open for the establishment of the Hungarian Soviet Republic. It fell to the new Communist government to face up to the consequences of the rejection of the "Vix note." Béla Kun's tough stand, however, forced the Paris Peace Conference to moderate its demands and to dispatch General Smuts to Hungary with the mission of negotiating with Kun. This fact later led Károlyi to write bitterly: "So what my Government had not been able to obtain in five months was granted to the Communists after a week, proving that the idea of standing up to the West was not such a bad one."[15]

Thus in the end it was the constant pressure on the frontiers that brought down the Károlyi regime. Danger to the territorial integrity of the country was most responsible for the radicalization of the population, for the growing popularity of the course offered by the Communists. The same pressures also brought to life the Hungarian counter-revolutionary movement.

The first of these counterrevolutionary groups, as we have seen, were formed in the most exposed frontier regions. As soon as occupation of Upper Hungary and Transylvania began scores of small, independent or semi-independent political and military organizations sprang up in the endangered areas. They aimed to resist the invading forces, regardless of official government policies. These groups were generally led by politicians of the old regime, by county or local officials, or by demobilized officers. Whereas the Károlyi government believed that loss of some territories was inevitable, these men would not acquiesce in amputation of the even predominantly non-Hungarian areas. They were soon forced to the realization that without an aggressive government in Budapest, willing to organize the military resistance, their efforts were doomed to failure. At first, these groups attempted to press the government into active military opposition. Failing in this they tried to mobilize the conservative and patriotic elements in the country against the regime. Aside from those in the immediately exposed areas, however, the response was extremely feeble. Leaders of these groups generally succeeded in gathering only a few dozen men willing to risk their lives in this hopeless enterprise. Aside from the Székely Division, which, as we have seen, did put up a determined fight, these groups could offer but a token resistance. They were easily pushed aside by the regular army units of the Successor States and were forced to withdraw to Budapest or to other cities of inner Hungary. There they joined other refugees in their loud denunciation of the Károlyi regime's cowardice.

In 1919 few among the refugees believed that their departure was permanent; they may have lost a battle but not the war. The idea of forceful resistance for the moment had to be abandoned, but only until the entire Hungarian nation should be awakened to the enormity of the crimes perpetrated against Hungary. The population's attention, therefore, had to be deflected from the heady dream of social revolution back to the true dangers which threatened the very existence of the nation. In other words, priorities of the refugees were temporarily reversed: for the moment reconquest of the lost territories had to be abandoned in favor of counterrevolution. These changes in priorities made possible the merger of the refugee and conservative opponents of the revolution into a single movement.

With rapid increase of the number of refugees in inner Hungary, the counterrevolutionary movement accelerated its momentum. In the refugees the movement found a group of reckless, radicalized men, willing to serve as its shock troops. During the last two months of 1918 alone, nearly 60,000 officially registered refugees arrived in inner Hungary. By the end of March 1919, when the flood of refugees temporarily slowed as a result of the establishment of the Hungary Soviet Republic their number was over 150,000. In addition, there were large numbers of civilians, soldiers, officers, and returning prisoners of war who were born in the lost territories but were caught by the collapse away from their homes and found their way home blocked by the occupying troops.[16]

In the major cities, especially along the new lines of demarcation, large refugee colonies began to appear, in Sopron, Győr,, Komárom, Miskolc, Debrecen, Szeged, and, most importantly, in Budapest. In some of these towns the size of the population suddenly increased by as much as twenty to forty percent. With the country's economy in ruins, local authorities were totally incapable of dealing with this influx of people. Perhaps the worst conditions prevailed in Budapest, where the prewar population nearly doubled during the war and revolution. There only the wealthier refugees were able to find decent accommodations and, thus, be spared the deprivations the majority had to endure.

Others, yet still the more fortunate, were crowded into the small apartments of tenement houses; thousands were totally unable to find any shelter for themselves. These unfortunates had to live, often for years, in the boxcars in which they arrived, at times three or four families per freight car, shoved to some abandoned track of a rail yard.[17] Others lived in converted schools, abandoned barracks used earlier as military hospitals, or in the hastily erected shanty towns which suddenly mushroomed around the capital, where refugee families survived often without even the most rudimentary heating or hygienic facilities.

Some families, especially the first arrivals, who departed in haste, panic-stricken, brought with them only their most essential and most valuable possessions. Even those who had adequate time to pack most of their belongings faced enormous deprivations. Without regular income, at a time of great food and fuel shortage when these items could be purchased only on the black market at inflated prices, they were forced to part with their valuables; one by one family jewels, paintings, rugs, and, finally, even furniture and clothing were sold or bartered away on the black market for food or fuel. The refugees also packed all public places, clubs, meeting halls, where for the price of a cup of coffee they could spend a day in warmth, and where they could commiserate with men of similar fate and similar background.

In view of these conditions, it is understandable that in the unstable and radical chemistry of Budapest the refugees acted as a catalyst agent, forming one of the most volatile and politically active groups. They were ready to support nearly any radical cause that promised to attack their enemies. At the time of their arrival they expected a warm welcome by their compatriots as victims of a common national tragedy. Also, as members of the old ruling class they were accustomed to deferential treatment. Now they were received at best with indifference or even hostility, mostly because the widespread misery caused by the war exhausted everyone's emotional and material resources. They responded with a deep resentment, which, at times, broke into destructive rage against the nation and government which passively watched the conquest of their homelands. They held the entire Hungarian nation responsible for the destruction of their lives and felt that the nation as a whole, therefore, owed them compensation for their sufferings and losses. Their minds were filled with righteous indignation and self-pity. They were quick to fix blame, ready to lash out against anyone or against any group which stood in their way, and eager to punish all those who they believed were guilty.

Under pressure of events, their old narrow class ideology disintegrated. No longer it could offer to the refugees a sense of direction or a solution to their grievances. These grievances cut across social and political lines: the refugees shared some of their tribulations with the conservative aristocracy of inner Hungary, some with the gentry, with the nationalists, or with the destitute middle class, but also with the unemployed masses of the country. It was a familiar sight to see large numbers of refugees participating in the nearly daily demonstrations, supporting every conceivable radical political, social, or economic cause, from the causes of the radical right to those of the extreme left: demonstrating for increased benefits to war veterans, for officers, for disabled soldiers, jobs for refugee civil servants, for national awakening, for a spiritual renaissance, or for the more mundane demands of food, shoes, clothing, or even for the release of arrested Communists.

Middle-class refugees, who were genuine supporters of the left, were a minority. Many joined the Socialist trade unions and even the Social Democratic Party, mostly out of opportunism. The majority of the refugees gravitated toward the right and the radical right. Many of the right-wing or counterrevolutionary organizations that sprang up during 1918 and early 1919 were originally regional associations of the refugees, though membership was generally open to anyone willing to support their cause. In these organizations refugees occupied most positions of leadership, but even in nonregional organizations refugees played an important and, at times, determining role. Many of these groups, though not all, were extremely small, at times consisting of not more than a leader and a few principal officers, but all had impressive patriotic organizational titles, inflated membership claims, and ambitious plans.

One of the most influential regional organizations was the Székely National Council formed in Budapest by such Transylvanian politicians as Count István Bethlen, Gábor Ugron, and Count Pál Teleki. Their aim was to mobilize public support for the defense of Transylvania, to gather supplies and military equipment for the Székely Division, to aid Transylvanian refugees, and to organize them into a powerful political pressure group. The Károlyi government sympathized with some of their objectives and gave financial aid to promote the work of the organization.[18] After the victory of the counterrevolution the Székely National Council concentrated most of its effort on political education of the nation and on propaganda, at home and abroad, on behalf of Hungarians in Transylvania and for the restoration of the province to Hungary. Its publications and propaganda were, perhaps, the most scholarly and intelligent that the right produced. A number of organizations also emerged from the Székely National Council. For example, the National Refugee Office (OMH) arose from the Transylvanian

Refugee Office of this organization; it always remained under the control of the most numerous and politically most active Transylvanian refugees. The Székely National Council also provided the leaders of most subsequent revisionist associations. For example, Emil Petrichevich Horváth led the Transylvanian Alliance, Pál Teleki was head of the Foreign Affairs Association and of the League for the Defense [of Hungarian Territory], and József Szörtsey, a Transylvanian landowner, was head of the Attila Alliance.

The Hungarian Christian Cultural League, the parent organization of the National Christian Unity Party, or KNEP, which was to become one of the most important counterrevolutionary groups in 1919 and during the early 1920s, was also originally brought to life by the Transylvanian refugees. It emerged from the Transylvanian Propaganda Committee, which was formed toward the end of 1918 by a few dozen enthusiastic young Transylvanian refugees, who took a solemn oath to defend the territorial integrity of Hungary.[19] Its original name, however, was abandoned in favor of Hungarian Christian Cultural League, when its leaders, Bethlen, Szörtsey, and Zsigmond Perényi, decided to shift the organization's priorities away from immediate military action against the Romanians to the support of purely counterrevolutionary activities.

Presence of the refugees was also strongly felt in the organization called the Hungarian National Defense League, or MOVE, which was formed on November 30, 1918, with membership open to all officers and noncommissioned officers of the old imperial army. Budapest was crowded with unemployed officers. At the end of the war 8000 career and 40,000 reserve officers were on active duty. By the end of December only 2700 career and 4200 reserve officers were kept on the payroll.[20] Many of the unemployed officers were destitute, especially those who found themselves cut off from their homes by the Czech, Romanian, or Serbian occupation forces. Originally MOVE was to be a nonpolitical organization. Its aims were, at first, limited to providing economic aid to refugees, impoverished, or homeless officers, and to organize their social activities.[21] The sharp turn to the right within MOVE was engineered by an alliance of rightists, mostly gentry officers from inner Hungary and the large number of Transylvanian officers in the organization. On January 19, 1919 Gyula Gömbös, captain in the Imperial General Staff and the future prime minister of Hungary, was elected as the president of MOVE; he quickly politicized and transformed the organization into a potent counterrevolutionary force. With Gömbös as president a new group of officers took over MOVE; they were men who were to play prominent roles in the next quarter-century as leaders of the political right. Gömbös came to the leadership of MOVE with ready plans. His basic aim was to create a nationwide network of officers who would rally all opponents of the Károlyi regime. He planned, first, to seize control of the countryside and, then, to isolate and thereby paralyze revolutionary Budapest. He wished to use the Székely National Council as the political center and the Székely Division as the military core of the planned counterrevolution.[22]

The regime was aware of the counterrevolutionary organizational activities. After January 19 the right openly attacked the moderate center. On that day the Transylvanian soldiers held a large demonstration and the Association of the Awakening Hungarians (ÉME) made its violent debut. The latter organization was made up of extreme right-wing university students, refugees, gentry officers, and civil servants. The Social Democrats counterattacked with a demand for banning these organizations. In a speech on February 7, 1919, József Pogány demanded active defense of the achievements of the revolution against the rapidly growing forces of counterrevolution made up of notaries, officials, gendarmes, officers, and "Székelys and pseudo-Székelys."[23] The government decided to attack in two directions: arresting Communist leaders and banning both the Communist Party and, on February 22, MOVE. The organization, however, was not dissolved; it merely went underground. On February 25 Gömbös fled to Vienna, which soon became the new center for the counterrevolution.

None of the various designs of these rightist groups to overthrow the Károlyi regime passed beyond the planning stage. It was the Communist Party, not the radical right, that capitalized on the weaknesses of the Károlyi regime and took control of the government in alliance with the Socialists. The right failed where the left triumphed, and not because of the Communist Party's size or ability to attract a larger number of active members; in fact, the Communist Party had no more than seven to ten thousand members, whereas the combined strength of the right was many times greater. It failed because, unlike the left, the right was incapable of generating broad popular support for its cause; its program appealed only to a narrow group of officers, refugees, and other beneficiaries of the old regime. It failed, too, in another very important respect: again unlike the left, it was unable to organize a disciplined party of its own, with a united leadership, and a membership dedicated to action.

The reasons for the failures of the counterrevolutionary organizations lay in the social origins and psychological state of their members. When they did join counterrevolutionary groups, they did so not in search for a new leader who would lead them to victory. In fact, an individual with strong leadership qualities was often looked upon with suspicion, as one who represented a potential danger to the independence and authority of the other members of the group. As gentlemen of the old order, its privileged elite, they were accustomed to give rather than to take orders. Nor does ideological opposition to the new regime account wholly for their motivation in joining right-wing groups. For the right was far from united ideologically; there was a general agreement on the desirability of destruction of the Károlyi regime and on the demand for a restoration of the prewar Hungarian frontiers. No agreement, however, existed on the political future of the country or on the social order that was to be established. They gravitated toward those organizations because they were deeply traumatized by the destruction of their old authority and the social structure which was its guarantee. Counterrevolutionary groups were attractive to the prewar elite, and especially to the refugees, because they offered certain psychological reassurances that their leadership was still needed by society, that their personal authority was still undiminished, and that their previous social status was still recognized by some individuals. Participation in these groups, in other words, affirmed what they wished to believe: their old identity was still functioning, even though, temporarily, the nobility was pushed into the background. In the group their sense of isolation and loneliness was replaced by a sense of security, of collective protection.

Because of the self-image of these men it was important to them not only to participate in organizations which planned the restoration of their previous social and political authority, but it was equally important to occupy a leading position in these groups. Thus they preferred to be independent generals or even lieutenants of a small group, ineffective as it might have been, rather than to be a disciplined silent soldier in a large, potent counterrevolutionary army. Comradeship of a few equals was preferable to subordination to a larger group. For similar reasons in those few organizations which nevertheless managed to attract a sizable membership discipline was impossible to enforce. Every counterrevolutionary group was wracked by constant petty personal jealousies, by a fierce competition among members for more illustrious and heroic roles. To gain personal recognition of their past social position, rank in society or army, and to protect signs and symbols of these seemed to be more important to many than the ultimate success of the counterrevolutionary enterprise. Thus many groups were not much more than political clubs, or gentlemen's casinos. Their meetings resembled more the chaotic noisy atmosphere of coffee houses, where indeed some of them were held, than gatherings of a determined army of conspirators.

Violent threats and impassioned patriotic pathos of these groups actually represented no real danger; rather they masked the passivity of the members. Incapable of galvanizing themselves into action, they hid behind make-believe preparations for action of these organizations. Baron Pál Prónay, who later commanded the most notorious officers' detachment, wrote the following about his own experience with those would-be counterrevolutionary groups: "Organizational activity went on only on paper, or not even on that. For if the authorities only as much as scared one or another individual, immediately they burnt their papers and fled to Austria. . . . These gatherings did not lead anywhere, only empty chatter flowed freely; everyone proposed some impossible plan, to be carried out in the most fantastic form, but which had no practical value whatsoever."[24] Little wonder, the right was neither able to overthrow, nor even to endanger the Károlyi regime, let alone prevent transfer of power to a coalition of Social Democrats and Communists.

Some of the refugees did drift to the radical left. They joined the various Communist-sponsored political organizations, such as the Association of the Unemployed, and later joined some of the terrorist groups. As Rudolf Tőkés put it: "They had nothing to lose but the unheated freightcar compartments that served as temporary shelter in one of the suburban freight yards. Communist recruiters found many eager converts among these unfortunates who were desperate enough to carry out any assignment in return for a bowl of soup."[25]

For a moment Béla Kun was able to capitalize on both social and national discontent of the population and on those of the refugees to take over the reins of government from Károlyi.[26] The Hungarian Soviet Republic's call to arms against the imperialist Romanians had a strong appeal to all strata of refugees, although the appeal was not uniform. For the working class refugees service in the new Red Army involved no contradiction; their national and class loyalties were in harmony with the aims of the Hungarian Soviet Republic, and their flight or expulsion from the occupied territories helped them to focus their anger on the Romanians and the Czechs.

A clearer indication of the radicalizing effects of the refugee experience is given in the case of refugee peasants. Workers in all parts of the country responded with equal enthusiasm to the recruiting efforts of the Hungarian Soviet Republic, so that the readiness of refugee workers to serve cannot be attributed solely to their refugee status. There was a sharp difference, however, between the attitude toward the Red Army of the peasantry of inner Hungary and that of refugee peasants. The former group, true to the suspicious and conservative nature of the peasantry generally turned a deaf ear to all appeals, whereas the refugee peasants formed a notable exception. They joined in large numbers; in fact, a majority of the peasant soldiers who served in the Red Army was recruited from the ranks of the refugee peasants. Most came from the Bánát and from the region just east of the Tisza River. It was a simple choice for them to join the Red Army, which promised to regain for them their lost homes and their lands, lying often just behind the Romanian front lines. To regain those lands radical steps had to be taken, and the sacrifices demanded of the peasants seemed meaningful to them.[27]

Somewhat more surprising was the participation in the Red Army of a significant number of officers and middle-class refugees. They served in spite of their ideological antipathy to the regime, for, in it, they saw replacement of a foreign policy based on pacifism with one of national resistance, even if Communist. In May and June 1919, during the highly successful northern offensive of the Red Army, these refugees fought with enthusiasm, not to save the regime but to regain the lost territories. When, under the pressures of Clemenceau, orders to evacuate Slovakia were issued, their reason and justification for a continued association with the Communist regime ceased to exist. Many of the refugees and officers suddenly discovered the dangers in their flirtation with the Béla Kun government and, to save their collective necks, deserted the Red Army for one of the counterrevolutionary organizations, the National Army, or some of the special officers' detachments.

In fact, the Hungarian Soviet Republic quickly squandered much of the popular support it gained through its firmness in foreign policy and boldness in military affairs. Withdrawal from the reconquered territories of Upper Hungary, however, was only partly responsible for the declining popularity of the regime. Some of its domestic measures and especially the introduction of a dictatorship of the proletariat contributed equally. Under the leadership of a group of former prisoners of war who participated in the Russian Revolution, the Hungarian Soviet Republic closely followed both the Russian model and method of revolution. As Tibor Szamuely said: "From the first step we followed the road of Soviet Russia. A ready plan, a ready example stood before us."[28] The goal of the Communist Party was a nearly instantaneous socialist transformation of society. To achieve that, in spite of the war against the Successor States, the regime also saw fit to unleash a class war against all opponents of the dictatorship of the proletariat.

Such policies as nationalization of the banks and industries were far less injurous to the popularity of the Soviet Republic than the excessive zeal of enforcement of some of its ill-conceived and naive social reforms. For example, though well intentioned, forced requisition of apartments and furnishings or ban on alcohol consumption caused widespread confusion and resentment without eliminating the underlying causes of social ills.

Fear of a counterrevolution led the government to treat all but the active radical minority as class enemies. To assure the population's submission the government embarked on a policy of taking hostages. In fact, according to József Pogány, every single member of the bourgeoisie was considered to be a hostage. Some even demanded the expulsion of the entire bourgeoisie from the capital. The newly established Political Investigation Bureau within the Ministry of Interior, and under the direction ot Ottó Korvin, conducted widespread arrests and interrogations of potential enemies of the state. It also introduced undercover surveillance of the populace in public places, coffee houses, sporting events, even in churches as well as through the use of informants. The bureau indeed discovered a number of secret political organizations; to deter others, some of the leading conspirators were executed.

Armed bands also contributed to the atmosphere of terror. Of those the activities of the Cserny detachment, under the command of József Cserny, a swashbuckling sailor, became the most notorious. His group of 180–200 men, made up of dedicated Communists, irresponsible sailors, opportunists and criminals, operated independently, without accountability. Cserny's men used their power to blackmail wealthy individuals, or simply to expropriate their property as well as to enforce the will of the dictatorship. The group took hostages, murdered at least eight to ten, and was responsible for the disappearance of an undetermined number of people.

The policy of intimidation failed to strengthen the regime. On the contrary, it helped only to alienate the middle classes and to erode support even among the industrial workers. For example, on July 10, when the workers of a large shipyard decided to vote on the form of government all but 27 voted to end the dictatorship of the proletariat.[29]

After the establishment of the Hungarian Soviet Republic the radical right was temporarily thrown into confusion. Some right-wing groups disappeared forever; others with greatly reduced membership were driven underground. Most of the leaders, fearing for their personal safety, departed in great haste either to Austria or to Szeged, where the French occupying forces offered a safe haven for them. Lesser figures of those groups melted into the crowds of Budapest or disappeared in the countryside. Many of the nobles simply withdrew from political activity and retired to their country estates. This last option was, of course, not open to refugees, who felt politically compromised; they either had to go into hiding or to flee to areas beyond the reach of the Communist government.

For the refugees it was easier to decide on a sudden second departure; they had already abandoned material possessions, homes and estates, and relatives and friends. Consequently, in the counterrevolutionary groups, which were formed in Vienna and Szeged, there was again a preponderance of the refugees from the lost territories. At the same time, as a result of the exodus of thousands of refugees and nobles from Communist-controlled territories, the makeup of the leadership of the clandestine counterrevolutionary groups within Hungary underwent some important changes. Aristocrats almost completely disappeared from the leadership; the proportion of the refugee leaders with gentry background was also greatly reduced. Their places were taken by army and police officers, by right-wing bourgeois elements and professionals, by doctors, engineers, lawyers, bureaucrats, mostly of non-noble origins, often from the assimilated German population.[30] At the same time among the rank-and-file membership the number of refugees from the Successor States still remained substantial.

Neither the bourgeoisie nor the military opponents of the Hungarian Soviet Republic were able to organize a mass following, which would have been necessary if they were to challenge the government with any hope of success. Civilian counterrevolutionary groups, though numerous, remained small in size and were isolated from each other. They were able to maintain only the most casual contacts with each other, with the counterrevolutionary cells in the army, and with the Vienna and Szeged groups. Isolation of these groups prevented or at least made coordination of their activities exceedingly difficult.

Even the officers still on the active list remained poorly organized. Counterrevolutionary headquarters were established at Székesfehérvár, but officers' effectiveness in mobilizing an army for the overthrow of the regime was at best minimal.[31] Most officers remained isolated at their posts; they were watched with suspicion and were frequently questioned about their associations and communications by Communist political officers. They could trust only their fellow officers, some subalterns, and virtually none of the soldiers. Many of them were arrested or held as hostages, and even a larger number were forced to flee across the border to Austria, or over the southern line of demarcation.

The first open counterrevolutionary attack against the Soviet Republic, in fact, came not from the radical right, but from the peasantry and some of the workers. The peasants, who in March 1919 greeted the new regime with an indifferent or suspicious silence at most, had by May and June begun to show signs of hostility toward the government. Once more disappointed in their hopes for land reform, incensed by the forced requisitions of their food reserves and draught animals, by the occasional senseless desecration of their churches, by the insults or arrests of their priests, and by the introduction of a new, virtually worthless paper currency (called white money since it was printed on white paper), the peasantry in many places reached the point of rebellion.

Already in April and early May violence had flared up in widely scattered parts of the country. Especially hard hit was the Tisza region along the demarcation line. In late May and June rebellion was rampant, a situation made even worse by a widespread rail and postal strike. The most intense fighting took place in Pest county, around the town of Kalocsa and in the region directly adjacent to the Austrian border. The rail strike paralyzed virtually the country's entire communication system and largely isolated Budapest from the rest of the country. It was triggered by certain economic demands of the workers and by their resentment over being drafted wholesale into the Red Army. In addition to draft exemption, the workers also demanded the resignation of the Communist-dominated government and the establishment of an all Socialist cabinet.[32] These demands, coming on the heels of major Romanian victories on the eastern front, led to the spread of not entirely unfounded rumors about the resignation or near collapse of the Kun government and the possible Romanian occupation of Budapest. The Romanian advance, in fact, was halted on April 27, and the regime not only survived but was even able to go on the offensive. Nevertheless, the peasantry responded to the rumors with a series of spontaneous risings.

Counterrevolution broke out in about seventy villages. The pattern of rebellion in nearly every village was the same. Upon hearing rumors about an imminent collapse of the Communist regime, the peasants, motivated by fear or aroused by some local grievance, armed themselves, determined to protect their property against one more final exaction, or to defend their village against roving bands of soldiers. They did not intend to march against the towns. It was sufficient for them to gain control of their village; they rarely even attempted to link up with neighboring villages similarly defending what was theirs. After disarming the local Red Guards and arresting members of the local Communist directory the peasants usually adopted a defensive position on the edge of their villages.

Generally both the nobility and the officers were absent from the early stages of these uprisings. Peasant counterrevolutionaries were led and organized by more prosperous villagers, or by local priests or other notables. Once it became clear, however, that these uprisings were not isolated incidents but a widespread phenomenon, hundreds of enthusiastic but irresponsible officers appeared on the scene, hoping to exploit the mass disaffection of the peasantry. They succeeded only in stiffening their resistance, but not in bringing down the regime.

Already, on April 21, the government established a Court of Summary Justice under the presidency of Tibor Szamuely. When the rebellions broke out Szamuely rode circuit court, accompanied by his detachment, the "Lenin boys." Most often the peasants surrendered at the first sign of force, but in some places loyal workers' battalions also had to be called out to repress the peasants. In other areas, especially where the officers were most successful in arming and organizing the population, fierce fighting took place before the regime's authority was restored. Officers and other nonpeasant leaders generally succeeded in escaping the consequences of their actions by fleeing to Austria or to Szeged, where they soon joined some of the officers' detachments of the fledgling National Army. The remaining peasants paid the price for rebellion. Of the five to six hundred people who were killed or executed during the Hungarian Soviet Republic, 73 percent were peasants, only 9.9 percent officers, 8.2 percent were members of the bourgeoisie, and 7.8 percent came from the landowning or former ruling stratum. But among all the victims none came from the aristocracy.[33]

The only serious attempt at overthrowing the Kun regime which was exclusively organized and carried out by middle-class counterrevolutionary groups, was the ill-fated Budapest *coup d'état* of June 24.[34] It was a debacle, just like all the previous attempts in which the right had participated. It failed, owing to basically poor planning, lack of manpower, and lack of coordination among different counterrevolutionary groups. The whole enterprise was doomed to failure from the beginning, because its success was predicated on a synchronized attack with the Social Democrats, who, as it was rumored, were also planning a coup of their own under the leadership of József Haubrich, the commander of the Budapest garrison.[35] The counterrevolutionary planners hoped to use the strength of the Social Democrats to overthrow the Soviet government and then to exploit the ensuing chaos to bring about a full-blown counterrevolution. As it turned out, at the appointed hour, in spite of the rumors, Haubrich failed to make a move; by the time his opposition to the counterrevolution became known, the uprising by the right-wing elements could not be called off.[36] In the confusion that followed most of the promised help from the different counterrevolutionary groups failed to materialize, partly because some of the leaders promised nothing but their paper armies. Even those groups which could have mobilized some armed men for the coup refused to respond to the opening artillery fire, signaling the beginning of the uprising, until they were assured of Socialist help. Thus, only a few officers, the cadets of the Ludovika military academy, and a few naval vessels on the Danube swung into action and began occupation or bombardment of some key government buildings.[37] Too weak to achieve much they were suppressed within a few hours. Most of those who actively participated in the uprising were quickly rounded up, but some of its leaders, ships with full crews, along with some who felt compromised by the incident managed to escape. In Vienna and Szeged, these new refugees, as all those who had come before them, were welcomed by the counterrevolutionary white government.

In Vienna and Szeged, as we have noted, these two groups, the refugees from the Hungarian Soviet Republic and the refugees from the Successor States, merged into a single counterrevolutionary force. From their refugee experiences a new radical ideology soon emerged. It was based on violent anticommunism of the refugees from the Hungarian Soviet Republic, fused with an extreme form of nationalism and national prejudice of the refugees from the Successor States. These became the cornerstones of the ideology of the Hungarian radical right, which during the Horthy era was proudly called: "The Idea of Szeged."

Chapter 7
Counterrevolutionary Movements in Austria and Szeged

With each failed attempt to overthrow the Kun regime the counterrevolutionary groups in Austria and in the French-occupied region around Szeged were reinforced by new refugees from Soviet Hungary. It was a highly mixed group that gathered in Vienna and Szeged. Virtually every stratum of old Hungarian society was represented: aristocrats, the gentry, politicians, landowners, some members of the non-noble middle classes, and even some workers and peasants. Nearly every shade of political opinion and every region of Hungary had representatives, archconservatives, liberals, and socialists from widely scattered parts of Hungary. Perhaps as many as 100,000 Hungarian refugees fled to Austria, most to Vienna, including between ten and fifteen thousand officers.[1] The vast majority were members of the prewar middle and upper classes of whom the aristocrats and the officers of the old Imperial Army were the most conspicuous.[2]

It was impossible to unite such a diverse group into a homogeneous counterrevolutionary movement. Personal jealousies, constant dissension, and passivity of the majority of the refugees prevented establishment of an effective organization. The Vienna refugee group was suffering from typical maladies of refugees.

All of these refugees were traumatized and radicalized by their experiences; yet, there were degrees in their radicalism. The degree of radicalization of a refugee was determined, aside from the natural variations between individual experiences and personal psychological makeup, mostly by his social and regional origins.

Members of aristocracy were generally less radicalized by their physical dislocation than those coming from the gentry or gentroid classes. This was especially true for magnates of western Hungary, including those from western Slovakia. Aristocrats of this region were the most cosmopolitan group among the Hungarian ruling classes. They frequently intermarried with the Austrian and Western aristocracy, and, for many of them, Vienna was their second home and German their second, if not their first, language. Many owned estates on both sides of the Leitha/Lajta River, consequently taking refuge in Austria did not mean even a change in their life style. They were wealthy, Catholic, and generally loyal supporters of the Habsburg dynasty. In the past, many were supporters of the aristocratic, conservative Constitution Party of Gyula Andrássy, Jr.; others were totally apolitical, and even during the revolutions some of them remained aloof from politics.

Aristocrats of Transylvania and eastern Hungary were poorer, traditionally lived on their estates, and intermarried with the lesser nobility. Many were Calvinists, some Unitarians, always more liberal. Historically, many of them were open foes of the Habsburg dynasty, champions of the idea of an independent Hungary, and some even of an independent Transylvania. Several had deep historical roots in the Transylvanian soil; hence, displacement made a profound impact on them. As a result they were more radical and more active in the counterrevolutionary movement than their fellow aristocrats from western Hungary.

The gentry and the middle classes shared only in part the attitudes of the aristocracy of their particular region. The gentry of western Hungary and the Slovak-inhabited north were also mostly Catholic, generally pro-Habsburg, and, at times, leaned toward a moderate form of Christian Socialism. The gentry of eastern Hungary and Transylvania was mostly Protestant, anti-Habsburg, and followers of what they believed was the liberal tradition of 1848 and Lajos Kossuth. Unlike the aristocracy, the gentry and the non-noble middle classes were not wedded to the idea of a complete restoration of the old regime. For them, to regain control of the state machinery, even if in a drastically different form, was far more important than the preservation of the old socioeconomic system based on the great estates in alliance with large-scale capitalism. In fact, many of the gentry were openly hostile to both and were willing to sacrifice the aristocracy's latifundia and the wealth of the capitalists in exchange for a restoration of their own political predominance. Some even harbored socialist ideas. Gyula Gömbös, one of the most prominent figures of the interwar period, offers a good illustration. In the April 2, 1919 issue of his newspaper the *Bécsi Magyar Futár* (Hungarian Messenger of Vienna), he boasted of his socialist convictions: "Yes, we are socialists, Hungarian national socialists." This socialism was different from that of Marx. To Gömbös it meant a kind of agrarian populism, with redistribution of the nation's wealth, thereby giving an opportunity to the lower classes to raise themselves out of poverty through their own initiative. It did not mean expropriation of all private property, nationalization of the means of production, or establishment of state capitalism. In his mind that was the greatest weakness of the Marxist system, for it sooner or later led to a destruction of national vitality and to dehumanization of man. "Marx's state," he wrote, "in the final analysis will be nothing but a bureaucratic state, without any dynamism, full of boring people who are nothing but lifeless parts of a great social machine."[3] He also rejected the Marxist concept of class struggle. Class conflict had to be replaced with class cooperation, where each class was to fulfill the role marked out by history and by the needs of the nation.

Gömbös's nationalist, agrarian social radicalism had wide appeal among the dispossessed officers and gentry officials, especially to those coming from the central and eastern regions of Hungary. These ideas, of course, could not be reconciled with the interests of the aristocracy. Nevertheless, for the moment at least, in face of the great common objective, that is, the overthrow of the dictatorship of the proletariat in Budapest, the ideological differences were blurred between the aristocracy and the gentry. Thus, in spite of the differences, it was possible to establish a common base for cooperation between the various refugee groups.

Conservative, radical Christian and radical nationalist points of view were well represented in both Vienna and Szeged. Vienna was overflowing with refugees of every nationality from all parts of the former monarchy, but according to Prónay, ". . . the largest contingent of these stateless persons was still made up of members of the Hungarian aristocracy, then of the landed gentry and of high-ranking officers, who had earlier fled from the red terror and communism in Hungary."[4]

These proportions hold true if we measure the weight of each group not by numbers, but according to political influence. Of the various refugee groups in the old imperial city, middle-class refugees from Slovakia were most numerous. In Szeged, on the other hand, the gentry and the refugees from Transylvania and from the Great Hungarian Plain formed the dominant groups. In Vienna counterrevolutionary leadership was in the hands of the aristocracy and the gentry from northern Hungary; in Szeged the radical-right gentry and the Transylvanian lesser nobility were most powerful.

An umbrella organization, which was to coordinate from Vienna all counterrevolutionary activities both within and outside Hungary, the *Comité de l'ordre et antibolsheviste hongrois,* the so-called *Antibolshevik comité,* or ABC, was formed on April 12, 1919, under the direction of Count István Bethlen. The organization found a home in the palace of Count Karl Schönborn-Bucheim who, though an Austrian aristocrat, was interested in the victory of the counterrevolution because of his vast estates in Hungary. The ABC claimed to be the legal successor to the Bourgeois Bloc, a coalition of all nonsocialist, nationalist, center and right-wing parties that was formed before the establishment of the Hungarian Soviet Republic, to run a single slate of candidates in the postponed national elections. Thus, the ABC claimed to represent not only the individual members present in Vienna but a broad spectrum of Hungarian society.[5]

The ABC was dominated by the refugee aristocrats and by the Catholic gentry or non-noble middle class refugees from Slovakia. Among them Counts István Bethlen, Pál Teleki, Kunó Klebelsberg, Zoltán Bánffy were Transylvanian magnates, Counts Gyula Andrássy, Jr., Aladár Zichy, János Zichy, and Géza Zichy were born on their estates in territories ceded to Czechoslovakia. Count László Szapáry was the wealthiest magnate from areas populated by Slovenes, including the Muraköz, lost to Yugoslavia; Count Antal Sigray and Count Zsigmond Batthyány were magnates of western Hungary; Count Gedeon Ráday and Margrave György Pallavicini came from central Hungary. The ABC's most prominent gentry or non-noble middle-class leaders were almost exclusively born in territories lost to Czechoslovakia. Among these, the best-known figures were György Szmrecsányi, Ödön Beniczky, Gusztáv Gratz, Sándor Ernszt, István Haller, and Elemér Huszár. In the past most had belonged either to Andrássy's Constitution Party, or to the Catholic People's Party, both opposing István Tisza. The Catholic People's Party was especially strongly represented among ABC leaders.

The ABC leadership's aristocratic wing had few illusions about their own strength. They realized that only with the aid of the Western Powers could they ever hope to regain control of Hungary. Bethlen, therefore, concentrated most of his energies on the establishment of contacts with the Western governments through either resident diplomats in Vienna, or through the extensive international contacts of some of his fellow aristocrats.[6]

Bethlen was most anxious to find out the attitudes of the Western Allies toward a possible counterrevolutionary government, set up on foreign soil, or in the Allied-occupied territories of Hungary. With this object in mind, Pallavicini contacted Colonel Thomas Cuninghame, the head of the British Mission in Vienna. Gratz approached the French representative Henri Allizé, others cautiously opened a dialogue with the Italian and American representatives; Bethlen submitted a memorandum directly to the Paris Peace Conference and to General Berthelot in Bucharest, urging the Allies to halt the Romanian advance at the line of the Tisza River and suggesting that the Great Powers overthrow the Kun regime. He also expressed his willingness to form a counterrevolutionary coalition government, in which one or two posts were to be reserved for members of the Social Democratic Party. He would exclude from this government only the Communists. The government, he proposed, would take over control of the country after the fall of the Communist regime, and immediately would hold elections based on universal suffrage. Finally, he requested a loan of between twenty and thirty million crowns that was to be used to maintain the counterrevolutionary government and to establish a small army.[7]

The Western Powers refused to commit their own military resources for the overthrow of the Hungarian Soviet Republic. They were also reluctant to finance a counterrevolutionary government in which the aristocratic element was dominant. They were suspicious of the attitudes of some members of the ABC, especially of the Andrássy group, which was believed to hold strong pro-German sentiments.[8] Additionally, they preferred to alter the composition of the Hungarian government through direct negotiations with the Hungarian Social Democratic Party. Indeed, during July, allied representatives in Vienna discussed the possibility of an all socialist government with Vilmos Böhm and other Socialist leaders.[9]

Nevertheless, the Western Powers through Henri Allizé held out a slender thread of hope by indicating their willingness to consider the question of recognition of a counterrevolutionary government if that government was composed of a coalition of the progressive parties, and if it was established on unoccupied Hungarian soil. The area where the non-communist government was to be established, even if it represented only a fraction of the total area of Hungary, had to be controlled exclusively by the counterrevolutionary government. Colonel Cuninghame conveyed essentially the same message to the ABC through his contacts.[10] In other words, the Western governments were willing to support a counterrevolutionary government only after its ability to function and to survive had been demonstrated, but they wished to refrain from overtly imposing a government on Hungary.

It was a clear challenge to the refugees to prove the viability of their movement by organizing a White Army. Bethlen was skeptical about the refugees' ability to establish a military force that was powerful enough to wrest even a small area from the Communist regime. Nevertheless, he urged the creation of a military force, not to use it for an invasion, but to hold it in readiness for the moment when the Kun regime would collapse, which he considered only a matter of time. The radical gentry and officer faction of the ABC, however, were eager to carry out an immediate attack on Hungary. They naively believed that the mere appearance of an anticommunist army, even if small, would have such a tremendous psychological impact on the entire population that it would trigger an immediate uprising all over the country.

In the absence of Western financial support the only alternative that remained open was to organize this counterrevolutionary army from the slender resources of the refugees. In the name of the Bethlen faction, Aurél Egry and Adolf Ullmann negotiated a ten million crown loan from a group of Viennese bankers, using as a collateral some estates of a group of Hungarian magnates. Some additional resources were secured from the thriving smuggling business across the Hungarian frontier under the direction of some of the aristocrats and officers, though the profits were not always used solely for the cause.[11] Most of the money for the counterrevolutionary army came from the famous Bankgasse robbery. On May 2–3, 1919, upon learning about a large shipment of cash from Budapest to the Hungarian Embassy in Vienna located at Bankgasse, the Szmrecsányi group first burglarized, and later, some forty or fifty officers ransacked the premises. The booty was quite substantial: about 140 million crowns in Austro-Hungarian bills plus an undetermined amount in Western currencies. Out of this sum about 69 million crowns were recovered by the Viennese police, but the remainder was divided among the various refugee groups. Szmrecsányi retained for his faction a lion's share, about 50 million crowns, the Szeged group received a mere 3 million; the rest was turned over to the Bethlen group.[12]

This coup made Szmrecsányi and his followers financially independent of Bethlen. From this point on, friction between the two factions drastically increased. Bethlen still insisted on an essentially diplomatic solution to the problem of Communist Hungary; Szmrecsányi and his officers pinned their hopes on military action. Szmrecsányi opposed any foreign alliance or foreign occupation of Hungary. He persisted in his belief that Hungary could be truly free only if it were liberated by a purely Hungarian counterrevolutionary army. The Western Powers' attitudes actually played into his hands. Their refusal to recognize a government-in-exile gave weight to his argument that it was imperative to invade Hungary with a refugee army first, before any aid from the West could be expected.

The most logical choice for such an invasion seemed to be along the western borders of Hungary, where the staunchly Catholic peasantry could be relied on to side with opponents of communism. Proximity of the area to military sanctuaries in Austria also made this region the favored target of the refugees in Austria.

To assure success of such an invasion careful organization and planning would have been necessary. Instead, after the "great victory" over communism in the Bankgasse raid, the impetuous Szmrecsányi with a small force of radical officers made an attempt at invading Hungary, thus setting off a counterrevolution. From the approximately 10,000 officers and 20,000 war veterans in Vienna only 44 men were willing to risk their lives in such an adventure. In a comic opera scene some of these enthusiastic and foolhardy conspirators rode in taxis to the border town of Bruck, only to be caught in the cross fire of waiting soldiers of the Hungarian Red Army and the Austrian *Volkswehr,* which returned the Hungarian fire. The counterrevolutionary invasion army was arrested by the *Volkswehr* without so much as setting a foot on Hungarian soil.[13]

After this fiasco the radical faction of ABC, headed by Szmrecsányi, Beniczky, and József Wild, shifted their headquarters to the politically more hospitable city of Graz, where they hoped to be free from the close watch of Socialist Vienna. From Graz, Szmrecsányi, somewhat sobered by his earlier failures, planned to direct a well-organized and coordinated attack against Hungary. The key elements in his plans were an uprising in border areas and a simultaneous invasion of Hungary from Austria by refugee officers' detachments, in cooperation with Austrian right-wing military groups. Early in May he opened negotiations with Willibald Brodmann, president of the Christian Socialist Party of Styria, and also head of the 10,000-man *Bauernkommando.* In exchange for a payment of five million crowns Brodmann promised that the *Bauernbund* would aid in the organization of the counterrevolutionary army.[14] In addition, Count Stürgkh, the brother of the murdered Austrian prime minister, promised that the *Heimwehr* would provide some 7000 weapons to arm refugee officers and peasants.

At the same time, agents of the ABC did everything in their power to encourage a Slovene separatist movement in Hungary. Large sums of money were made available for support of secessionist Slovenes. To an independent Slovenia, foreign aid was promised, also diplomatic and military aid, plus full support of the right-wing officers both in Hungary and in Austria, was guaranteed. In Vilmos Tkalecz, head of the Communist Slovene District Directory and also a Slovene nationalist, a willing local leader was found. Tkalecz, a teacher by profession who served as an officer during the war, was willing to use the aid offered to him by the refugee officers in Austria, but it is not clear what his own plans were and to what degree he was aware of the plans of Szmrecsányi to use the secessionist movement to establish himself on Hungarian territory. There is some indication that with a sudden declaration of independence of the Slovene population he intended to force the intervention of the Belgrade government.[15]

At any event, the ill-disguised preparations for the coup and the large-scale smuggling carried out by Tkalecz and his supporters, as well as some of his other financial abuses, aroused the suspicion of the Kun regime. This forced the conspirators to show their hand prematurely, before all preparations were completed. Thus on May 29, Tkalecz suddenly decided, before he was assured of all the aid that was promised to him, to declare the establishment of the independent Mura Republic. Tkalecz became president of the new republic and in this capacity he appealed to the Hungarian Soviet Republic to respect the Slovene people's right to self-determination. He also requested aid from the Hungarian regime to help his people in their efforts to establish a Socialist state. He expressed his desire to live in friendship with the Hungarian Soviet Republic, but also threatened an appeal to the Western powers, should Hungary decide to use military force against the Mura Republic.

This hasty declaration of secession caught the Szmrecsányi group totally unprepared. As a result, the promised military assistance could not be delivered in full, and even those detachments that were dispatched and crossed over to Hungary arrived too late to affect the outcome of the struggle. At the outset Tkalecz had at his disposal a force of some 600 regular troops and 300 mercenaries.[16] It was believed that this force was sufficient to hold the territory until the arrival of reinforcements from Austria. At first, this small unit was indeed successful against local Red Army units; some of which refused to fight, others sided with the rebels; but the unexpectedly swift and violent counterattack by the hastily transferred loyal workers' battalions forced the rebels, after some heavy fighting, to retreat toward Austria. Once in Austria they were disarmed and interned in a prisoners' camp at Feldbach, which soon became a new center for counterrevolutionary activities. Feldbach served as the gathering point for all those officers and men who after the failure of subsequent coup attempts in Hungary managed to escaped to Austria. It became a major recruiting ground, from which Colonel Baron Antal Lehár drew the manpower for his detachments that were to operate in western Hungary after the collapse of the Hungarian Soviet Republic.[17]

Failure of these invasion attempts convinced many that Austria was not the proper place for organization of a counterrevolutionary army. Efforts to create a military force that would be capable of penetrating Hungary never ceased, but no significant new attempts were made after early June. Increasingly the focus of counterrevolutionary activities shifted to Szeged. Many of those officers who were dissatisfied with poor organization in Austria concluded that the next decisive move would not come from the refugee groups in Austria but that it would be made by the Szeged counterrevolutionary government.

Counterrevolution in Szeged

In 1939 during celebrations commemorating the twentieth anniversary of the 1919 counterrevolutionary movement, Count Pál Teleki said: ". . . since that time there are anticomintern pacts, antibolshevik movements but who were the originators? We were, here at Szeged."[18] During the Horthy era the name of Szeged acquired a special mystique, a special place in right-wing nationalist mythology. Szeged was celebrated as the birthplace of national rejuvenation and as the city where the "Idea of Szeged," the ideology of this national renaissance, was first given concrete form. In the eyes of right-wing chroniclers of this period Szeged appeared as the new Mecca where, at the moment of deepest despair and humiliation of the nation, when Hungary lay prostrate before her conquerors and devoured by flames of revolution, a few thousand patriots, undaunted by many defeats and by heavy odds against them, gathered to form a national government and a national army. From there they marched forth to recapture Hungary and to cleanse her of the alien and anti-Christian usurpers of power and, then, to rededicate the nation to its true national and Christian principles.

Szeged, itself, was not a radical or conservative town. Although the second largest city in Hungary, it was still predominantly agricultural, with a strong commercial and official stratum generally of non-noble origins, and a relatively weak working class mostly employed in the agriculture-oriented industries. This social makeup, plus the location of the city on the Great Hungarian Plain, where the tradition of Kossuth was always strong, went far to determine the political attitudes of its population. Throughout the Dualist Era Szeged had remained faithful to the liberal principles of 1848. After the October Revolution the population generally backed the moderate democratic course advocated by Károlyi.

Szeged, therefore, owed the dubious distinction of being the celebrated birthplace of the Hungarian radical right not to any traditional right-wing radicalism of its native population, but to the fact that in mid–1919 it was the only Hungarian city which could offer a safe haven for both the thousands of displaced persons from the Successor States and for those fleeing from the Communist-held territories. The city's favorable geographic location and the special status that made it attractive and safe for the refugees. Wedged between the occupation zones of

Romania and Serbia and the territories of the Hungarian Soviet Republic, Szeged was easily accessible from all three areas. At the same time, due to French military presence in the city, it was outside the jurisdiction of the Successor States and after March 29, 1919, beyond the reach of the official Hungarian government.

French occupation began in December 1918 and by January 1919 the number of French troops rose to approximately 3000.[19] The presence of these troops became especially significant after March 21, and the establishment of the Hungarian Soviet Republic. Following that event, in Szeged, as almost everywhere in Hungary, control of instruments of state power passed to a hastily formed directory. Neither the populace nor the local French military commander opposed that move. Unlike anywhere else, however, French presence made dissolution of the directory possible after only six days of existence, and the disarming of the local Red Army units a few weeks later.[20] This did not alter the legal status of the city; nominally it still remained under Budapest's control, but, in reality, it attained an independent status, subject only to the authority of the city's French commander. The French generally refrained from interfering in the city's day-to-day operation. Thus the old city administration functioned more or less as an independent government.

It would be an error to date the beginning of the counterrevolutionary movement with the overthrow of the Szeged directory. This coup was essentially a local, isolated incident, made possible by special circumstances and carried out by local officers. These officers were not members of the radical right. Most of them were recruited from the ranks of local moderate and liberal elements, with only a sprinkling of radical refugee officers. The large number number of Jewish officers among the participants is especially noteworthy. It indicates that active opposition to the Communist regime was not the exclusive concern of the right. Also, it demonstrates that in early May the moderate and liberal forces still held the upper hand in Szeged. Moreover, at that time, cooperation between moderate and right-wing elements was still possible, and anti-Semitism was not a factor as long as the refugee officers were in the minority.[21] Even the establishment of the ABC's Szeged branch, in April 1919, was strictly a local affair, without national significance.

The counterrevolutionary ideology became dominant and the counterrevolutionary movement began to acquire momentum only after the refugees began to arrive in sufficiently significant numbers to tip the balance of power in favor of radical right-wing elements.

In March 1919 there was already a sizable number of refugees in Szeged. They came mostly from the southern, Serbian-occupied territories, but, being largely unorganized, their political impact on the city was negligible. After March, however, their numbers were rapidly reinforced by waves of new refugees, especially from Romanian-controlled areas. These refugees did not dare go to Hungary for fear of less than generous treatment by the Communists who considered them enemies of the people owing to their class origins and association with the old regime. Szeged, therefore, was the only place where they could find safety. The flow of refugees toward Szeged accelerated after mid-April, when Romania renewed her offensive and brought under her control large strips of additional territory. The same offensive also broke the back of the Székely Division. Scores of Székely officers and men who refused Romanian internment and no longer wished to serve in the Red Army gradually found their way to Szeged.[22] During May and June thousands of additional refugees escaped to Szeged from central Hungary, some, mostly politicians of the old regime, as a precautionary measure, but much larger numbers fled after each of the many unsuccessful counterrevolutionary attempts, to escape the draconian justice of Tibor Szamuely. For example, from Kalocsa and its neighboring villages alone several thousand individuals fled to Szeged after the collapse of the counterrevolutionary attempt.[23]

From Austria, hundreds of refugees were sent in small groups across Yugoslavia by ABC's recruiting officers. They were mostly radical officers. Others, such as Gömbös and László Magasházy, were sent there to establish contact between the various counterrevolutionary groups in Austria and Szeged. A third group of officers, such as Prónay, left Vienna on their own; they were disenchanted with the Austrian groups' failures and grew skeptical about the success of any attempt directed against the Hungarian Soviet Republic from Austrian territory. They were also opposed to the conservative, aristocratic leadership of the Vienna ABC.[24] Prónay, who was never short of malice, wrote about this migration to Szeged: ". . . From every corner of the country the opportunists, frauds, condottieri descended on [Szeged] like wasp on to honey, because they knew the different opportunities which such times opened for them. All offered their services and wished to become somebody."[25]

Precise figures on the number of refugees who thus gathered in Szeged are not available. By the summer of 1919, however, their numerical strength and their political impact on the city were considerable. It may be estimated that by the beginning of August around 35,000 refugees were living in the city, out of which approximately 12,000–14,000 came from the Successor States, mainly from Yugoslavia and Romania, and most of the rest from inner Hungary.[26] As we have noted, the social background of the refugees in Szeged differed from that of the Vienna group. The aristocratic group was weak; the more radical officers and Protestant gentry elements from central and eastern Hungary, dominant. The Szeged group, therefore, held more radical social views, were less attached to the old land-tenure system, and were more intensely nationalistic. Some were also anti-Habsburg, although the question of Habsburg restoration had not yet divided the forces of the right.

The political impact of these refugees on Szeged was far greater than their actual number would have warranted. For one thing these refugees were politically more conscious and more active than the average citizen of Szeged. Most were members of the old ruling elite and, as such, they were accustomed to think in political terms and felt that it was their responsibility to offer an alternative to the nation more in tune with their own traditional ideology. They were generally young, well educated, at least in those subjects that were deemed appropriate for their class, and psychologically prepared to take drastic measures to recapture their previous positions in society. Many of them had served in the army as officers, some saw long combat duty; all had witnessed an increased political influence of the military. These experiences had prepared them to accept violence as the method and dictatorship as a political form when dealing with a crisis situation.

At first, the population of Szeged welcomed the refugees with generosity and with compassion. Prominent citizens opened their homes to upper-class refugees. Leading ladies of the city organized charity drives for their benefit. The city council ordered conversion of schools and other available public buildings into refugee hostels, set up free kitchens and, for others, made loans available guaranteed by the city treasury.[27]

With the growing number of refugees this hospitality gradually gave way to irritation and finally to open resentment. Complaints about housing shortages and crowded conditions grew louder with each passing day. In fact by mid-summer many refugees were incapable of finding any accommodations within the city and spilled over into adjacent villages. There at times reluctant peasants opened their gates to the uninvited guests only under police pressure. Food shortages and scarcity of other supplies and a necessity of having to share these with an army of refugees and opportunists caused additional frictions.

A more important conflict arose because of the right-wing radicalism of the refugees, which stood in sharp contrast with the moderate and liberal views of the local population. Liberals, local trade unions, and non-Communist Socialists were apprehensive about the increasing domination of the city by refugee extremists. These groups were opposed to dictatorship in whatever form. In their view a genuine alternative to the dictatorship of the proletariat was to be found not in a dictatorship of the right but in a liberal or, perhaps, socialist, democracy.

The liberal press such as *Délmagyarország* (Southern Hungary) openly attacked the extremist tendencies among the refugees and the more and more frequent physical street attacks on peaceful citizens.[28] Another paper, the *Szegedi Napló* (Journal of Szeged) in an editorial entitled "White Bolshevism" raised the specter of an irresponsible white terror should the right be allowed to triumph. It also called for expulsion of those refugees who could not prove an overriding necessity for their presence in the city. The nationalist press indignantly rejected these charges and defended the refugees as innocent victims who suffered for the whole nation. This followed up with an acrimonious and venomous campaign of their own against the liberal press.[29]

With rapid increase of refugees in the city the right radicals acquired sufficient strength to silence the disunited local moderates. But French occupying forces proved an obstacle which this new power could not overcome.

The French generally did not intervene in the day-to-day squabbles in the press and between liberals and refugees, but they did in clashes over the makeup of the proposed counterrevolutionary government, and the struggle became three-sided. On this issue as well as on questions concerning the counterrevolutionary army, the French had an important and, often, deciding voice. To the counterrevolutionaries at Szeged, French policy toward Hungarian opponents of the Kun regime contained some curious contradictions. The French seemed both to support and oppose the counterrevolutionary movement. First, French-occupying forces turned Szeged into a safe haven for all reactionary and right-wing elements. They openly encouraged the gathering of refugees in that town; they were instrumental in sending hundreds of officers and other refugees from Austria to Szeged. Also, although they turned a deaf ear to Count Bethlen's proposal for the establishment of a counterrevolutionary government-in-exile, the French were responsible for the existence of the first counterrevolutionary government of Count Gyula Károlyi at Arad. This government was brought to life on May 5, at the express urging of two French officers, General Paul de Lobit, and the commander of Arad, General Henri Gondrecourt. The composition of Károlyi's cabinet was also prescribed by the French. It had to be a moderate, anticommunist coalition government with both the liberals and conservatives participating, that is, not unlike Bethlen's proposed government.[30] The French, too, engineered its transfer to Szeged after realizing that Serbian and Romanian occupation of the surrounding countryside isolated Arad, thereby making it unsuitable for uniting opponents of the Hungarian Soviet Republic. Similarly, the French instigated cabinet changes, and, finally, they were responsible for the formation of the counterrevolutionary National Army under Admiral Miklós Horthy.[31]

At the same time, the French had no intentions of negotiating with, let alone recognizing, Károlyi's cabinet as the legal government of Hungary. Although the French fashioned the artificial environment in which the refugees could organize in safety its protective shield around the town soon became a prison for both the counterrevolutionary army and government. Without French permission, supplies, and military cooperation, no counterrevolutionary attack could be contemplated against the Hungarian regime. Such permission was withheld until after the collapse of the Kun regime. The French also prohibited expansion of the National Army, and they refused to release the needed captured arms. Thus the counterrevolutionary government was paralyzed and its will remained constantly fixed on its French masters' wishes.[32] In short, the whole Szeged counterrevolutionary movement became an instrument, an appendage of French foreign policy; the movement could triumph only if its victory could be fitted into the greater French foreign policy designs for East Central Europe.

Neither the French nor the other Western Powers had specific long-range plans for Hungary. After the establishment of the Hungarian Soviet Republic the country aroused international attention only as a Western outpost of Bolshevism. The major aim of French policy was to destroy that regime, and, if necessary, use force. The counterrevolutionary movement was not suited for that purpose. It lacked the necessary military strength to make even a significant contribution; the overthrow of the Hungarian Soviet system had to be achieved either with French forces or with those of France's East Central European allies, the Czechs and the Romanians. At the time when the first proposal for formation of a counterrevolutionary government was made, the French were, it seems, momentarily considering dispatching some of their own troops to Budapest to overthrow the Communist government.[33] In that event a Hungarian government, representing a broad coalition of the noncommunist parties, in tow of French forces, could have been useful. Even after this plan was discarded, French control of the counterrevolutionary movement promised some solid diplomatic advantages. By keeping the Szeged government firmly in their orbit France could curtail diplomatic contacts between Hungarian refugees and other powers, could limit the influence over the refugees of other powers, especially Great Britain and Italy.[34]

Control of a Hungarian counterrevolutionary government also offered

France a leverage against its own East Central European allies, specifically Serbia and Romania. Both Belgrade and Bucharest looked upon signs of friendliness toward Hungary by a great power with utmost anxiety. They realized that premature normalization of relations between the Western Powers, and especially between France and Hungary, would jeopardize chances of securing their maximum territorial claims against Hungary. Unconditional support of France could not be taken for granted after France decided to permit organization of a new Hungarian government. This policy, therefore, had a moderating influence on Belgrade and Bucharest *vis-à-vis* each other, and their strained relations over the disputed province of Bánát were kept below boiling point.

Belgrade chose to follow the French example and adopted a correct, and even at times friendly, attitude toward the counterrevolutionary government of Szeged. Various high Serbian officials repeatedly received with courtesy Count Teleki, Admiral Horthy and other representatives of that government. As another gesture of good will permission was granted to refugee groups to travel across Yugoslavia from Austria to Szeged. The Yugoslav government also hinted that, at a future date, it might even consider granting diplomatic recognition to the Szeged government. As a result, the Gyula Károlyi government, as well as its successor headed by Dezső Ábrahám, became strong advocates of pro-Serbian policy. Just before the Hungarian Soviet Republic's collapse the Yugoslav government did recognize the Ábrahám government and promised to send official representatives and arms to overthrow the Kun government. It also promised aid to the counterrevolutionary government once it came to power. The question of an economic union of the two countries was also seriously considered. Some politicians, both Hungarian and Yugoslav, were even toying with the idea of a personal union of the two countries under the Serbian dynasty.[35]

It was more difficult to establish a *modus vivendi* with the Romanian government. Károlyi as a Transylvanian magnate was personally unacceptable. The Károlyi family was to lose in Romania 106,000 yokes of land, out of which Gyula Károlyi and his wife owned about 14,000 yokes. The foreign minister in Károlyi's cabinet, Baron Gyula Bornemissza, was also a member of the Transylvanian nobility. The rest of the ministry came mostly from Arad and Temesvár; both cities were claimed by Romania. Thus most of the cabinet was strongly opposed to Romanian occupation of eastern Hungary; this made cooperation with the Romanians most difficult. International recognition of a Hungarian government and normalization of relations between the Western

Powers and Hungary presented a greater danger to Romania's territorial ambitions. The first response of Romanian authorities to the establishment of the Arad government, therefore, was simply to arrest, in spite of the safe conduct pass issued by the French, nearly the entire Károlyi cabinet as they travelled across Romanian controlled areas from Arad to Szeged. Between May 13 and 22, Károlyi and his entourage remained in Romanian custody and were released only after strong and repeated French protests. Subsequently Romania modified its position and made some overtures to the Szeged government, suggesting that if the Hungarians were willing to subordinate themselves to the Romanian high command, interned Székely units could be released and would be allowed to join the Hungarian National Army and to participate in a joint offensive against the Hungarian Soviet Republic. The French approved this plan and promised arms if the Hungarians aided the Romanians, but Count Teleki, foreign minister in the second and third Szeged governments, indignantly rejected the idea of killing Hungarian soldiers, even if Communist, in service of Romania. The National Army, however, was willing to engage in simultaneous, but totally independent operations against the Red Army, but no agreement to this effect was ever worked out between the Romanians and the counterrevolutionary government.[36]

Initial French enthusiasm about the idea of a counterrevolutionary government rapidly waned as it became apparent that it was virtually impossible to bring together under one roof all the Hungarian feuding factions. To be useful, a counterrevolutionary government not only had to be viable, but capable of gaining control and restoring order within Hungary. It had to demonstrate through its makeup and policies a clear break with the prewar regime. In the French view, only a broad-based government could claim to be representative, and only such a government would have sufficient strength to give some assurances that the country would accept the verdict of the Paris Peace Conference. For this reason the French never ceased to press for a broadening of the Szeged government and for exclusion of those politicians or soldiers who were considered to be pro-German or too closely identified with the old order. They repeatedly urged the formation of a *"union sacrée,"* a coalition of all political parties, with a strong representation of liberals and Socialists.[37]

Chances of a moderate government in Szeged, however, proved rather slim. In the radical atmosphere of Szeged, only the right could hold together. Refugees from inner Hungary and from the Successor States vigorously resisted pressures for moderation and all suggestions for cooperation with liberal or Socialist political groups. They also refused to compromise on the territorial issue; in fact, they rigidly lined up behind the principle of Hungary's complete territorial integrity. Thus, in spite of French pressúres, a shift in the Gyula Károlyi government toward the right was more likely than toward the left.

After Károlyi's arrival in Szeged, he immediately ran into strong opposition from various right-wing groups, from officers, refugees, and especially from the ABC's Szeged branch. In fact, the ABC's first reaction to news of the formation of the Arad government was to reject it outright, to declare it illegitimate. Károlyi, therefore, if his government was to survive, had to mollify the Hungarian right before he could defer to the wishes of the French.[38] A compromise had to be reached to meet the major objections of the Szeged counterrevolutionary groups; concessions had to be made both in terms of personnel, and in the political composition of the government. The Szeged groups complained that the Károlyi cabinet lacked prestige because it contained too many unknown figures, whose only claim to fame was that they happened to be in Arad at the right time. More important, the Arad government included some liberal politicians who, in their eyes, compromised themselves during the presidency of Mihály Károlyi. Resentment was also voiced about participation in the government of supporters of Archduke Joseph, symbolizing to many a continued Habsburg claim to the Hungarian crown; and a legitimist or Habsburg restoration was not the most welcome idea in Szeged.

A compromise was finally struck, after the arrival of Count Pál Teleki who represented the magnates in the Viennese ABC. The supporters of Archduke Joseph and some liberals of the Arad government were sacrificed and were replaced by more illustrious members of the Szeged and Viennese refugee groups. The only man with genuine liberal credentials to remain in the cabinet was Lajos Varjassy, a member of Oszkár Jászi's Radical Party. He had to be retained, in spite of a strong antipathy toward him in right-wing circles, because he was the only man in the government who enjoyed the confidence and whole-hearted support of the French. The Foreign Ministry, after Bethlen refused the post, was taken over by his friend and confidant and fellow Transylvanian, Count Pál Teleki. The Interior Ministry went to the leader of the Szeged ABC, Béla Kelemen, and the officers were appeased by calling Horthy to Szeged to head the Ministry of Defense, with Gömbös, the president of MOVE, as his second in command.

This was a clear victory for the right. Nevertheless, in its first proclamation "To the Hungarian Nation," the new government preached moderation. It declared itself the representative of all political parties and of all classes; it called for reconciliation within the country and with the Western world; and finally it promised social reforms and a general amnesty.[39] In actual fact, the list of political leaders, who in the name of the various noncommunist political parties signed a supporting proclamation, left little doubt about the political position of the government. Eight of the fourteen were aristocrats, and all but three were refugees from areas occupied by the Successor States. Also, in their public statements some government members, or their close supporters, made it clear that the right was in a triumphant mood.

This was not as much a victory for a political ideology as for the radical frame of mind of the refugees. It was a victory for the spirit of revenge against their enemies both social and national.

As we have noted earlier, manifestations of open terror increased after the counterrevolutionary government took control of Szeged. Intimidation through threats, violent attacks by gangs of officers, through arrests, and, at times, even through murder, rapidly became the order of the day. Socialist workers when caught were beaten on the spot and then dragged into the barracks for more punishment. "On these occasions," brags Prónay, the chief perpetrator of these crimes, "I ordered an additional fifty strokes with the rod for these fanatic human animals, whose heads were drunk with the twisted ideology of Marx." Or he personally slapped the face of a victim until, as he complained, his arm was more painful than the prisoner's face. Those newspapermen who dared to raise their voices in protest were threatened with arrest or with expulsion from the city.[40] In an open memorandum to Gyula Károlyi Jews of Szeged rejected the charge of the officers that they were responsible for sins of their coreligionists in Budapest and for the outbreak of Bolshevism. All over the country, they argued, noncommunist Jews suffered as much at the hands of the Communists as any other religious group.[41]

Gyula Károlyi merely replied to the Jewish delegation delivering this memorandum that although he regretted the anti-Semitic outbursts as long as some Jews remained opposed to his nationalist government, it was natural that the nation should look upon even patriotic Jews as destructive, internationalist enemies of Hungary.[42]

The extreme right, and especially Transylvanian refugees, remained dissatisfied and embittered, and continued to press for a more intensely nationalistic government. Many felt that their own particular interests were neglected or sacrificed in the struggle for reconquest of Hungary. The Székely National Council, therefore, as a minimum concession, demanded the creation of a new ministry dealing with Transylvanian affairs. The function of this new department was to be threefold: to aid those thousands of refugees who were forced to leave their native towns

and villages; to organize an international campaign to ease terror against
the Hungarian population in Romanian-occupied territories and to aid
the thousands of dismissed persons who lost their jobs because of their
loyalty to the Hungarian nation, which led them to refuse the loyalty
oath; and, most important, to make the necessary political and military
preparations for reconquest of Transylvania. Such a ministry, the
Székely National Council argued, was necessary to restore partially the
Székelys' lost faith and confidence in the Hungarian nation, which up to
that point had not lifted a finger to save Transylvania for Hungary. They
warned that if the Hungarian nation stood by passively once more, at a
time when the Székely nation cried out in desperation for help, the
Székelys would rise up alone in revolt and would be either destroyed
totally or would surrender to Romania. In either case Transylvania would
be lost to Hungary forever. Károlyi, however, had to reject these
demands. The establishment of such a ministry would have run into
strong opposition from the Romanians and the French, since its
irredentist purpose would have been transparent.[43]

The Szeged government and some refugees, mostly teachers, officials,
and other public servants, also clashed head on over the refugees' angry
demands for the payment of salaries by the new national government.
The government was also besieged with applications from other old state
employees still in Transylvania for positions within the new government.
These demands finally forced the counterrevolutionary government to
come to grips with the refugee problem and somehow halt the flood of
refugees to Szeged. From its meager resources the new government was
obviously not able to maintain an army of state employees. The Károlyi
cabinet, therefore, resolved not to assume responsibility for the salaries
of the refugees, but it held out a slender hope to the refugees by hinting
that once the counterrevolution was victorious the contribution of the
refugees would not be forgotten and there would be sufficient employment for all.[44]

The Károlyi government also decided to discourage the flight of the
Hungarian population from the occupied areas. It urged everyone to
remain in their old residences, and to take the oath of loyalty to the new
government there. The Minister of Interior went even further. In his
view, to flee from the lost territories was cowardly and unpatriotic.
"Every refugee public employee," he argued, "is like a soldier, who at the
moment of danger abandoned his post; with his departure he weakens the
Hungarian minority in the occupied territories and thus weakens the
cause of the whole Hungarian nation."[45] During subsequent years this
argument became a recurrent theme and a constant source of conflict
between refugees and the population of inner Hungary.

For those already in Szeged the government could only suggest that they should hasten the day of victory by joining the National Army where, incidentally, they were to receive regular pay — a suggestion that, in fact, was followed by the refugees in increasing numbers. Thus the National Army became the melting pot where the most radicalized men from inner Hungary and from the Successor States joined hands to impose their radical frame of mind on the whole counterrevolutionary movement, and ultimately on the country.

Some of the more astute politicians in Szeged realized that growing radicalism in the National Army and in the government paralyzed the counterrevolutionary movement. Defiance of French wishes for a more democratic government may have been emotionally satisfying for the frustrated officers, but these actions merely increased French opposition to the Szeged government. Such men as Teleki and even Gömbös realized the utter helplessness of the movement in the face of French opposition. They knew that the strength and the ultimate success of the movement depended not on the particular makeup of the Szeged government but on the power of the National Army. Nowhere else were the Hungarians more dependent on the goodwill of the French than in military affairs.

Gömbös, the spokesman of the radical officers, therefore, tried to negotiate a compromise with Lajos Varjassy, the leader of the liberal faction and the only man who had free access to French officers. Gömbös promised to restrain the most extreme officers, while Varjassy agreed to muzzle the liberal press and to gain permission for expansion of the National Army.[46] Neither of the two, however, was able to make good on his promise. Relations with the French continued to worsen to the point that the Károlyi government was in constant fear of imminent arrest and internment by the French.

By the beginning of July the Károlyi government realized that its position had become untenable. It had to make room for a new government that was more in harmony with French wishes. Thus, on July 12, the most objectionable individuals were removed from the cabinet, namely Károlyi, Horthy, Kelemen, and Gömbös. The latter was even expelled from Szeged.[47] Horthy, however, was allowed to retain control of the National Army by becoming its Commander-in-Chief.

The new government of Dezső Ábrahám was more moderate. The result was that relations with the French and the local population improved, but only at the cost of alienating the radical right. The right distrusted and held in contempt the new government, and looked only to the army for leadership. The Ábrahám government lost control of the army, which was willing to obey none but its Commander-in-Chief,

Admiral Horthy. From the time of the establishment of the Ábrahám government Horthy became independent all but in name, though he did not formalize this break until August 9, 1919.[48]

The loss of the army's confidence proved to be a death blow to the Ábrahám government. With loss of the army's support the very reason for its existence had also vanished. Since this government was a forced mixture of divergent views, this body was without character or prestige; because it tried to reflect most of the political ideologies and factions competing for power, it became representative of none. In the public's mind the Szeged government was closely identified with the counterrevolutionary army. Once this government ceased to represent the radical attitudes of the army officers, it could no longer survive. Consequently, on August 19, on the eve of the triumph of the White Army, it quietly expired, less than two weeks after the collapse of the Hungarian Soviet Republic.[49]

The Establishment of the National Army

Success or failure of the counterrevolutionary movement was predicated on the strength of its military forces. The newly established army had three basic aims: to defeat communism in Hungary; to restore the prewar elite to power and to revive the nobility's lost self-confidence; and, finally, to regain the thousand-year frontiers of the Kingdom of Saint Stephen. This last goal, as long as the Hungarian forces at Szeged were under French supervision had to be deemphasized, but for the refugees from the Successor States it was the main rason for joining the National Army.

The fact that this was a class army of the nobility was immediately and widely recognized. In it, the gentry mentality dominated and trappings and symbols of gentry power and virtues were immediately restored. To mention but one example: Gömbös's first act as undersecretary of defense was to reestablish duelling and the noble code of honor in the army. Horthy whole heartedly approved this move, remarking, "As long as the laws of the state fail to protect completely the manly honor of a gentleman, he should and he must be free to resort to illegal weapons."[50] This principle of legitimacy of illegal means at times of crisis was not limited to duelling alone, but became the governing principle of Horthy and his army.

The goals and the prevailing mentality in the army necessarily limited its appeal to a narrow segment of society, principally to the upper classes, to the gentry, and specifically to the refugee nobles, officials and officers. At first, immediately after the establishment of the first Szeged government, broad mass participation in the army was not deemed essential. As long as it was believed that the French would move against the Communist regime, it seemed that a token force would be sufficient to accompany the French.[51]

It soon became apparent, however, that the French were unwilling to spill the blood of their own soldiers as long as other means were available. Various French officers made it clear to the Szeged government that if the Hungarians wished to challenge the supremacy of the Budapest government they had to do it with their own resources, though the French held out the possibility of some material aid once the offensive was under way.[52] In view of the French ban on expansion of Horthy's army, such an offensive was not likely.

Organization of a large invasion force, within the limited confines of Szeged, proved to be an arduous task. For various reasons the size of the counterrevolutionary army remained small. First, the French refused to permit expansion of the army and rejected appeals for arms until after the collapse of the Hungarian Soviet Republic. Also, the limited financial resources of the Szeged government seriously handicapped the recruiting efforts. Finally, the manpower itself was lacking for organization of a larger army.

The French commanders, in spite of repeated requests, refused to permit the expansion of the army beyond the original officially approved force of 1300 officers and men. Political considerations played the most important part in this refusal; but the French were also reluctant to permit the creation of an army that was larger than their own. Nevertheless, by August 1919 the counterrevolutionary army was surreptitiously expanded well beyond its official size.

By controlling much of the local military supplies, namely the weapons seized at Szeged after the Communist takeover at Budapest, the French acquired additional leverage over the National Army. Without these munitions the Hungarians could not arm their forces, nor launch an invasion against the will of the French.[53]

The financial weakness of the Szeged government was only slightly less important in limiting the size of the army. The Szeged government was able to maintain itself financially only with the greatest difficulties. Since its tax revenues were limited, it had to finance most of its operations from contributions by private individuals, from those three-million crowns that Count Teleki had brought from the *Bankgasse* booty as a peace offering to the Szeged group, from the two million crowns contributed by the Székely National Council, and from loans taken from various sources. The twenty-four million crowns collected was woefully inadequate for maintaining, let alone expanding, the National Army.[54] To maintain this counterrevolutionary army was more expensive than usual, since regular pay and good food were major incentives to many of the volunteers, and especially because of the high proportion of officers who insisted on drawing regular-officers' salaries.

The most important problem, however, was shortage of manpower. Since the French military command prohibited a regular draft within its jurisdiction, the White Army had to be made up entirely of volunteers. This seriously handicapped all efforts to expand and limited the volunteers to those who hoped to benefit from participating in such an endeavor. It almost completely excluded all workers, peasants, and much of the local middle class. Even a cursory examination of the social composition of the army reveals its extremely narrow class base of middle- and upper-class refugees, army and especially cavalry officers, members of the police and *gendarmerie*, and to a lesser degree the nationalist middle class students, teachers and state officials.

On June 5, 1919, Horthy issued his order for recruiting this army from the trustworthy elements in the country.[55] Count Aladár Zichy was appointed head of the recruiting committee. Contrary to his committee's expectations and to its deep disappointment, the local population failed to respond in the expected numbers, in spite of all the patriotic appeals and even of some coercion.[56] Especially disappointing was the response of the landed peasantry, to whom the army leaders made special appeals. For it was this stratum, in fact the only one, which the counterrevolutionary leaders believed to be sufficiently trustworthy and conservative to provide a mass base of support in the struggle against communism. Father István Zadravecz, a member of the recruiting campaign, bitterly complained about the lack of enthusiasm on the part of the peasantry of Szeged.[57]

The total of 6568 individuals heard the call for volunteers, a far smaller number than originally anticipated. Less than ten percent belonged to the peasantry, and most were from the ranks of refugee peasants. At one of the smaller recruiting stations out of 281 volunteers only 21 were peasants. At the largest station 3320 persons signed up to serve, but only 147 were peasants. The native population of Szeged, with the notable exception of the state and city officials, showed little enthusiasm for the White Army. Again, out of these 3320 volunteers only 1019, that is, less than a third, were old residents of Szeged, and the balance, some 2301 individuals, refugees.[58] At other stations the proportion of peasants, local residents, and refugees were roughly the same. In short, refugees made up over two-thirds of the counterrevolutionary army. A third to a half of the entire army, at least 2000 men, but perhaps as many as 3000 were officers,[59] and a significant portion, perhaps as many as 800 men, came from the *gendarmerie,* mostly from Transylvania.

Manpower shortage forced the recruiting committee to go to tortuous lengths to collect and transport at considerable expense all willing officers to Szeged from other parts of the country and from as far as Vienna. As these officers arrived they were immediately taken to a recruiting station, carefully debriefed, classified according to their political reliability, and assigned to an appropriate unit. The three categories of classification were: totally trustworthy; politically not cleared; politically unreliable, that is, a politically criminal past. Those in the first group were assigned to the officers' detachments, those in the second into special officers' units were placed under the surveillance of trusted officers, and those in the third group were immediately arrested.[60]

Concentration on recruitment of officers was partly a necessity, since they formed one of the few groups to whom the counterrevolutionary movement held a special attraction, and, moreover, because their skills were deemed essential to the army's success. Officers were to form its nucleus, which could be rapidly expanded when opportunity arose. Until the march from Szeged commenced most battalions and regiments remained in a skeletal form. The great surplus of officers also made it necessary to set up special elite companies, made up exclusively of officers.

These officers' detachments formed the backbone of the White Army — they were the driving force which propelled the counterrevolutionary movement and Horthy forward to victory. They were the first to depart from Szeged, acting as the shock troops of the National Army; they were most responsible for the terror that soon followed.

Baron Pál Prónay's detachment was the first to be established in early June. It was soon followed by the formation of Gyula Ostenburg-Moravek's special assault officers' company.[61] Subsequently a special officers' battalion was established with six companies. For a time both Prónay and Ostenburg were part of this unit, but later they seceded and operated as independent detachments, or more precisely, as terror groups subject only to Horthy's personal command. In July another special unit was established on the insistence of the Székely National Council. All the Transylvanian soldiers, except officers, after July, were to be enrolled in this special Székely infantry battalion. Another, the Bárdoss Company, commanded by Béla Bárdoss, was brought to life toward the end of June, mostly by city and county officials of Szeged and from the large number of refugee officials in the city. This group's prime function was to operate as a special, mostly political security detachment, patrolling the streets of Szeged.

These units and especially the officers's detachments formed the most extreme wing of the Szeged radical right. The Prónay detachment must be singled out as the most radical, the most uncompromising supporters of all right-wing causes. In many ways, Prónay and his specially selected officers personified the essence of the "Idea of Szeged." The detachment's flag blessed with great pomp and circumstance on July 15, symbolically reflected the two main objectives of the movement. Inscribed on one side, around the embroidered picture of the Virgin Mary, the patroness of Hungary, was the device: "*Cum Deo, pro Patrie et Libertate.*" On the other side, the sentence was to continue, but only after the detachment marched into Budapest "*et pro Rege nostro Apostolico.*" That is, the first goal was to liberate Hungary and then to abolish the republic and restore the Apostolic Kingdom of the Crown of St. Stephen to its rightful ruler. The symbolism was complete when the soldiers swore their oath to this flag. They were the sons of the old noble elite who were determined to recapture the country of the forefathers and to lead a punitive expedition against all those who dared challenge the supremacy of their class within Hungary.

A closer look at the social composition of the original Prónay detachment bears out the essentially gentry character of these officers' companies. Out of the initial 163 members 86 were identified as belonging to the Hungarian nobility, and only 26 as commoners. An additional 32 were German, either Austrian or assimilated Germans; some also had noble titles. Virtually the entire detachment was composed of refugees from various parts of Hungary, but 58, that is, over a third, were refugees from the Successor States,[62] mostly petty nobles from Transylvania. It was precisely this segment of the nobility which came to be dependent on the state during the last decades of the former monarchy, the stratum whose survival was most intertwined with the fate of the old state bureaucracy. The lower nobles, too, were those who were most traumatized and radicalized by the upsurge of the national minorities, who had the most to lose by the loss of the minority areas. Their privileged position within the state was also the most endangered by the social revolution and the challenge from the radical and liberal intelligentsia.

Additionally, these officers were young: few over thirty-five, most below the age of thirty and some under twenty. The leading figures were only captains, such as Hussar Captains Pál Prónay, Miklós Kozma, József Görgey, Captains on the General Staff Gyula Gömbös and Gyula Toókos, and Captains Gyula Ostenburg and László Magasházy. Older officers in the higher ranks were noticeably few. The younger officers came from a new generation of nobles, whose *Weltanschauung* and emotional makeup were distinct from those of the preceding generation. Born during the 1880s and 1890s they reached maturity in the turbulent decade before the war or during the war. Their future was clouded, their identities less secure. As a result, throughout their lives, they existed in a defensive atmosphere. They were defending a disintegrating social order and the noble world view. They were also fighting for preservation of the nobility's warrior self-image, which, in the past, had served to justify their privileged position. The brutality of the war and the callous disregard for the value of life weakened past moral restraints. In their view, military control of society and the use of terror had become justified, and even necessary, as the only means to end society's ills.

The officers' companies first flexed their muscles within the Szeged counterrevolutionary movement, where they managed to gain political power. The Prónay detachment became the strong arm as well as the arms and ears of the Horthy faction within the government. Prónay collected information for Horthy and for himself; he organized a spy system both in Szeged and in Hungary where he maintained regular contacts with right-wing officers' groups. He sent out regular patrols to guard secret routes to Szeged with order to arrest anyone suspected of bearing any clandestine messages from the Communist government. Those who were caught in his net were taken into Prónay's "laboratory," as he called his torture chambers, where the victim was frightfully and sadistically tortured until he confessed everything, "even that which he never knew."[63] No one was secure from his officers' suspicion, not even members of the counterrevolutionary government or army. The French presence at Szeged served as the only restraint on this group's violence, but even repeated French protests could not eliminate their activities.[64]

It was this White Army that descended on Hungary after the Soviet regime's collapse. It emerged not as a victorious army triumphant in combat over the Red Army. The first unit of the National Army, the Prónay detachment, had to steal its way across the French lines in the middle of night. While they had to wait with impatience in Szeged, the Romanian Army, attacked by Soviet forces, went into counterattack, forcing Béla Kun to yield power on the first day of August to an all Social Democratic government.

News of these events reached Szeged on August 2, 1919. It was received with both enthusiasm and anxiety. The opportunity of the moment was great, the dangers were clear. It was imperative to begin the march toward Budapest before the new government had an opportunity to consolidate its forces or before other political groups could make their bid for political power.

The attitude of the French held the key to the fate of the counterrevolutionaries in Szeged. Without their permission to depart the White Army might have remained bottled up in Szeged. The French, however, no longer had any reason for restraining these forces. The collapse of the Communist regime in Budapest eliminated the reasons for maintaining a strict cordon around Szeged. Thus the French yielded to the demands of the National Army and granted permission for departure.

The White Army's haste was necessary in view of the Romanians' rapid advance. For the main Romanian force was marching in a northwesterly direction toward Budapest. It was only a matter of days before Romanian troops were in position to fan out toward the south-west as well as toward the Yugoslav demarcation line, and occupy the entire region between the Tisza and the Danube Rivers. The danger of encirclement, capture, and even internment was genuine.

Thus in the early hours of August 4, even before the final French permission was granted, the first advance companies of the National Army crossed the French lines. This first unit was the detachment of Prónay, followed by three other officers' companies. The main force, several battalions and the officer cadre of several future regiments, some 1200 men followed a few days later.[65] Other units as they were outfitted followed the White Army's main force. In all, some 2400–2600 men marched out of Szeged. By the time, however, the White Army got under way the Romanians already occupied Budapest. Hence original plans had to be altered and, instead of heading for Budapest, the National Army marched to the Danube in the hope of crossing it before the rapidly advancing Romanians cut their road. Once in Transdanubia they were joined by the 3500-man Székely Brigade, that remnant of the Székely Division which never surrendered to the Romanians and had remained a semiautonomous force within the Red Army. In addition, a 9000-man force from the Red Army with headquarters at Székesfehérvár, under the command of General István Horthy, brother of Admiral Horthy, subordinated itself to the National Army.[66] On August 5, the forces' first units organized in Feldbach, under the command of Colonel Antal Lehár, also entered Hungary from the west. Regular Hungarian units stationed in west Hungary recognized Lehár's authority, and the forces under his command soon reached division strength, nearly 18,000 men.[67] Shortly after the occupation of Budapest the advance of the Romanian army was halted under Western pressure; but, by that time, they occupied the northern districts of Transdanubia as far as the cities of Győr, Veszprém, and Székesfehérvár. In the unoccupied regions, however, the various refugee and other right-wing military groups were given an opportunity to consolidate their power.

The experiences of the Vienna and Szeged refugee groups proved, once more, that the old ruling classes when relying upon their own strength were impotent; they were incapable of defending the country against the Successor States after the October Revolution; they proved unable to organize a successful counterrevolution against Mihály Károlyi; they could not even seriously challenge the Communist government, though it was internationally isolated and gradually lost its popular support. In spite of their seemingly feverish counterrevolutionary activities, loud oratory, the vast majority of the refugees remained passive observers. Their activities were often only make-believe, without consequence or import except to themselves, serving only to shield them from admitting failure. For the opportunity to return to Hungary from Austria and Szeged the counterrevolutionary aristocracy and gentry owed gratitude to the much despised Romanians, whom, even if only for a brief period, they had to consider their benefactors and allies.[68] This was their final humiliation.

The refugees in Szeged and Vienna, if for no other reason than to cleanse themselves of this last stigma and to demonstrate their independence, had to prove to the nation, but above all to themselves, that they, as the old elite, still had the strength and determination to assume control of the country without foreign help. With the defeat of the Hungarian Soviet Republic all dangers and all penalties for action were eliminated. This permitted the refugees to swing from passivity into violent action. From their sense of weakness and powerlessness sprang the terror which they let loose against those who dared to challenge their supremacy. Openly and proudly they discarded humanism and promised retribution. As one of the officers, Miklós Kozma, wrote at the beginning of August 1919:

> Both the red and the pink eras are over. We shall see to it . . . that the flame of nationalism leaps high. . . . We shall also punish. Those who for months have committed heinous crimes must receive their punishment. It is predictable . . . that the compromisers and those with weak stomachs will moan and groan when we line up a few red rogues and terrorists against the wall. Once before the false slogans of humanism and other 'isms' helped drive the country to its ruin. This second time they will wail in vain. . . .[69]

Chapter 8
The Struggle for Power and the White Terror

Collapse of the Hungarian Soviet Republic on the first day of August signaled the beginning of a scramble for political power by the various counterrevolutionary groups. Those people who went into hiding during the Kun period, magnates, gentry officials, members of the bourgeoisie, politicians of the old order, suddenly surfaced and threw themselves into the struggle for control of the country. All the refugees who at one time or another had fled to Austria or to Szeged, the conservative aristocrats, the Bethlen-Teleki, the Szmrecsányi-Beniczky groups, and the radicals of Szeged, plus the various independent little armies, such as those of Baron Lehár and above all of Admiral Horthy, descended upon the country and demanded a voice in the new counterrevolutionary government.

The fierceness of the struggle that ensued between these factions is, however, misleading. The perpetual government crisis of the next two years, formation of countless political parties, fragmentation and mergers of these parties all tend to give an impression of a bitter ideological conflict. In reality no sharp difference existed between the groups. What is remarkable, in fact, is how close these groups were in their political and social outlook. Nothing is more indicative of this than the fact that the only issue which polarized the new political elite into two opposing factions was the question of Habsburg restoration. The legitimacy issue turned essentially on personalities; it did not involve any fundamental social or political problems. This is understandable, since nearly all the participants in the political struggles came from only one end of the political spectrum, from the right. The democratic center was reduced to impotence; the left was decimated, its members were either killed, arrested, fled abroad, or moved underground.[1]

With the victory of the right the Hungarian political arena came to resemble a large exclusive club filled with quarrelsome people, where each member paid his dues in real or imagined counterrevolutionary activities. In this, the pool of visible political leaders numbered in the scores, each surrounded by a narrow circle of like-minded friends; the constituency of active supporters, on which the entire counterrevolutionary edifice rested, was only a few hundred thousand. Consequently, the fall of a government or reshuffling of a cabinet never really signaled a change of course or adoption of new policies, but merely a change of personalities. Nor did removal from office mean exclusion of the fallen members from the club. The same faces kept reappearing a decade or even two decades later.

The narrowness of the political base permitted the refugees from the Successor States to exercise a far greater influence in Hungary's political life than their actual numbers in relation to the entire population would have warranted. Tens of thousands of politically active refugees, by permeating virtually all right-wing organizations, were often able to assume a commanding position or at least exercise a *de facto* veto power in national issues. As members of different factions these refugees may have clashed with each other, mostly over personalities, but they remained essentially united over the broader issues and specifically over those which affected them as a group.

The price which the refugees extracted for their support was very high, but no government dared to alienate such a large segment of its basic constituency by ignoring their vital economic or political interests. The refugees' discontent and their radical attitudes greatly hindered the country's return to normalcy. The White Terror, in which many of the refugees participated, within months after victory of the right, became an increasing political liability. Refugee economic claims upon the state treasury became an excruciating burden which slowed down the rate of economic recovery of the entire country. Their reciprocation of the hostility of the leaders of the Successor States and their universal opposition to the Treaty of Trianon isolated the country and paralyzed its foreign policy. Not until Bethlen, himself a refugee, assumed control of the government, was a compromise found between the interests of the state as a whole and those of the refugees. As we shall see, this compromise favored the refugees.

On August 1, the all-Socialist or trade-union government of Gyula Peidl was formed; it had only a slim chance of survival. The political pendulum, which since the October Revolution was steadily moving toward the left, suddenly turned and threatened to sweep the country toward the opposite extreme. Although the Social Democratic Party purged its radicals, it was too closely identified with the revolution, and with the Hungarian Soviet state, to be able to survive in power. Several cabinet ministers in the new government, even if during the previous months they had consistently opposed the radical course of the extreme left, were vulnerable to charges of communist sympathies. The Peidl government's weakness was compounded by the fact that it had to function without a coercive force. The working class was exhausted in the struggle of the past months and the workers' battalions were dissolved.

If this government was to survive, it needed time to dissociate itself from the Soviet regime's radical policies, thereby gaining support of the peasantry and the moderate bourgeois elements. This was, in fact, the basic thrust of the new government's policies. In rapid succession it issued a series of edicts, all aimed at dismantling the system built up during the Hungarian Soviet regime. Under the terms of these edicts the government released all imprisoned counterrevolutionaries, abolished the revolutionary courts, restored the prewar judicial system and the old city police and the *gendarmerie*. It restored to their previous owners all nationalized private property, such as apartment houses, industrial or commercial enterprises; reduced wages; lifted rent control; and finally, in a secret memorandum, it ordered the arrest of all fleeing Communists.[2] All of these measures were designed to reassure the bourgeoisie of the benign character of the Socialist government. At the same time, as a gesture toward the peasantry, the confiscated estates were not restored to their previous aristocratic owners. Simultaneously, Peidl, with a coalition government in mind, opened negotiations with the various liberal parties and on August 5 with the leader of the Smallholders' Party, István Nagyatádi Szabó.[3]

By these steps the Social Democrats also wished to demonstrate to the Western Powers that the new government had broken with the past and was determined to follow a moderate course. The government realized that only with the firm backing of the Allies could it remain in power and stem the rising tide of counterrevolution. Yet, although the government was created after negotiations with Allied representatives in Vienna, the Allied and Associated Powers refused to recognize it, since it was comprised of representatives of only one party.[4] The Romanian government's attitude also became an important factor, since Romanian troops occupied Budapest. The anticommunist Romanian government remained hostile to the idea of a Socialist government in Hungary and refused to protect this government against the right-wing counterrevolutionaries. Without substantial allied support, the Peidl government's fate was sealed. It fell easy prey to the counterrevolutionary groups at the first sign of force.

On August 6 a small band of counterrevolutionaries, taking advantage of the government's isolation, simply marched into a cabinet meeting and informed the Peidl government that its brief tenure of office had come to an end. This *coup d'état* was the work of a Budapest-based counterrevolutionary organization known as the White

House group. Its members were mostly non-noble, professional or bourgeois residents of the city, supported by a group of police and army officers. They acted with boldness since they were assured of, at least, some Western backing. The Romanians, who were informed of their intent, remained neutral, while the British and the Italian representatives in Budapest gave their tacit approval. On the day before the coup General Reginald Gorton, head of the British military mission in Budapest, and Prince Livio Borghese, head of the Italian mission to Vienna, arrived in Budapest and immediately held a series of conferences with some of the leaders of this group, as well as with Archduke Joseph.[5] The upshot of these negotiations was that on August 7, claiming Western support, Archduke Joseph proclaimed himself governor of the country. In this capacity he immediately appointed a temporary caretaker government headed by István Friedrich, his chief supporter and a member of the White House group. The rest of the cabinet was composed of other participants of the coup and of leading bureaucrats in the various ministries.

The Friedrich government's position was even weaker than that of the Social Democrats. It represented no great political bloc, but merely that small group of adventurers who actually carried out the *coup d'état*. Nor could Friedrich rely upon the military backing of his Western supporters. The Italians had only a military mission in the capital; the British had a tiny force at their disposal only after August 25, when a small flotilla sailed up the Danube and landed a few troops along the west bank of the river. The entire country east of the Danube, the city of Budapest, as well as the northern counties of Transdanubia east of Győr, remained under Romanian military control. The Romanians refused to recognize the Friedrich government and, with French encouragement, they maintained that a state of war still existed between the two countries. Until a ceasefire agreement went into effect, Romania reserved, for itself, the right to deal with Hungary as a belligerent power; to extend its zone of occupation whenever the security of her forces demanded it; to disarm any Hungarian military unit, including those of the right; and to arrest all those judged dangerous by the Romanian military authorities.[6] Only in deference to Britain and Italy did they not arrest the Friedrich government.

The new government, almost immediately after its formation, came under strong pressures from two other quarters. Both the French and the excluded counterrevolutionary groups were determined to overthrow the Friedrich cabinet or, at least, to alter drastically its composition. The swift diplomatic action by the British and the Italians caught the French unprepared; for the French were backing the Szeged counterrevolutionary government, which precisely at this moment was in process of disintegration. The French could not recognize a government that was established without their consent and against their will. France objected especially to Archduke Joseph as the head of the new Hungarian state. In this Paris was strongly supported by all the Successor States, who saw a danger to their very existence in a Habsburg restoration anywhere in Europe. Under these circumstances the British and the Italians began to retreat from their earlier support of Archduke Joseph and tried to shift the blame on the Romanians for the overthrow of the moderate Socialist government.

For Friedrich this opposition to the person of Archduke Joseph presented a dilemma. It was made clear to him that as long as Archduke Joseph was head of state no peace negotiations could commence. At the same time the prestige that the Archduke lent to his government helped to legitimize it. Joseph, finally, had to recognize the hopelessness of his position and agreed to yield to pressures by resigning on August 23. It was not possible for anyone to fill his position immediately. That rather delicate question of electing a new head of state had to be postponed until after the evacuation of the Romanians and the election of a new parliament.

Removal of Joseph did not earn Friedrich recognition by the Allies. Although the Western Powers set no specific conditions, they demanded formation of a coalition government capable of restoring peace, and of maintaining itself in power. Some Western Powers were especially anxious to establish a strong anticommunist government in Budapest as rapidly as possible so that the occupation of the country could be terminated. They planned to transfer the released army of occupation to Romania's eastern frontiers to join the Denikin Army in the fight against Soviet Russia.

The Western Powers realized that only the radical right was in a position to organize the necessary military forces to assure a permanent liquidation of the leftist revolution in Hungary. At the same time these powers, especially France, wished to guard against, mostly for domestic reasons, the introduction of an open military dictatorship. They urged creation of a coalition government formed from political parties right of the moderate Social Democrats to which the various right-wing military groups were to be subordinated. Thus they simultaneously pressed for formation of a moderate government and aided expansion of the counterrevolutionary police and army.[7]

As long as the right remained fragmented no such solution could be brought about. Friedrich possessed neither the skill nor the political stature to bring about a reconciliation of the feuding factions. He was able to seize power from the Peidl government only because at the time his was the only counterrevolutionary force in Budapest. As the refugees from Austria and from Szeged returned to the capital they exerted increasing pressure for reorganization of the government. Indeed, Friedrich's first cabinet rested on an extremely narrow base, excluding most of the potential supporters of even the extreme right. Friedrich, himself a factory owner, may be considered a representative of the wealthy bourgeoisie;[8] some other members of his cabinet, András Csilléry, a dentist, and Jenő Polnay, a Jewish lawyer friend of Friedrich, represented Budapest's right-wing professional bourgeois elements. Generals Gábor Tánczos and Ferenc Schnetzer represented the officer corps and the other ministers the bureaucracy. The entire cabinet lacked luster; it was composed of political unknowns. It was without strong gentry representation and without one aristocrat, which was almost unthinkable in Hungarian politics. Political leaders of the old regime were excluded as were the representatives of the major refugee groups. Most important, the National Army did not identify with the Friedrich government. In truth, what is remarkable is the length of time Friedrich was able to maintain himself at the head of the government. Paradoxically he was greatly helped in this by the occupation of Budapest by the Romanian army. The National Army could not and did not want to enter the capital due to the presence of the Romanians. Friedrich tried to seize this opportunity to establish a military force loyal to him, but his efforts were largely frustrated by the Romanian army's violent opposition to a Hungarian military force in Budapest. Therefore, only organization of his potential supporters into a powerful political bloc and experimentation with different political combinations in his cabinet remained open to him. As it turned out, this strategy was not sufficient for recognition by the Allies.

Generally, the regular police forces were loyal to the government, but the Romanians refused to consent to their reorganization and relented only under strong pressure from Paris. When a small police force, under Allied supervision, was at last organized it was feared that it might prove to be insufficient to protect the government against the working class. Too, for political reasons, the government was eager to line up behind itself the middle class by organizing from its ranks military or paramilitary units. The government especially welcomed the spontaneous clandestine efforts of right-wing university students to arm themselves. The first "University Battalion" was established at the School of Engineering on August 7, 1919, followed by the "Medical Student Battalion," which was soon renamed "School of Science Battalion." On August 12, the formation of these units was officially endorsed by an

order of the Ministry of Defense.[9] During the next few weeks the size of
the student battalions was rapidly expanded from an initial 300–400 to
1200 by the beginning of September, to 2400 by December, and, finally,
to 3000 by the fall of 1920. A majority of the volunteers were older
students, whose education had been interrupted by the war. Most
served in the army as reserve junior officers. In the student battalions,
just as in the other counterrevolutionary armies, the size of the refugee
contingent was quite large. In the fall of 1920, out of approximately 3000
student soldiers 930 came from the lost territories; in the battalion of the
School of Sciences 38 percent of the volunteers were refugees.[10]

The refugee students identified with the Friedrich government's
Christian and nationalist ideology. But their enthusiasm for service may
be also attributed to the generous salaries the government agreed to pay
to them. Penniless, without any income, often without as much as a
change of clothing, these refugee students were saved from starvation
by a monthly pay of over 800 crowns.

Though numerically the battalions represented a significant force with
considerable political weight, their military value was limited. In December the battalions had sufficient number of rifles to arm less than
half their numbers. As a result, they were used mostly to guard military
installations and major utilities or were held in reserve against a potential workers' uprising. Indeed, subsequently the battalions were called
gendarme reserve battalions. In other words, the university battalions
were helpful as an internal security force and temporarily helped the
Friedrich government to remain in power, but could not guarantee the
government's long-range survival. In fact, after Horthy entered Budapest most of the battalions transferred their loyalty to him.

During August and September 1919 Friedrich made every effort to
organize a powerful political bloc. Between mid-August and September 11, he had reshuffled his cabinet three times, only to be informed by
the Allies that each new combination was still unacceptable.[11] First, he
dropped most of the political unknowns, trying to open his government
first to the left and then to the right. He appointed the Liberal Márton
Lovászy as foreign minister, István Nagyatádi Szabó, the Smallholders' Party leader, as minister of agriculture, and, from the old
Catholic People's Party, he included in his cabinet István Haller and
Károly Huszár. This combination proved unworkable. After a minor
cabinet reorganization toward the end of August, a major government
change took place on September 11. Lovászy and Nagyatádi were
excluded, their places taken by legitimist radicals or conservative supporters of the aristocracy. Ödön Beniczky from the Szmrecsányi-
Beniczky ABC faction took over the ministry of the interior, and with it

control of the police. To Count József Somssich, a wealthy Catholic aristocrat, went the foreign ministry, and Gyula Rubinek, a gentry politician from northern Hungary and head of the *Országos Magyar Gazdasági Egyesület* or OMGE, the powerful association of the great estate owners, became the minister of agriculture.

One result of these changes was that politicians who returned from Austria were given a voice in the government. With each of the successive government changes the number of those members born outside the reduced territory of Hungary steadily increased as well. In the first cabinet only three out of eleven such individuals served, including Friedrich himself, who, although born near Pozsony, was a long-time resident of Budapest. In the government formed in mid-August this number rose to eight out of fifteen; in Friedrich's final cabinet nine of the sixteen. This last government was no more successful in gaining Allied recognition than its predecessors due to Social Democratic refusal to join it. Nevertheless, it made some important gains in another direction. Under its auspices, and with the aid of refugees, a strong political alliance was formed, which became one of the two major parties of the "Christian bloc."

The Christian National Unity Party,[12] or KNEP, was formed during October 1919 representing the merger of the Christian Social Economy Party, successor to the prewar Catholic People's Party and of Friedrich's own Christian National Party. The old People's Party was strongest in west Hungary and the Slovak areas. It was the party of the Catholic Church and of Catholic magnates and was led by Count Aladár Zichy and István Rakovszky, a member of a prominent gentry family from northern Hungary. A large number of well-known refugee politicians belonged to this party. It was the party of György Szmrecsányi, Ödön Beniczky, Sándor Ernszt, János Bartos, all born in northern Hungary, of István Haller, from Szatmár county, lost to Romania, and Károly Huszár, who was born in Austria. This group took over the leadership of the new Christian National Unity Party. They were strongly backed by the refugee aristocrats from Slovakia, by men like Count Gyula Andrássy, Jr., the Zichy family, Count Albert Apponyi, the dean of the Hungarian aristocracy, along with most of the legitimist aristocrats of western Hungary. The Catholic bishops closely identified with the refugee aristocrats and lined up behind a restoration of Hungary's lost territories. The church was in danger of losing over forty percent of its flock, a majority of them to Czechoslovakia, and the bishops stood to lose about sixty percent of their estates. Catholic prelates looked upon this party as their own and lent it their considerable prestige. The Bethlen-Teleki group also participated in the negotiations leading to the formation of the KNEP; Count Kunó Klebelsberg, a friend of Bethlen from Arad, and the Catholic Count Pál Teleki joined the party. Some Transylvanians, however, stayed away, for as Protestants and Transylvanians, they could be at best only mildly enthusiastic about the idea of a Habsburg restoration.

The wealthy, conservative bourgeoisie of Budapest, including some Jewish capitalists, also supported the party, or, at least, wished to attach themselves to it. It seems that their aim was to create the symbiotic relationship between large capital and large estate that served so well both strata during the 1867–1918 period. Aristocrats were expected to restrain the anticapitalist propaganda of the radical right; Jews hoped that the Church would use its moral authority to end attacks upon Jews.

In short, the KNEP was roughly an alliance of the refugee group that returned from Vienna, the Church, the bourgeoisie of Budapest, and counterrevolutionaries of the capital. During Friedrich's tenure of office this coalition did everything in its power to prepare itself for the moment when the Hungarian right would rule by itself, without the hindrance of the occupation forces. They were also preparing for the political struggle that was certain to ensue within the right itself. Supporters of the party, therefore, were entrenched in the various centers of power, in ministries, police, and judicial system. The manpower for this was drawn partly from the ready pool of refugee office seekers. To assure control of the countryside and to carry out the program of the KNEP the government appointed trustworthy individuals with extraordinary powers to head the administration of the various regions or counties of unoccupied Hungary. These plenipotentiaries came mostly from the ranks of the legitimist aristocracy. Most prominent among them were Count József Károlyi, Count István Zichy, Margrave György Pallavicini, Count Antal Sigray, and Count Gedeon Ráday. Some members of the gentry were also appointed, among whom the best-known figures were Gaszton Gaál and György Szmrecsányi.

The coalition seemed strong enough to establish itself in power once the Romanians withdrew fom the country. It spanned most of the right, embracing conservatives, radicals, as well as most of the aristocrats, segments of the gentry and nationalist bourgeoisie. Its principal weakness was its lack of military force, though the gravity of this shortcoming was not immediately realized. There was no reason to believe that Admiral Horthy would not support the program of the Christian Nationalists. The Szeged government, which brought to life the army of Horthy, had already resigned in favor of the Friedrich government. Admiral Horthy was also known to be a loyal supporter of the Habsburgs. He spoke often of his great admiration for Emperor Franz Joseph that he had developed while serving as his *aide-de-camp*.[13] In conversations with legitimist aristocrats he repeatedly assured his listeners of his loyalty to the dynasty. Hence, understandably, many unsuspecting legitimists, though not all, were lulled into believing that Horthy was indeed their man. It is doubtful, for example, that Baron Lehár, an ardent legitimist, would have been willing to subordinate himself to Horthy had Horthy's subsequent attitude toward King Károly been known at the time. It was wise for Horthy to conceal his real views and ambitions even from his own officers among whom some, such as Ostenburg, also held strong legitimist sentiments. It is also conceivable, however, that, at that time, Horthy, indeed, felt as he publicly stated.

The Friedrich government tried to appease Horthy by recognizing him as the Commander-in-Chief of the Hungarian Army, but Horthy and, even more likely, the men in his entourage, had higher ambitions. He already exercised the powers of the Commander-in-Chief without any government sanction. The Friedrich government could offer him nothing that would have induced him to abandon his freedom of action. He gratefully acknowledged the government's recognition of his title, but steadfastly refused to reciprocate in form of subordinating himself to the minister of defense or to the cabinet. He also refused to transfer his command post to Budapest — he was to enter that city only on his own terms at the head of his army. Until then Horthy was satisfied with remaining at his headquarters at Siófok on the shore of Lake Balaton.

Expansion of the National Army

There is little doubt that from the time of the National Army's arrival in Transdanubia the aim of Horthy and his circle was to establish a military dictatorship, to make Horthy the unchallenged master of Hungary.[14] He was unable to match the political strength of the KNEP, especially with its impressive array of well-known political and public figures. His only weapon was the army, but he used this to his maximum advantage. From Siófok, until the Romanian evacuation of Budapest, he carefully orchestrated its expansion and made a determined effort to bring under his command the various independent military groups in the country. Concurrently, he extended his authority to most unoccupied territories of Transdanubia, and, thus, effectively outflanked the Budapest government. Horthy ruled in these areas through his officers and not through the regular local administrative agencies, which took their directives from the Friedrich government. Only in western Hungary, in the

Szombathely, Sopron, Kőszeg area, where Baron Lehár controlled most of the military forces, did the military and representatives of the government cooperate smoothly. In most other areas, except in some of the larger towns,[15] whenever disagreement arose over contradictory orders from Siófok and Budapest, the military was able to force its will upon civilian authorities.

Between mid-August and November 1919, when Horthy finally marched into Budapest, the size of the military forces recognizing his supreme command in Transdanubia had increased from less than three thousand to roughly fifty thousand.[16] The National Army's expansion did not drastically alter its political outlook and only slightly its social composition. It remained a hotbed of radicalism and continued to be dominated by young officers, by the gentry and gentroid elements. The proportion of refugees also remained nearly as high as in the Szeged Army. Although the population at large was less than enthusiastic about the White Army, Horthy, freed from the close supervision of the French, was able to recruit from the larger pool of potential counter-revolutionaries in Hungary. The old officer corps and noncommissioned officers remained the prime target of his appeals for volunteers. They were the only people whom Horthy could genuinely trust and expect to follow his lead. Many officers who remained in Hungary during the Soviet regime now surfaced and eagerly grasped at the opportunity for advancement promised by the National Army's imminent victory. In most parts of Transdanubia when the Red Army collapsed left-wing soldiers deserted their units, leaving behind in the barracks only a skeletal force of commissioned and noncommissioned officers. They were anxious to demonstrate their right-wing sympathies and immediately recognized Horthy as their commander. Sons of the nobility were equally eager to join. Whenever one or another officers' detachments appeared in an area they were always able to beef up their ranks with recruits from this group and then use their knowledge of local conditions to seek out all those who were considered to be Communists or Communist sympathizers. In widely scattered parts of the country, during August, a number of independent terror groups also sprung up. These were also gradually linked to the National Army.

Service in the White Army held a special appeal to the younger generations of refugees. One of the first refugee groups to recognize Horthy's authority was the Székely Brigade. Many of their comrades from the Székely Division were already in the National Army, and some of the units were almost exclusively made up of Transylvanians. In addition, to many it seemed that only Horthy promised to follow a determined policy to regain the lost territories. They were welcome in the army since their refugee status provided them with good nationalist credentials. In fact the Székelys were virtually the only group that was trusted without reservation. A February 15, 1920 report on the political reliability of the so-called Berényi special *gendarmerie* group in Budapest is a good example of this trust. Out of its four companies only the first company, made up exclusively of Székelys, was to be considered totally trustworthy. The rest, recruited mostly from residents of the city, could not be relied upon.[17] In every major city in the country there were groups of radical refugees without any livelihood who were eager to participate in any military adventure. The army promised them regular and decent pay, special severance pay upon completion of service, a family allotment while in uniform, and possibly a new career.

The large number of Transylvanians in Horthy's army caused considerable anxiety to the Romanians. The Allied Military Mission, therefore, ordered Horthy to cease drafting them into his units and to dismiss all those already serving in the National Army. In a top-secret memorandum Horthy informed his commanders of this order but instead of compliance he ordered the circumvention of the directive. He wrote to his officers: "According to the decision of the Entente generals the Székelys could not be drafted, nor used in any form. . . . The District Command must explain this in the proper manner to the various Székely units. They must be warned that as long as the Romanians are here, it is in their interest to keep their Transylvanian origins secret, otherwise the Romanians will demand their extradition and they will be interned. . . ."[18]

The Székelys were to remain within the army, only the proud "Székely" designation of their units had to disappear. Thereafter, they were to be referred to only by the number of their regular army unit.[19]

Just as in Szeged, Horthy still hoped to fill the ranks of his army with recruits from the conservative peasantry. But only some of the wealthier peasants were willing to join voluntarily; the rest had to be drafted into the army, at times forcefully.

During September, with the Friedrich government's cooperation, Horthy ordered a call-up of the age groups between 25 and 35 years, effective in unoccupied territories of Hungary. In a series of secret orders he ordered a careful screening of all volunteers and draftees. Only the most loyal and most dedicated persons could be drafted; only peasants were to be called up, preferably the wealthier, land-owning peasants, rather than the landless day laborers or peasants from the large estates, that is, "only those elements whose moral and political viewpoints were totally unimpeachable."[20] From the new recruits a special oath was extracted. They had to swear to fight against Bolshevism and had to take an absolute oath of obedience not to the government or to the constitution, but personally to Horthy.

Horthy made several attempts to bring under the control of the Army High Command all law enforcement agencies, including the regular city police, the rural *gendarmerie,* the border police, and the treasury officers. In this, he was only partially successful. The Friedrich government, and especially Beniczky, the minister of interior, vehemently opposed this attempt. In a letter to Beniczky, Horthy argued that a united command for all coercive forces of the state was necessary since the primary task of all armed and police forces was to wage war against the remnant forces of Communists, and to prepare for the reconquest of the lost territories. The border police, for example, in addition to their regular functions, were to maintain constant contact with the Hungarian population across the frontiers and were to aid them in their clandestine operations. Furthermore, Horthy expressed his intentions to purge, with the aid of the army, all police units in the country which, in his belief, during the revolutions had become infected with Socialist sympathies. He wished to replace all untrustworthy and disloyal elements with military officers, commissioned and noncommissioned. Finally, Horthy argued that the police's subordination, its restraint, and reorganization along military lines, were advisable for yet another reason. He expected that in the final peace treaty the size of the Hungarian army would be curtailed sharply, and, therefore, a large police force was necessary to augment the army.[21]

In this proposal Beniczky discovered a poorly disguised attempt by Horthy to deprive the government of all of its enforcement powers, thereby making it totally dependent on the Army High Command.[22] The promised purge threatened to replace all individuals opposed to Horthy even if their counterrevolutionary credentials were otherwise in good order. Beniczky, therefore, refused to yield on the issue of control of police; instead, he proposed an increase in police strength from the prewar level of 8960, which was sufficient at a time when Hungary was three times as large, to fifteen thousand.[23] This larger police force was required not only to make possible an intensified supervision of the working classes, but also to strengthen the hand of the government *vis-à-vis* the army.

The White Terror in Transdanubia

In spite of these differences the Friedrich group and the army agreed in one respect. Both believed that the first and most important task was to eliminate all traces of revolutionary spirit, to punish the guilty parties, and to restore the nobility to its previous position in the villages. Their solutions, however, differed. The government, in deference to Western opinion, preferred to use the judicial process to force the population into submission, whereas Horthy and his officers' detachments used a much more direct method. Both the police and the army arrested all those who were in the slightest way implicated in the revolution or who were suspected of Communist sympathies; but, the police generally turned these individuals over to the public prosecutors; officers dispensed with judicial niceties and often took their revenge on the spot.

In the history of the White Terror, therefore, the army played a far more important, and especially a more visible, role. The army also had a high concentration of the less prominent and most radical refugees. Protected from retribution by the uniform and by Horthy, they could freely vent their anger and release pent-up hostilities and frustrations against a population that dared to rise against them. Horthy fully shared his officers' prejudices and hatreds and agreed with them that at times, the most violent methods were necessary and justified against the rebellious elements in society. Only through ruthless intimidation and terror could the army and Horthy become supreme in the country. Consequently, Horthy imposed few limitations upon his officers, with the result that the officers' detachments operated as virtually independent little armies.

Emergence of independent or semi-independent military or terror groups was not unique to Hungary. Most defeated countries experienced a similar phenomenon. The makeup and motivation of these groups, however, were not the same. The most striking differences between, say, the German *Freikorps* movement and the Hungarian White Army was that the former was bourgeois in origin, while the latter bore the imprint of the Hungarian gentry. Also, unlike the Germans, the Hungarian counterrevolutionaries were less interested in reshaping the world along some vaguely defined abstract ideals than in constructing or reconstructing a society which restored the nobility to its past preeminent position.

The prewar privileged stratum, however, was far from united in its conception of post-revolutionary society. To the aristocracy and their followers the arrangements of the Dualist Era appeared to be ideal. But to many among the gentry and gentroid groups the broken pieces of that world could never be fitted together again. Only a surface restoration was possible. Within the reduced territory of Hungary it was impossible to accommodate all who laid claims. The refugees from the Successor States could never be completely satisfied. The surplus gentry in inner

Hungary and large segments of the non-noble gentroid elements remained excluded from the centers of political power. The discontent of these groups rapidly crystallized into demands for a fundamental change in the social order. During their search for an ideological alternative some of them turned against the aristocracy and began to espouse, already in 1919, an ideology akin to Italian fascism; a typically modified version still within the context of the old noble national ideology which led some to characterize it as gentlemen's fascism (*Úrifasizmus*). At its core we can still discover the old agrarian feudal conception of society. In 1919, however, these differences were still subsurface and did not prevent the entire nobility from marching in step against peasants and workers.

The nobility's aspirations to dominate society left a deep imprint on the character of the White Terror. The terror was, in fact, the work of the returning nobility trying to rebuild their past paradise. Paradoxical but typical of the mentality within the officers' detachments was that the military feared the working classes less than the essentially passive peasants. The working class had provided soldiers for the Red Battalions; the peasantry generally remained neutral or even sympathetic to the right. Nevertheless, harsh as treatment of the workers was, villagers bore the brunt of the terror.

Repression of the workers was left to the government and to the regular police or *gendarmerie*. The officers' detachments preferred to operate in the villages, small towns, and especially on the great estates. Consequently, the retaliatory measures against the workers were generally applied collectively,[24] while rebellious peasants and villagers were singled out for individual punishment. Hence, in the countryside a sympathetic word for a Communist cause might have resulted in immediate execution; many industrial workers or miners suffered no greater punishment for even serving in the Red Army than those that were inflicted on their class as a whole. To be sure, most workers subsequently suffered some form of persecution, but, at least, they survived the worst months of the White Terror. This greater circumspection, it is true, was partly due to the organized strength of the workers and to the greater watchfulness of the Western Socialist parties who tried to protect the Hungarian workers, but also to the obsession of the organizers of the White Terror with restoring peace in the villages.

The most notorious and most bloodthirsty of all the terror groups was that of Baron Pál Prónay, but the detachments of Gyula Ostenburg-Moravek, Antal Madary, Baron Jenő Jankovich-Besán, Iván Héjjas, as well as of the lesser-known commanders, lagged behind the officers of Prónay only in number of victims, not in cruelty. Prónay,

Ostenburg, and Madary marched into Transdanubia from Szeged; the other terror groups were formed after the overthrow of the Hungarian Soviet Republic. Of these only Prónay left to posterity any written record of his activities, but it is easy to surmise that the thoughts and motivations of the other commanders were similar to his. In his journals Prónay catalogued some of his exploits. He relates these without a shred of remorse, without ever attempting to excuse himself. Rather the story is told with sadistic delight, in which some of the worst crimes of his men appear as nothing more than innocent pranks of lively children. From the pages of these journals emerges the stark naked picture of a terrorist: a hallow, emotionally deadened, empty man who is incapable of any human sentiment other than rage, a man who incorporated in his person all the faults and anxieties of his class, but without preserving its virtues. Prónay claims that authorization for the terror came directly from Horthy. Consequently, he merely followed orders. In view of the special relations that existed between Prónay and Horthy this is likely.[25] Prónay's instructions before leaving Szeged were specific and came from Horthy's Chief of Staff, General Károly Soós. These were: restore order, execute all Communist leaders, protect and restore to their offices all the prerevolutionary officials, and seize all state property.[26]

Horthy in his memoirs claimed that the headquarters of his army "never issued a bloodthirsty order." However, he meekly admits to terror and excuses himself by endorsing the opinion of his German biographer. "A soldier," he quotes, ". . . cannot be reprimanded for every trifle; the officers who exceed competence cannot always be shot or even disciplined, not, that is to say if the danger of mutiny, or worse, is to be avoided. In times of disturbance, the military cannot be too softhearted. Hell let loose on earth cannot be subjugated by the beating of angels' wings."[27]

Horthy did issue precisely such "bloodthirsty" orders. He also demanded from the government that its officials should not hinder his officers. To all county government plenipotentiaries he sent messages demanding the intensification of the terror. He wrote: "I call upon all military and civilian authorities to commence immediate suppression of all operating centers of Communism, and to arrest all agitators and all participants in the criminal Communist regime who are still free, and to sentence them forthwith. . . . On this issue I will not accept any excuse."[28]

He threatened with dismissal those officials who were found to be soft on Communists. In a letter to Friedrich, Horthy demanded an immediate declaration of martial law for the entire Transdanubia. "We need extraordinary laws," he argued, "which are rigorously enforced by the judges." He warned Friedrich that:

> Excesses of military authorities will be avoided only when everyone knows that arrested Communist leaders, even if it is not possible to prove any ordinary crime against them, will receive their just punishment. It hardly needs an explanation why it is necessary to use severe procedures to create terrible examples. I find it also necessary . . . to examine the procedures of the . . . judges, because so far the High Command had sad experiences with the behavior of the judiciary, especially concerning their laughably soft treatment of Bolsheviks.[29]

Prónay and his officers, as well as the other detachments, hardly needed encouragement from their chief. This becomes evident as one follows, through the pages of Prónay's journal, their terrible journey across the Hungarian countryside. From Szeged the officers' detachment fanned out in Transdanubia. They went from village to village, from estate to estate. Everywhere they recruited new officers, requisitioned food and other supplies, acquired new weapons, motor vehicles, airplanes, artillery pieces, and even armored trains. Their numbers rapidly increased. Within a month, for example, the original 160-man company of Prónay rose to around 400, and by January to 1600 men. Ostenburg's company also reached that size about the same time. The other detachments were similarly expanded. Prónay explained his aims in his journal: "My prime objective was to restore the earlier good relations between lords and servants on the great estates. For in an agricultural country such as Hungary . . . unhindered agricultural production is very important."[30]

Once across the Danube Prónay began to work on the restoration of those "earlier good relations" by organizing the first of his many "people's judgment," which was a euphemism for lynching. These events were reported to the public as spontaneous outbursts of the peasantry against Communists, but usually Prónay's men were the chief instigators.

Wherever these officers went the local landowners eagerly welcomed them; others sent urgent invitations to Prónay to visit their estates. At Cece, for example, Prónay was the guest of the gentry landowner Dénes Szluha. After Prónay visited the neighboring estates and silenced the uppity peasants with "well-measured canings," the grateful landowners of the district honored the officers with a feast and an all-night party. As he went from estate to estate his troops beat or executed arrested Communists, peasants and estate employees. Other detachments were equally brutal in the "pacification work."

Most victims of the White Terror were poor peasants or servants on the great estates and a minority were Jews. Some of the latter were punished for their real or imagined roles during the Soviet Republic; others were caught in the web of suspicion that surrounded the Jewish community after the fall of the Kun regime. The reasons for those suspicions are not hard to see. The sizable Jewish community of the country played a highly visible and seemingly contradictory role in Hungary's modern history: the leading capitalists as well as Communists came from its ranks. As a result the Jewish community came to be identified with both the prewar and wartime abuses of the capitalist system and those of the postwar communist regime.

During the Dualist Era Jews achieved virtual equality. Jewish industrialists and bankers were primarily responsible for Hungary's rapid industrialization, playing a prominent role in the modernization of its economy. A substantial percentage of the country's non-noble middle class also came from the ranks of Jews. By the first decade of the twentieth century, the community as a whole, with the blessing of its most prominent leaders and without effective opposition by the rest of Hungary's society, was well on the way toward full assimilation.

The war and the postwar revolutions changed attitudes toward the Jewish community. The deprivations the population was forced to endure necessarily intensified resentment against the more prosperous classes and during the Hungarian Soviet Republic in the popular conception and especially in the not too subtle minds of such men as Prónay, Communism was linked with Jews. The prime cause for that linkage is to be found less in some widely felt need for scapegoats than in the image that the radicals and especially the Communist Party projected. The most prominent and visible leaders of the party, all but a few of the people's commissars and their deputies were Jewish; so were a majority of middle-rank officials, many of the radical publicists and, above all, such well-known and dreaded proponents of terror as Ottó Korvin and Tibor Szamuely. As György Száraz pointed out, some of the victims of the Red Terror were also Jewish, about 70 of the hostages held by the Communist regime were leading Jewish industrialists and bankers.[31] The counterrevolutionary movement also enjoyed the political and financial support of a segment of the Jewish community. But these facts could alter but little the popular perception of Jews. Not surprisingly most Jews were suspected as potential Communist sympathizers, as responsible for the reckless policies of the Soviet regime, and the Red Terror was laid at the doorstep of the Jewish community.

Uncontrolled terror in the countryside, however, proved to be an ever-increasing embarrassment to the Allies. The Western Powers needed Horthy's military strength to replace the Romanian occupying forces, but the Western liberal and especially Socialist press increasingly opposed recognition of Horthy as the man who was most responsible for the terror. It was necessary, therefore, to impress on Horthy that these activities must cease. At the same time, the Allied Military Mission was willing to cooperate in proving that his troops were not responsible for the murders, that they were the work of independent groups or the result of mass outrage against the Communists. In the name of the Allied Military Mission, therefore, a Jewish-American officer, Colonel Nathan Horowitz, was dispatched to Horthy's headquarters to investigate allegations of terror. Horthy was well warned of this visit. Consequently, Horowitz's tour was carefully prepared and the investigation, from Horthy's point of view, was a total success. In Horowitz's report which was transmitted to the Paris Peace Conference, he denied the existence of White Terror, and especially the responsibility of the National Army for some of the incidents.

> I visited Siófok, headquarters of National Hungarian Army . . . and . . . investigated reports of mistreatment and murder of Jews and pogroms. I went thoroughly into the subject both with Jews of the neighborhood and with Hungarian officers and found that although there were several authenticated cases of mistreatment and even murders, that these could not be traced even remotely to Hungarian Army authority. On the contrary the authorities are doing their utmost to prevent injustice and disorder in territory under [their] control. Every case reported is investigated and guilty offenders severely punished. I am convinced that rumors regarding so-called White Terror are unfounded. I consider the officers of the National Hungarian Army to be patriotic and inspired with most liberal sentiments of duty and justice. No well-behaved Jews or Christians need fear anything at their hands. They represent the visible and tangible support that Hungary now has and should be received with acclaim by the Hungarian people instead of with suspicion and dread.[32]

This report remained the principal document to which the Horthy regime repeatedly pointed to refute the charges of terrorism. To allay public fears the Allies decided to publish this report, though the last phrases were omitted.[33]

Horthy himself gradually came to the conclusion that terror must be moderated. Horthy approved the harshness of his officers. He did not wish to end the terror completely, but he began to urge his officers to be more cautious in selecting victims and, above all, to be more skillful in covering up their tracks. Even Horthy had difficulty in convincing many officers of the advisability of this course. Many officers had an emotional investment in the terror which they were reluctant to yield. Prónay was especially opposed to moderation. He considered it a sign of cowardice to yield to the pressure of the Allies or to the liberal press of Budapest. According to him, there was nothing to be gained from moderation.

From several directions pressure was exerted on Horthy to end the terror. Not only the Allies and Western press found its continuation intolerable, but many within Hungarian conservative circles were equally opposed to it. Hungarian prelates, aristocrats, at times the very same aristocrats who had invited the officers to their estates to restore order, were shocked by the unexpected violence of the officers. Even older members of the officers corps, temporarily outside the service or attached to regular army units, expressed their revulsion, considering terror by officers a stain on the honor of the officers corps and the nation. Baron Lehár, for example, fell into this category. On August 6, 1919, upon crossing the Austrian border, in a proclamation, he reassured the population that his troops were under strict order to refrain from violence.[34] As a result, his forces established army control in west Hungary with few incidents.

During negotiations about formation of a new government that would be acceptable to the Western Powers, next to subordination of the National Army to the civilian government, the question of terror was the single most important issue. By the first weeks of November the Romanians were ready to withdraw from most of the country, and the task of occupying Budapest and the region between the Danube and the Tisza Rivers had to be assumed by Horthy's troops. The Allies were also pressing Hungarian political leaders to form a broadly based coalition government so that peace negotiations could begin. On October 23 a special envoy of the Entente, Sir George Clerk, a British diplomat, arrived in Budapest to direct negotiations between contending parties.[35] Horthy's attitude, however, remained a question mark. If he intended to carry the terror into the capital he could not be acceptable either to the KNEP or to the Allies. Already at the beginning of September a prestigious delegation, composed of Beniczky, Count Bethlen, Count József Károlyi, Count Andrássy, Count Batthyány, and Margrave Pallavicini visited Horthy, and tried to convince him of the inadvisability of terror. They also tried to seek out Horthy's plans for the time after he marched into Budapest. To Beniczky's question: "If the National Army marches into the capital will there be a pogrom, yes or no?" Horthy replied: "There will not be a pogrom! But a few people will have to take a swim!"[36] On this issue Horthy's attitude remained the same during the Clerk negotiations.

On the question of the coalition government Horthy's opposition to inclusion of Liberals and Socialists remained one of the major stumbling blocks. In this he shared the views of the KNEP representatives, but, while KNEP leaders were extremely susceptible to Western pressure, Horthy was able to hold out.[37] Nevertheless, on November 5, a compromise was reached between Horthy and the Liberal and Socialist parties. Horthy agreed that the army's march into Budapest would not lead to the establishment of a military dictatorship. The army would subordinate itself to the representatives of the Entente and to the government that was established with its cooperation. At the same time Horthy reserved the right to crush all manifestations of communism.

Thus the door was opened to formation of a coalition government as well as for occupation of Budapest by the National Army. The first units to arrive in the capital were actually those of Baron Lehár. These, however, as the only fully combat-ready forces, were soon ordered to leave the city, to follow the retreating Romanian army, and to occupy central and eastern regions of Hungary. On November 16, Admiral Horthy himself, between walls of his troops, accompanied by the Prónay and Ostenburg detachments, mounted on a white horse, triumphantly rode into Budapest.

Chapter 9
Political Assimilation of the Refugees and the Triumph of Horthy

The refugees from the Successor States played a vital role in the radical politics of 1919. Their presence was conspicuous in every extremist group and, on most issues, they staked out for themselves a position on the right side of the political spectrum. The contribution of these refugees to the development of Hungarian right radicalism is not lessened by the fact that they were less visible as refugees than as extreme nationalists or as members of the old ruling elite. Their effectiveness, in fact, would have been much diminished had they chosen to act always as a refugee group *per se,* with special goals and special claims upon the rest of Hungarian society. Instead they chose to participate in larger groups, where they could hope to enlist the support of a broader segment of the population for their grievances. In this they were successful. As conditions returned to normal the population of truncated Hungary ceased to look upon them as refugees; they were accepted as *bona fide* Hungarian citizens.

In Austria and in Szeged these refugees joined hands with those who fled from Communist Hungary. Both refugee groups were dispossessed and displaced. They were radicalized by their experiences. But once the road to return to Hungary was open those who fled from Communist terror ceased to be refugees. They attained their primary objective: they regained their lost properties and their previous position in the state. They returned to their estates or resumed their careers and began to yearn for a return to normalcy. Some of them withdrew from political activities altogether; others, their desire for revenge sated, began to oppose the continuation of the revolution in white.

For the refugees from the Successor States the causes of their radicalization could not be removed so easily. Their lives were still in ruin, their position and status in Hungarian society remained in doubt. For them, returning to Hungary was only the first step toward regaining their lost positions and properties in their native lands. Thus, they searched for new allies among the other discontented elements in Hungary and aimed to continue the counterrevolution until they either regained the lost areas, or at least until the state had found ways to accommodate or absorb them.

Between November 1919 and June 1920, the focal points of political struggle were the parliamentary elections and the choosing of a new head of state. The refugees, as the most politicized and the single most radical group in the country, threw themselves, with vigor, into the conflict, and ultimately emerged triumphant. Almost without exception they lined up behind the two right-wing parties, the majority of them, though not all, behind the candidacy of Horthy as the regent of the realm. Hence, the victory of the right in the parliamentary elections as well as that of Horthy was also a victory for the refugees, especially for the gentry and gentroid elements.

In November 1919 the question of an open military dictatorship lay heavily on everyone's mind. It did not, however, follow the arrival of Horthy and the National Army into the capital. Contrary to urgings of his officers Horthy chose to exercise some caution. Budapest was still in the stage of latent revolution; its population had to be treated with greater circumspection than the people of the villages. Among the workers there was still present an often-expressed desire and hope for a second Socialist revolution. Although such a revolution was no more than a hope, in reality no one was working for it, the right still feared it.[1] Horthy, therefore, was anxious to avoid taking drastic steps which might rekindle the revolutionary fire thereby jeopardizing his own position. A forceful seizure of government, too, would have aroused the opposition of other right-wing groups, mostly represented by KNEP. Their opposition would have endangered the unity of the military forces under Horthy's command, and an open civil war between the various right-wing factions was not an impossibility. Most important, Horthy feared the sanctions of the Western Powers, who, up to this point, expressed full confidence in his abilities and who supported the expansion of his army.[2] In other words, the Clerk mission was only a partial failure. It failed to guarantee reintroduction of genuinely democratic institutions. Nor did it break the power of the National Army. But it did prevent the establishment of an open military dictatorship and forced upon the right a degree of moderation. Concern about Western reaction to terror, to introduction of open military dictatorship, was also responsible for the creation of a dual system of government, where political power was jointly exercised by a constitutionally elected government with a parliamentary system and by a network of hidden organizations, by a parallel civilian and covert military hierarchy.

Instead of open military dictatorship, Horthy chose a less perilous course, which nevertheless safeguarded just as effectively his and the army's carefully constructed central position in Hungary's political life. He did not oppose formation of a coalition government was temporarily satisfied with remaining somewhat in the background. Contrary to his promise during the Clerk negotiations, however, he refused to permit any interference in army affairs or a curtailment of the army's police powers by either the ministry of defense or the ministry of interior. Thus, while retaining control of the army and slowly increasing its strength, he gained additional time to organize a political bloc that was willing to back his candidacy for regent of the state.

With the establishment of a coalition government legality was maintained. Seemingly all political factions in the country gained representation in the new government. The Christian National Unity Party, claiming to be the largest party in the country, retained five seats in the cabinet; counting its one independent ally, it had six. The interests of the peasantry were to be represented by the two agrarian parties, each holding two seats, and the liberal, urban, and working classes were nominally represented by the Liberal Party, the Democratic Party, and the Social Democratic Party, each receiving one seat.[3] The KNEP, nevertheless, remained all powerful in the cabinet. It retained, for itself, the most important cabinet posts. István Friedrich yielded his office to Károly Huszár, a man without great stature or power base. Most KNEP leaders would have preferred Count Albert Apponyi, who came to Hungary from his Slovak estate just for the purpose of heading the government. He enjoyed the support of most of his fellow refugee nobles and aristocrats from northern Hungary who, jointly with the Catholic aristocracy of inner Hungary, effectively controlled the party. Apponyi's stature as an elder statesman would have been a major asset against Horthy's ambitions, but, for precisely that reason, Horthy's supporters objected to his candidacy. Friedrich took over the ministry of defense, Beniczky retained control of the ministry of interior, and Count József Somssich, a KNEP supporter, though nominally independent, retained the ministry of foreign affairs. The Friedrich-Beniczky group believed that, by controlling these key ministries, they would be in effective control of the country, which indeed would have been the case had Horthy kept his promise.

Judged from other surface appearances it also seemed that Hungary was well on the way toward establishing a democratic regime. Only the Communist Party was outlawed. A wide variety of newspapers continued publication including Socialist papers. Democratic elections were decreed; to be held within two months. For the first time in the country's history women were given the right to vote; in fact, no one was denied the right to vote under the new universal franchise law.[4] To assure participation of all classes voting was made mandatory. Even some progressive social reforms were promised along with land reform.

In the rural areas, however, terror continued unabated, with the difference that now it was extended to the region between the Danube and the Tisza Rivers as soon as it was freed from Romanian occupation. The Romanian military already arrested and executed a large number of suspected Communists.[5] After the withdrawal of the Romanians the area was to be combed once again for functionaries of the defunct Béla Kun regime. The arrests, followed the pattern established in Transdanubia. The most extreme case was the "Orgovány Affair." A *gendarmerie* reserve unit, made up mostly of local counterrevolutionaries operating around the town of Kecskemét, under the command of Iván Héjjas, a friend of Prónay, arrested 26 individuals, dragged out of prison another 36 suspected Communists, and, at Orgovány, slaughtered them all. This mass murder received worldwide attention, and the facts of the case were fully substantiated by both an international investigative commission and by the local police. Other incidents, though on a much lesser scale, were frequent during most of 1920.[6]

To intimidate the population Horthy increasingly relied on the army's political section or, as it was called, the "national defense" sector. This was in effect an elaborate spy network crisscrossing the country, reaching all the way down to the village level. Its functions were: supervising all political organizations, reporting on the mood of the people, observing state officials, supervising all publications and their circulation, maintaining clandestine postal censorship, preventing circulation of opposition papers of Budapest in the countryside, and finally, aiding the organization and operation of Gömbös's MOVE. A similar though less extensive spy network was already established by the government, which at the time tried to counter the effectiveness of the army propaganda officers.[7]

The judiciary was also under intense pressure from both the government and the army to participate in the reprisals, in the process of intimidation. The regular judicial process was suspended, the rights of the accused greatly curtailed, the appeals procedure was made difficult. According to Gratz, through regular judicial procedures 97 Communists were found guilty and sentenced to death, 68 of them executed.[8] Thousands of others were sentenced to lesser punishment.

Every prison in the country was teeming with political prisoners. Wholesale arrests commenced with Friedrich's seizure of power, but the arrests were intensified after Horthy's arrival. On November 16 alone, the day Horthy marched into the capital, 350 persons were rounded up. By mid-August the jailers were complaining about the intolerable overcrowded conditions in the prisons.[9] The solution to this problem was found in establishment, by the army, of concentration camps, among others at Hajmáskér and Zalaegerszeg. All those prisoners who were considered dangerous but against whom no specific criminal charges could be filed were ordered to be delivered in sealed boxcars to one of these camps.[10]

Precise figures on the exact number of individuals arrested and interned are not available. At the time, the Social Democratic Party claimed that about 60,000 persons were held in custody; no one of the right challenged these figures.[11]

The government issued the internment edict on December 5, 1919. All those individuals who were considered "dangerous" or "suspected to be dangerous," as well as those who were believed to be "damaging to the economy of the country," were ordered to be deported to the villages with all their dependents and kept there under close police surveillance.[12] But still, the army demanded more arrests; it still feared a second revolution. As one of Horthy's officers bluntly wrote: "The only solution for this problem is a timely mass arrest and internment of the disorderly element. I urgently ask authorization for this! . . . Objections of the Entente must be ignored! A choice must be made between mass arrests and mass internment and a bloodbath and perhaps downfall. . . ."[13]

In this atmosphere of terror the country was preparing for its first democratic elections. All political parties except the Communist Party were allowed to run their candidates, but, in fact, the election boiled down to a contest between the two major political factions of the right, that is, between KNEP and Horthy supporters.

In spite of the army's strength and political muscle in the electoral competition, Horthy was at a disadvantage. The KNEP already staked out its claim as the principal political party of the right, but the KNEP was not likely to elect Horthy as head of state. The majority of the party's leadership was legitimist, although a significant number of the younger radicals and refugees were not. The leadership's first choice was King Károly (Emperor Karl). Even if he could not have returned to the throne, the KNEP was more likely to turn to a man like Apponyi than to Horthy. Horthy needed an alternative party that was capable of returning a majority to parliament and which was opposed to a Habsburg restoration.

The logical choice was István Nagyatádi Szabó's Smallholders Party. Among the peasantry the House of Habsburg was unpopular, and, consequently, their representatives were not likely to be enthusiastic about the king's return, but it was a moderate party; it was deeply committed to land reform. Therefore, it had to be transformed from within before it could become a useful instrument for Horthy. On the land reform issue some concessions had to be made to the peasantry. Since the October Revolution no other issue stirred the peasantry so deeply as this. Their hopes were dashed by Mihály Károlyi's timidity and the collectivizing policies of the Hungarian Soviet regime. At the same time it was not possible to promise a far-reaching land reform since that would have alienated many of Horthy's own supporters. It also would have made a subsequent reconciliation with the aristocracy impossible.

The harnessing of the Smallholders Party was achieved through a forced merger with the conservative Agrarian Party, headed by Gyula Rubinek, a gentry politician from Slovakia and President of the OMGE, the association of the Hungarian landed aristocracy. His presence in the Smallholders Party, and at the head of the ministry of agriculture, stilled the fears of aristocracy. At the same time many of Horthy's own supporters, including Gömbös and Horthy's own brother, joined the Smallholders Party and ran as its candidates in the parliamentary elections. Thus the Smallholders Party was transformed into a party leaning strongly toward the right and toward Horthy.

Simultaneously the Horthy group made several attempts at undermining KNEP unity. Leaders who were unalterably opposed to Horthy were attacked and some, such as Friedrich, were isolated through a political smear campaign.[14] Others, who were less committed to the legitimist cause or who were legitimists only in principle but realists in politics, were quietly approached and won over. This task of softening the opposition primarily fell to the various secret societies which suddenly came into prominence during the electoral struggle. Some of these societies played a vital role in the 1920 and in subsequent elections, as well as in elevating Horthy to the regency.

During 1919 and 1920 scores and indeed hundreds of semisecret or ultrasecret right-wing organizations mushroomed all over Hungary, though only a few were powerful enough to leave a permanent mark on its history. The most influential were The Twelve Captains, The Blood Alliance of the Apostolic Cross, The Alliance of Etelköz, or EKSz, or merely "X," The Resurrection, better known as the Wolff-group.[15] With the exception of the last-named group the original core membership of each of these societies consisted of officers loyal to Horthy, but gradually the so-called theoretical legitimists and other right-wing factions were also admitted.

In effect these organizations formed a closed circle. They shared ideals, purposes, and often membership. The Twelve Captains, for example, headed by Gömbös, formed in July 1919 in Szeged, were recruited entirely from the most prominent young officers in Horthy's immediate military entourage.[16] These same officers were also members of the EKSz, as well as of The Blood Alliance. Prónay and several other detachment leaders were also active members in the EKSz and The Blood Alliance. Bishop Ottokar Prohászka, and later even István Bethlen and Pál Teleki, became prominent figures in both the Wolff-group and the EKSz.

The least is known about the makeup and activities of the so-called Wolff-group. Most of its leaders were born in the lost territories, among them Károly Wolff, head of the Christian National League, Counts Bethlen and Teleki, Bishop Prohászka, and the two Protestant bishops, the Transylvanian Calvinist theologian, László Ravasz, and the Lutheran Sándor Raffay. It also embraced some of the top civil servants and jurists in the country. Its size was not impressive, it had no more than perhaps 300 members, but what it lacked in size it made up in political skill and astuteness. Zadravecz claims that this group was even weightier in political matters than the EKSz.[17] Although this may be doubtful, it is true that ultimately the Bethlen-Teleki group triumphed and, through a secret alliance, managed to harness the EKSz for their own purposes.

The largest of all these secret societies was the EKSz. It operated under the legal cover organization of Hungarian Scientific Race Defending Association.[18] Through its nationwide network of local chapters, with some 5000 members, the EKSz stretched across a broad spectrum of the political right and united the radical elements from various parties, especially those of the Christian Nationalist and Smallholders Parties. It also linked the officer corps with civilian leaders of the right. In addition to the younger officers represented by The Twelve Captains, many of the senior army officers supporting Horthy were EKSz members. Most of the detachment commanders also played a prominent role in the organization, among them Baron Prónay, Ostenburg, Count Jankovich-Besán, Iván Héjjas, and György Hír, along with many of their officers. Among the other members some were prominent clergymen, such as Prohászka, the two radical Franciscans, Bishop of the Army István Zadravecz and Arkangyal Bónis. The aristocracy was represented by the young Archduke Albrecht, whom some of the EKSz leaders wished to elevate to the Hungarian throne, Count Gedeon Ráday, Count Imre Károlyi, Prince Lajos Windischgrätz, Prince Károly Odescalchy, and Count Miklós Bánffy, a Transylvanian magnate from Bethlen's inner circle. Some of the Arrow Cross Party's future leaders, men like Ferenc Szálasi and Baron Berchtold Feilitzsch, were also members. Later even Counts Bethlen and Teleki joined this group.[19]

The EKSz was headed by seven chiefs, among them Gömbös and Zadravecz. Each of the chiefs led a tribe. These tribes in turn were subdivided into clans, and the clans into families. The position of Chief of Chiefs was reserved, according to some, for the head of state, that is, for Horthy, although it seems that Horthy refused to assume official control of the society. Still, he was the "invisible leader." From 1920 the EKSz held its meetings at the national headquarters of MOVE, which occupied the spacious national lodge of the Free Masons. With the physical facilities they also took over much of the ceremonial trappings of the Masons. Zadravecz wrote: "In its organization [the EKSz] kept in view the Free Masons and it wished to save the country using methods the Masons had used to destroy it."[20] New brothers were recruited after careful screening.

In any political equation the decision of the EKSz was a major factor. During its meetings the issues of the day were regularly and hotly debated. Often, the fate of one government or another was decided in these meetings, at least until Bethlen took over direction of the government. A vote of no confidence by the EKSz often amounted to dismissal of a government, especially since many cabinet ministers, as members of the society, were bound by its decisions. The EKSz, while serving Horthy, also had a hold upon him. According to Zadravecz, "the soul and backbone of the Ex was . . . Horthy loyalty."[21] At the same time the members knew that it was largely the EKSz that raised and maintained Horthy in power. Consequently they exploited their considerable political influence for their own benefit and pressed Horthy to adopt policies favored by the EKSz. At times they even sent brisk ultimatums to Horthy, which he had to obey.

During elections the society campaigned vigorously for the election of brothers, regardless of their party affiliation. In this they were always highly successful. In 1922, for example, about seventy EKSz members were elected to the National Assembly,[22] that is, the EKSz captured nearly a third of the assembly seats.

Since the Szeged days the program of the radical right changed little; it still consisted of only two points. The first goal was the destruction of Communist and Free Mason, that is liberal, influence in the country; the second, reconquest of the lost territories. By early 1920 the first goal was achieved and, therefore, the attention of most radicals increasingly shifted to the second objective. These secret societies stood at the center of the irredentist movement; in fact, several of them were brought to life precisely for that reason. This was especially true of The Blood Alliance of the Apostolic Cross. It was formed in Szeged and headed by an officer of the Székely Division, Major, later Colonel, Tihamér Siménfalvy. Its sole function was to organize a clandestine army, the so-called Free Troops, which could be used against domestic enemies but especially as guerilla forces in Slovakia and Transylvania. The leaders of The Blood Alliance assumed that such an army, composed mostly of dedicated refugees familiar with the terrain of the lost provinces, would be able to penetrate Czechoslovakia and Romania undetected and, then, acting as dissatisfied members of the Hungarian minority, organize and lead an uprising. The plan was to attack Slovakia first; when the situation became intolerable, the regular Hungarian Army would have to be sent in to protect the minorities against retaliation by the Czechs and restore order.[23] The *Felvidéki Liga*, or the Upland League, was established for the same purpose. It carried out propaganda and made strenuous efforts to organize a Slovak Legion from separatist Slovaks.[24]

Understandably, to the refugees from the Successor States, these societies were tremendously appealing and, indeed, they were fully represented both in the leadership and among the members. Through these societies the refugees formed an alliance with the ultranationalist right of inner Hungary or, perhaps more accurately, they maintained the old alliance that was forged at Szeged and Vienna, in order to assure that the question of their return to the lost territories would never be removed from the public agenda and, at the same time, to ensure that the economic plight of their fellow refugees would not be lost from sight. Most of the irredentist groups maintained close ties with the EKSz and the other groups.

In addition to the army and the secret societies, the presence of the refugees was also strongly felt in virtually every other right-wing radical association. The refugees who joined these were less prominent, the forgotten refugees. They were those whom the economic collapse of the country hit most severely, who, therefore, were ready for radical action.

Conditions of life since the middle of 1919 failed to improve. On the contrary, in many areas the situation had drastically deteriorated. Unemployment reached the critical point in most parts of Hungary. Entire industries came to a halt owing to coal and raw material shortages, to the long Allied blockade, or to wholesale looting by the retiring Romanian Army, which carted away at times whole factories.[25] Food shortages were noticeable everywhere in the country, but especially in the larger cities, where the distribution system was in a constant danger of collapse. A report by the ministry of food supplies of January 4, 1920 illustrates the magnitude of the problem. According to this report, Budapest was without flour reserves and the limited supplies that were still arriving were totally inadequate to meet the city's needs. The daily food allotment under the system of rationing was reduced to about four ounces of bread (12 dkgs.), but even this could not be satisfied. For weeks no potatoes were available, since the limited supply arriving in the city barely sufficed to satisfy the needs of the hospitals and the army. There was absolutely no fat available, no meat, no sugar. The milk supply was insufficient even to provide for the needs of hospitals and infants.[26] The city command on January 17 reported:

> Everyday after the curfew hour, sad and dangerous events occur. Already at 8 o'clock in the evening somber crowds begin to line up before the bakeries . . . so that in the morning, around 7 or 8 o'clock, they would be able to buy some bread. Amongst humanly unimaginable sufferings, want and cold, they wait for arrival of the bread shipment. The human mass, which grows into the thousands, often stretches to the third and fourth street. They wait sadly and silently, they shiver, they are cold, and with truly Christian patience stand the frightful rains, snow, and winds of the nights of these days.[27]

Under these economic conditions, the plight and desperation of the masses of refugees is understandable. Families without prominent names, influential friends, or without ties to the officers' detachments, were often on the point of starvation. The housing shortage had already reached the critical point during the first part of 1919. Yet refugees continued to pour into the country, and especially into the capital area. During the months following the Romanian troops' evacuation from Budapest and the Danube-Tisza regions, the rate of their flow even accelerated. The refugee influx reached its peak around mid-1920, when, after imposition of several government restrictions, it gradually began to decline. The number of officially registered refugees by the end of 1919 was about 170,000. During the next twelve months an additional 32,000 arrived from Slovakia, about 71,000 from Transylvania, and over 10,000 from Yugoslavia, that is, their numbers had increased to a minimum of 280,000,[28] and according to our calculations close to 350,000.

The worst conditions prevailed in the Budapest area, yet about half of the refugees were still heading for that city. It may be estimated that by the end of 1920 there were in Budapest proper, excluding its suburbs where some of the shanty towns were located, around 125,000 refugees. That is, at least one out of every seven residents of the city was a refugee.[29]

The new arrivals were no longer the affluent Hungarians. A large number of them were students from the closed gymnasiums and universities of Slovakia and Transylvania. For example, a majority of the Hungarian students and faculty from the universities of Kolozsvár, Nagyvárad, Pozsony, and Eperjes decided after their old institutions lost their Hungarian character to continue their studies or teaching careers in Budapest. A majority of new refugees came from the ranks of the lower state civil service, of the lesser county officials, teachers, and other groups, who exclusively depended upon their salaries. Some held out even after their dismissal in a vain hope of some sudden reversal of events. By 1920, however, their economic situation became hopeless. Thus, their departure was no longer politically motivated, it was a simple matter of survival.

The refugees' situation was critical; the solutions they demanded were radical. Understandably, soon after their arrival they were drawn into the ultraradical right-wing politics of the city, which afforded them an opportunity to vent their outrage against the miserable conditions of their lives. They had little patience with the constant political squabbles between the various parties, which deflected the energies of the nation from its true national goals. They demanded unity and wished to silence all opposition. Many preferred the order promised by a military dictatorship to the chaos offered by the even limited political freedom. The most radical of these refugees, and especially the students and the Protestant Transylvanians, supported the army and Horthy, who seemed to possess all the right qualifications, held the right attitudes required as the leader of the country. Like most eastern refugees Horthy was a Protestant. He also stood in the way of a Habsburg restoration. He was a man who was seemingly determined to establish a strong authoritarian rule and who also had the stature to lead the nation to a military reconquest of the lost territories.

Right-wing organizations in which the radical refugees had a prominent voice usually lined up behind the army and Horthy. Such were MOVE and the Awakening Hungarians, or ÉME. MOVE became the principal political association of the officers, which was originally brought to life to aid the refugee officers. On December 13, 1919, Horthy virtually ordered all army officers to join MOVE.[30] Subsequently state, city, and local officials were also recruited. In 1920, MOVE claimed to have had about 100,000 members — certainly an inflated figure; nevertheless, the organization did wield considerable power. Its leader, Gyula Gömbös, boasted vis-à-vis Italian and German fascists that MOVE was the first fascist organization in Europe. In 1920, in reference to contacts with Hitler and Ludendorff, he stated: "In other countries, following our example, the Christian renaissance also began." And later, courting Italian fascist favors, he said: "We also have fascist organizations. First of all, the MOVE is such . . . also the ÉME and the TESZ."[31] MOVE established a nationwide spy network and a far-reaching propaganda system. It continued to aid families of refugee officers, organized escapes of officers and their families from the lost territories and promoted their irredentist cause.[32] MOVE's extensive organizational activities led to charges in the National Assembly that it was becoming a state within a state, which used its network of officers to supervise and pressure the regular government agencies. In January 1920, Gömbös, in a letter to Horthy, offered MOVE's help in the upcoming elections. He wrote: "We will achieve our goals not with catchy slogans but through genuine organization, stubborn persistence and if necessary through the murderous tools of the 'Narodna Obrana.'" Moreover, he suggested to Horthy that MOVE should be entrusted with the execution of all those domestic tasks which, for whatever reason, the office of the Commander-in-Chief could not carry out.[33]

The Association of the Awakening Hungarians united the most unruly and desperate extreme right-wing elements of the country with the equally desperate refugees. Most of the Awakening Hungarians were young, many of them ex-officers and university students. Its president until 1921 was the irrepressible György Szmrecsányi; he was then replaced by István Pálóczy Horváth. The other prominent figures in the organization were about equally divided between the radical refugees and those from inner Hungary.[34] Among the Transylvanian Awakening Hungarians we find some of the most impulsive members of the First National Assembly, such as the young radical lawyer, Ferenc Ulain, János Koródi Katona from Nagybánya, the Székely Menyhért Kiss, László Budaváry from Ugocsa County, Vilmos Pröhle, a professor from the University of Kolozsvár, and one of the founders of EKSz, Tibor Eckhardt, a former Transylvanian county official of Tordaaranyos.[35] Károly Wolff and some of his followers were also members. From inner Hungary some of the most notorious radicals were likewise members of the ÉME, among them Iván Héjjas, György Hír, István Lendvai. Fittingly, in 1920, Prónay also became a member.

The Awakening Hungarians maintained a nationwide organization of local chapters; members were enrolled in its paramilitary companies. These groups were ready to participate in any radical or wild adventure or in intimidation of the population. According to its leadership, it had about one-million members, a grossly exaggerated figure. Even if it had only a tenth of that number as active members it was a large and a politically influential organization with great powers.

A main part of the hoped-for national awakening was irredentism. The leader and many of the so-called Free Troops (*Szabad csapatok*) and Ragged Guard (*Rongyos gárda*) who rose against the Treaty of Trianon during 1921 and fought in Burgenland under the command of Prónay, came from the ranks of the Awakening Hungarians. The companies of Awakening Hungarians were also instrumental in saving Horthy during the second legitimist putsch, when a large segment of the army deserted him or at least could not be trusted. In 1923, however, they formally broke with Horthy, who, they believed, abandoned their radical cause and postponed a military reconquest of the lost provinces in favor of a compromise with the aristocracy and the Jewish bourgeoisie. At that point much of ÉME moved into opposition in alliance with the Race Protecting Party (*Fajvédő Párt*), headed by Gömbös. Ulain, Hír, Lendvai, and Héjjas became the principal leaders of this party and won seats in the National Assembly.

The refugees from the Successor States also established their own organizations. Such were the *Felvidéki Liga* (Upland League), *Délvidéki Liga* (Southland League), *Erdélyi Magyar-Székely Szövetség* (Transylvanian Hungarian-Székely Alliance). Various regional groups were brought together in the organization called *Magyarország Területi Épségének Védelmi Ligája* or *Területvédő Liga,* or TEVÉL (League for the Defense of Hungary's Territorial Integrity). Another umbrella organization was the *Menekülteket Védő Szövetség* (Alliance for Refugee Defense), established in April 1920 under the sponsorship of Archduke Joseph and the Prince Primate, Cardinal József Csernoch. Similar organizations representing smaller groups were the *Székely Hadosztály Egyesület* (Association of Székely Division) and the *Bocskay Szövetség* (Bocskay Alliance). In the 1920, and subsequent, elections these and similar organizations worked to guarantee that only candidates sympathetic to their cause would be elected; in general, to assure their influence on the country's foreign policy. Before signing the Treaty of Trianon some of these organizations actively promoted the creation of a massive army drawn first and foremost from the refugees to reconquer the lost areas. After the signing of the treaty their main goal was to make certain that the nation did not drift into complacency, return to normalcy, and, in the process, acquiesce in the partition of the country. Especially the more radical refugees placed great emphasis on the preservation of a sense of national crisis. Only in such an atmosphere could the militarization and ultranationalistic re-education of the country, and especially of the youth, take place.[36] Bishop of the Army István Zadravecz summed up this view in 1922 when he said: "Only a fanatic can be irredentist. An irredentist country does not recognize a 'legal order.' The irredentists should not be held back; it is not legal order but a sin to protect from their rage those who endanger the nation."[37]

These groups were the chief supporters, the mainstay of Horthy's power: the officers' detachments, the army intelligence and propaganda network, and the secret and open right-wing societies and associations. Since, in each of these organizations, the radical refugees participated in great numbers, they formed a powerful bloc behind Horthy in the elections. These groups staffed the election machine that began to campaign all over the country to assure the triumph of the most radical right-wing candidates and the most loyal supporters of Horthy. The particular party label under which a candidate ran was less important to them than the degree of his commitment to the anti-Communist and irredentist crusades, and the degree of his support of Horthy. The Army High Command gave specific instructions to key officers about their role in the elections. They were to assure, regardless of party affiliation, that only supporters of Horthy would be elected.[38] The chief of the army's propaganda division warned officers that the army could not let the leadership of the country slip from its hands as a result of the election. The army propaganda machine therefore had to convince the public that Horthy was "the most suitable person to hold the leadership of the country." When "we search for a dedicated leader," wrote Miklós Kozma, "our eyes, no matter how long we look, will finally come to rest on one man, Miklós Horthy."[39]

The significance of the outcome of the January 1920 elections was not lost upon any of the political factions. It was a struggle for control of the country. For the makeup of the new National Assembly shaped the new society, the foreign policy of the state, and set the whole tone of the regime that was to follow the revolutionary and counterrevolutionary epoch. This National Assembly, possessing constitutional authority, was to decide upon the question of a head of state, who, in turn, would appoint the government from the parliamentary majority to carry out the task of reconstruction. This assembly was also to decide on some vital social and economic questions, the most important of which was land reform.

As a result, the election struggle was conducted, simultaneously, on three fronts: between the right and the left, that is, between the two right-wing parties, on the one hand, and the liberal and Socialist parties, on the other; between the two major parties of the right, the Christian National Unity Party and the Smallholders Party; and finally, between the radical and conservative wings of KNEP and the Smallholders allied with each other, making party labels quite meaningless.

At the opening of the campaign there was considerable uncertainty on the right, since the ultimate outcome of the election was far from clear. No one could predict how the newly enfranchised masses would use their vote. It was not even certain that the two right-wing parties together would be able to muster a parliamentary majority. Party leaders, therefore, in order to prevent splitting of right-wing votes, decided to come to some kind of electoral agreement. Accordingly, a vague reciprocal agreement was worked out, whereby, in each district, the candidate of the weaker party was to withdraw in favor of the other. In 41 districts, partly due to this agreement and partly to the threats against the nominees of the moderate parties, rightist candidates ran unopposed.[40] In the majority of districts, however, the agreement broke down because of the two parties' inability to agree on the degree of their candidates' popularity. Thus, in most parts of the country, the election became an all-out struggle between all parties and all factions. In the end both parties tried to outdo each other in right-wing radicalism, swamping virtually all other issues under the flood of slogans denouncing Socialists and Communists, and supporting chauvinism and restoration of the territorial integrity of Hungary.

The atmosphere that the government, the Army High Command, and the right-wing groups created effectively paralyzed the campaigns of the moderate and Socialist parties. None of their candidates or meetings was safe from assaults of officers or Awakening Hungarians. The Socialists were especially hard hit. They soon realized that it was totally pointless even to attempt to field candidates in districts outside the capital, but even in Budapest their campaign was constantly disrupted, their press severely censored, their candidates and campaign workers arrested or sent to concentration camps. On January 15, therefore, in protest the party decided to withdraw from the coalition government and from the election race.[41]

With all instruments of power behind the two right-wing parties, the outcome of the elections was a foregone conclusion. It surprised no one that both in the January 25 and in the February 13 run-off elections they won with a landslide. The Smallholders Party emerged as the majority party with 79 seats, while KNEP captured 72. Thus, out of a total of 164 seats the two right-wing parties held 151; the others were scattered between the Democratic Party, which gained six seats, the other minority parties, and such independent candidates as Counts Andrássy and

Apponyi.[42] In June, an additional 43 deputies were elected in the Trans-Tisza region, which at the time of the January elections was still under Romanian occupation, but these elections did not significantly alter the makeup of the National Assembly. The Smallholders Party captured most of these seats; yet it failed to become a party of absolute parliamentary majority. The reason for this failure was that almost immediately after the February elections both parties of the right began to fragment, especially KNEP. Friedrich split with KNEP and established his own party with some of his followers. Nineteen other deputies from both parties who were supporters of Bethlen established a faction called *Dissidents,* under the leadership of Count Klebelsberg. Seven dissatisfied Smallholders formed a splinter Smallholders Party; the number of independent deputies rose to 17. Thus, after the June elections, in spite of its victory, out of 207 seats, the Smallholders still held only 91 seats, KNEP 59, the Dissidents 19. Nor was this alignment permanent. Party strength was constantly shifting, factions splitting off and merging with others, making most estimates of actual party strength meaningless.

Soon after the elections the refugees made an attempt to gain direct representation, thereby gaining an absolute majority within the National Assembly. Already, towards the end of 1919, politicians from the lost counties and cities began to organize and to demand legal recognition as representatives of Hungarian territories under temporary occupation. During February 1920, they came forth with the demand that the refugees should be allowed to elect delegates to the National Assembly, arguing that without such refugee representation the National Assembly would represent no more than a third of the nation. Moreover, they argued that to deny representation to the lost areas was tantamount to an acceptance of the country's dismemberment.[43] Had this been allowed, the refugees would have gained an absolute majority in the National Assembly. Yet, even without direct representation, the victory of the right was also their victory.

Within the right the elections represented a victory for the right radicals, that is, for the gentry and gentroid alliance, for Horthy, and for the army. It was a defeat for the legitimists and, partially, for the aristocracy and the bourgeoisie.

The National Assembly's first order of business was election of a new head of state and a definition of his constitutional powers. For this post, the first choice of the legitimists was of course King Károly, who according to them, had never legally abdicated his throne and, therefore, was still the legitimate ruler of the country. They would have been willing to settle for his young son Otto with a regency during his minority. If even that proved to be impossible, they preferred Archduke Joseph. All these options met with the firm opposition of the Successor States and the Western Powers. Early in February their cause suffered a major setback when both France and Great Britian, in order to dispel all rumors about Western support for the King, delivered strong notes of protest to the Hungarian government, leaving no doubt about their unqualified opposition to a Habsburg restoration in whatever form.[44] As a substitute candidate the legitimists put forth Count Albert Apponyi, whom they could trust to step aside should the international situation become favorable to the Habsburg cause.

Had the attitude of the Western Powers been the opposite, or even if they had maintained a benevolent neutrality on the issue, there is little doubt that Károly would have been returned to the throne by the National Assembly. Even Horthy would have had to acquiesce. The opposition of these powers made the cause of the legitimists hopeless and paved the way for Horthy. It was a major boost to the "free electors," that is, to those who argued that, with the dissolution of the Habsburg monarchy, the Pragmatic Sanction lost its validity; that Hungary had regained her ancient right of electing her own sovereign.[45] Horthy felt free to apply pressure on both the Huszár government, where the legitimists had a majority, and on the newly elected members of the National Assembly. In a letter to the government Horthy wrote: "The discipline and patriotism of the National Army and law enforcement agencies serve as my guarantee that I will carry out my intentions whatever the circumstances may be."[46] Horthy did nothing to discourage perisistent rumors that if he were not elected and on his own terms there would be a military *coup d'état*. The legitimists tried in vain to exploit Horthy's last minute embarrassment over the mass murders at Kecskemét, and especially the murder by members of the Ostenburg detachment of two prominent Socialists, Béla Bacsó and Béla Somogyi.

Apponyi, realizing the hopelessness of his candidacy and fearing outbreak of civil war if the army were thwarted, informed KNEP leaders that he was withdrawing his name from consideration. After stormy debates in both party caucuses, Horthy's opponents were disarmed; both parties agreed to vote for him. Resistance to Horthy was especially strong in KNEP, which, nevertheless, finally came around after Prime Minister Huszár bluntly summed up the situation by stating: "I understand your indignation, but you should be conscious of the fact that if tomorrow you do not elect Horthy as regent, they will forcefully scatter the National Assembly."[47]

Horthy's election was no longer in doubt. Some of his opponents put up a last-ditch effort to curtail his powers, but Horthy insisted on virtually all the traditional prerogatives of Hungarian kings. On election day, to assure absolute compliance with his wishes, Horthy ordered the Prónay and Ostenburg regiments into action. They closed off all streets leading to the parliament building and escorted Horthy to the Assembly. The cornered Assembly leaders had no other choice but to allow Horthy to dictate his terms. Out of the 141 deputies voting, 131 voted for Horthy, and only seven diehards for Apponyi.

Horthy's election was a victory for those refugees who since the days of Szeged saw in him their principal hope for carrying out their program. The radical irredentists triumphed through Horthy; through the National Army, the officers' detachments, the secret societies; and through the Awakening Hungarians who ran Horthy's election campaign and elevated him to the regency.

Most ultraradicals, however, soon came to be disappointed in Horthy. Once secure in his possession of supreme power, Horthy began to search for ways to dissociate himself from the radicalism and the radicals of the 1919–20 period. He was, essentially, a conservative man who turned to radicalism only under the trauma of the times. He preferred authoritarian rule to totalitarian dictatorship. Within a year of his election, he began to search for a compromise with the defeated aristocracy, and even with the Jewish upper bourgeoisie. This was not possible until the legitimacy issue was finally put to rest. The archlegitimists, led by Andrássy, Beniczky, and the Catholic aristocracy of western Hungary and Slovakia, twice attempted to depose Horthy. First during Easter week 1921; then during October 1921 when King Károly suddenly appeared in Hungary to claim his rightful throne. Both times Horthy was able, with the aid of Western pressure, to persuade the king to depart.[48] The politicians and aristocrats responsible for these coup attempts had to be destroyed politically before a compromise could be achieved. Also, some of the worst perpetrators of terror had to be removed from the center of the political scene. Thus one by one the chief terrorists were quietly let go, or forced into oblivion, or opposition. Such was the fate of Prónay, Ostenburg, Héjjas, and even of Gömbös.

The Bethlen-Teleki group was best situated to bring about a compromise on the right. First Horthy turned to Teleki, who in June 1920 became prime minister. The Teleki government was generally ineffective, though it made some progress in normalizing conditions in the country. It was, however, not until April 1921 that the return to normalcy began in earnest when Count Bethlen, finally judging the time ripe, decided to accept Horthy's mandate to form a government. Bethlen was, at least in part, acceptable to most factions of the right. He was a man of personal stature, puritanical, stoic, and phlegmatic in his personal habits.[49] A shrewd, artful politician who knew how to wait for the right moment, to exploit the weaknesses of friend and foe alike. As an aristocrat, he was acceptable to most of the aristocrats of inner Hungary, except to the extreme legitimists. His conservatism stood as a guarantee against any diminution of the aristocracy's economic and political power. His motto was: "The revolution had ended. Let us terminate the revolutionary spirit. . . ."[50] This meant not only an end to all social experimentation and the restoration of prewar conservatism, but also an end to the revolutionary spirit generated by the right. This policy opened the way for a reconciliation with the bourgeoisie, including the Jewish bourgeoisie. As a Transylvanian and as a Protestant, he was also acceptable to Horthy. Bethlen could be trusted to oppose all attempts at a Habsburg restoration. Eventually Bethlen was able to sign a secret pact even with the Socialists. The Social Democratic Party agreed to end republican agitation, stop denouncing atrocities, condemn their fellow Socialist émigrés, refrain from political strikes, and cooperate in foreign policy. In exchange Bethlen guaranteed their right of assembly and association, and promised to reduce the number of interned persons, end the state of siege and martial law, and return the confiscated property and treasury of the trade unions.[51]

Bethlen was also one of the principal leaders of the refugees. Until he became prime minister, he was one of the leading figures in the Peace Preparation Commission. He was also the head of the National Refugee Office and, as such, was highly conscious of the plight of his fellow refugees. He constantly championed the idea of compensation for the refugees, from which, incidentally, he himself was to gain. In addition, Bethlen was president, or honorary president, of literally scores of revisionist, irredentist organizations. Thus, with him at the head of the government, the "Transylvanian Mafia," as his group was at times called, triumphed. The refugees could trust that he would not miss an opportunity to destroy the Treaty of Trianon and to regain the lost territories.

Not only in the government but also in the National Assembly itself the refugees became a major power. The 1920 elections, in fact, signified the assimilation of the refugees into Hungary's party and political life. During the 1920s, refugee strength in parliament remained remarkably constant. In spite of some major party shifts and realignments, they supplied roughly the same proportion of deputies in the 1920, 1922, and 1926 elections. Their consistent strength in the First and Second National Assemblies and, after 1926, in parliament, assured that no issue would be decided contrary to the interests or inclinations of the refugees.

We have been able to collect biographical data on 239 deputies who were, at one time or another, elected to the First National Assembly.[52] From this number 79 deputies, or about a third, were born outside the reduced territory of Hungary: 40 in areas ceded to Czechoslovakia, 30 in Transylvania, 7 in Yugoslavia, and the remainder in the Burgenland or Austria proper. That is, although in the total population, those born outside of Trianon Hungary represented only 6.9 percent, in the National Assembly, they captured 33.1 percent of the seats.

Distribution of the Deputies in the First National
Assembly According to Place of Birth

Party	Number of Deputies Born in						
	Slovakia	Romania	Yugo-slavia	Austria	Lost Areas	Trianon Hungary	Total
KNEP	26	16	4	1	47	52	99
Smallholders	11	11	3	1	26	91	117
Independent, Other	3	3			6	17	23
Total	40	30	7	2	79	160	239

This group's power was especially felt in the Christian National Unity Party. Out of a total of 99 deputies who were elected, at one time or another, on KNEP lists, or on the lists of its associated parties, 47 or nearly half were born in the lost territories. The figures for the Smallholders Party were 26 out of 117, that is, about a quarter of the deputies. There were several reasons for the greater strength of the refugees in KNEP. First, it enjoyed the backing of the Catholic Church and the wealthier classes of the country. A majority of the Catholic, and therefore, most of the refugees from Slovakia naturally looked upon it as their own party. Similarly, the wealthier refugees from all parts of the country, including some of the Protestant landed gentry and aristocracy also gravitated toward this party. In the National Assembly at least 18 refugees had lost substantial gentry and aristocratic estates located in the Successor States. Eleven of these initially joined KNEP, three remained independent, and only three decided in favor of the Smallholders Party. KNEP also enjoyed the advantage of being the first party to capitalize on right-wing radical issues, which made it attractive to the radical gentry. And, finally, it cannot be ignored that KNEP was the party of the government at the time of the elections, which drew into the campaign large segments of refugee officials, a group which always preferred to support the election of the government party, since an office-holder's or office-seeker's fate always depended on the favors of the various ministers.

The high percentage of refugees in KNEP was also partially responsible for its decline. The refugees were less likely to remain within the party, especially the Transylvanians, and were always present in every splinter group. They were more volatile and more easily changed party affiliations.

The Dissidents, for example, were led by the Transylvanian faction, but they were also the group which pressed hardest for the merger of the two parties. It was the "Transylvanian Mafia" of Bethlen, Teleki, Klebelsberg, and Bánffy that ultimately succeeded in forcing the fusion of the two right-wing parties, and in establishing a firm majority for the Bethlen government. This merger clearly worked to the advantage of the refugees.

The number of individuals in the National Assembly from the lost territories, large as it was, still does not accurately reflect the strength of the group. On the whole, they were younger, more vigorous, better educated, and generally had enjoyed a higher social status in prewar society than the rest of the National Assembly. About 43 percent of the deputies born in the lost territories were under forty years of age; only 33 percent of those born in Trianon Hungary. In fact, according to our calculations, the 1920 National Assembly was the youngest elected between 1892 and 1931, in spite of a higher minimum age requirement for candidacy than before the war. Educational advantage, too, was clearly on their side.

Distribution of the Deputies in the First National
Assembly According to Education

Place of Birth	Law and Pol. Sc.	Milit. Acad.	Theology		Professions	4–8 years Education	Gymnasium Educated	Total
			Prot.	Cath.				
Successor States	50.6	3.9	2.6	9.1	27.3	1.3	5.2	100
Trianon Hungary	36.4	3.7	4.3	6.2	21.6	21.6	6.2	100
Entire Assembly	41.0	3.8	3.8	7.2	23.5	15.1	5.6	100

Slightly above half had studied law or political science, that is, subjects which best prepared a young man for political life. Only 36 percent from Trianon Hungary were thus educated. Even more important, in the category of individuals with less than eight years of education, the first group, the refugees, had only 1.3 percent; the second had above 21 percent. In nearly every area of education, the group born outside the reduced territories of Hungary enjoyed an advantage.

Taking the National Assembly as a whole, the strength of the gentry and the aristocracy sharply declined in comparison with prewar parliaments, but among the deputies from the Successor States, their proportion remained as high as ever. Out of the 239 deputies who served in the First National Assembly only 12 were aristocrats, but seven of these were born in the Successor States. A large number of the refugee gentry politicians were seasoned politicians who enjoyed high prestige among the other deputies. Thus, from their ranks, the National Assembly elected its principal officers. Rakovszky, for example, became the president of the House, Szmrecsányi, its vice-president. As we have seen they also captured the leadership of KNEP; even in the Smallholders Party, they were well placed. After the formation of the Unity Party — the merger of these two parties — the leadership was clearly in the hands of the refugees, and specifically in the hands of the Transylvanian nobles.

Additionally, refugee political and parliamentary strength had a strong effect on the makeup of all governments during the 1920s. Of the thirty-five ministers, for example, who served between November 1919 and April 1921, the first Bethlen cabinet inclusive, only eighteen, that is about half were born in Trianon Hungary. Of the other seventeen, eight were Transylvanian, seven born in Slovakia, and two in Austria. Even more indicative of the domination of the politicians from the lost territories is the distribution of offices. Only one of the five prime ministers, between Friedrich and Bethlen, came from Trianon Hungary. The three most prestigious and powerful ministries, that is, interior, defense, and foreign affairs, were similarly dominated by politicians born in the lost territories. From that group came three of the five ministers of defense, four out of seven ministers of interior, and six of the seven ministers of foreign affairs.

The political strength that the refugees demonstrated during the early months of the counterrevolution had a lasting effect on the refugees' role in Hungary's subsequent political life. The refugees eagerly grasped the opportunity opened to them by the fluidity of the situation and, as a group, they succeeded in deeply entrenching themselves in Hungary's political institutions. Some of the most radical, or ultralegitimist groups, to be sure, were politically destroyed by Bethlen and Horthy, or were forced into opposition. The refugees from Slovakia and the Catholics were partly pushed into the background while the Protestants and the Transylvanians rushed to the fore. Some of the deputies retired after the end of the term of the First National Assembly; others were rewarded with high government posts or with appointments in the diplomatic corps.

In spite of these changes, the overall strength of the deputies from the lost territories remained constant during the next two assemblies — the 1922 Second National Assembly and the 1926 parliamentary elections. In 1922, their proportion was 33 percent; in 1926, about 35 percent. The 1922 assembly was much more manageable and subdued, in spite of occasional violent debates, than the First National Assembly. For, in 1922, the aristocracy regained its previous strength — their numbers rose sharply from twelve to twenty-eight — whereas many of the peasant deputies along with some of the radical priests and pastors disappeared. Even those radical refugee politicians of 1919 and 1920 who were reelected had moderated their positions by 1922. With their assimilation into the social and political fabric of society their lives became more secure, and they regained or even increased the social prestige they had enjoyed in the lost territories before 1918. With at least the partial restoration of the noble domination of the country and their own personal political successes assured, their once endangered noble identities again began to function. They did not give up the dream of returning to their old homes, of regaining their estates, this remained an *idée fixe* with them, but they were less willing to risk the security they enjoyed in a foolhardy adventure.

It was, however, relatively easy to satisfy economically and assimilate politically the most vocal and most prominent members of the refugees. The assimilation of the great masses of the refugees was a task which was beyond the strength of any government. In spite of tremendous efforts they were only partially satisfied, with the result that the masses of refugees remained susceptible to political and subsequently to social radicalism.

Chapter 10
Economic and Social Assimilation
of the Refugees

One of the persistently repeated slogans of the post-revolutionary period, and indeed of the entire Horthy era, was: "Save the middle class," or more precisely, save the intelligentsia, the dispossessed, and unemployed official class. The long-brewing crisis in the life of the gentry and gentroid strata finally reached the crisis point; society was no longer capable of absorbing the vast surplus of educated people. But the gentry refused to recognize that as a class it had become superfluous and insisted on viewing itself as the "nation-sustaining historical class," entitled to special claims and special rights within the Hungarian state. During the 1920s and 1930s, scores of publicists, historians, sociologists, and politicians trumpeted the grievances of the intelligentsia and analyzed the causes of the gentry's demise.[1]

The fate of the middle classes was always a burning issue which no political leader dared to ignore lest he alienated precisely that class on which the counterrevolutionary edifice had been erected. It is not at all surprising, therefore, that Prime Minister Bethlen in his inaugural address to the National Assembly chose to single out the revitalization of the middle class as one of the prime tasks of his government. His speech both mirrored the attitude of the gentry and set the tone for the policies of the state for the next two decades.

In addition to the historical circumstances, Bethlen attributed the decline of Hungary to the decline of its middle class, which in his vocabulary meant the landed gentry. During the Bach era, he argued, "the Hungarian landed class was destroyed and the problem was that this class, instead of entrepreneurship, sought improvement of its life through office holding."[2] This economically weakened class was no longer capable of fulfilling its historical role of leading the nation, and, with it, the nation also declined. The main task of the new government, therefore, was to diversify the middle class by encouraging it to move into commerce and industry, thereby strengthening it economically. As Bethlen put it: "The government, therefore, must initiate a large-scale middle-class oriented politics. We will take the first step when, for those officials who are left out of state offices, and for those refugees who come home from territories torn away from us, we organize retraining courses and establish such an organization that through its own efforts will be capable of providing employment for these officials."[3]

The problem, nevertheless, defied simplistic solutions. In fact, most government efforts to transform the intelligentsia into a productive part of society were doomed to failure. The economic chaos brought on by war, revolution, and partition of the country, forced a wide-scale reduction in economic activities everywhere in Hungary, with a corresponding reduction in employment. The sheer size of the unemployed or underemployed officials made the solution more difficult. Finally, and most importantly, its mentality and its training made the gentry unsuitable for few jobs other than government employment.[4]

Changing over from war to peacetime production in itself would have caused major disruptions in the economy, but, within Hungary's reduced borders, this changeover became a monumental task. The new frontiers sliced across old lines of communications, separated industries from raw materials and markets, and forced a sudden severance of the banking and currency ties with Austrian financial institutions. Simultaneously, in a somewhat unusual pattern, at the time when the country had a contracting, deflationary economy, it was also hit by a high rate of inflation. The consequences of all these factors was massive unemployment in industry and commerce, with some 300,000 workers at the end of 1919, not counting other groups, without jobs.[5]

The refugees could not find employment in private industry or commerce; they had to look to the state for providing them with jobs. We have already had occasion to discuss the rapid rise of the numbers of gentry officials in the Dual Monarchy. By 1914 Hungary's bureaucracy had far exceeded the needs of the country, according to some estimates, by threefold. In 1919, the territory and population of the country sharply contracted. Hungary lost about 64 percent of its previous territory; its population was reduced from about eighteen million to eight. Yet, the size of the group that had a claim to state employment was reduced only slightly. The reason for this phenomenon can be attributed only to the flight of the officials from the Successor States.

Reliable figures on the occupational breakdown of the refugees were never compiled. The Refugee Office's records are far from complete; they merely give some sketchy information about the occupations of 350,000 refugees, but as we have estimated, an additional 75,000 refugees must have escaped registration. According to the *OMH Report,* among 350,000 refugees, 104,804 were wage earners; 245,196, dependents. Occupationally they fell into the following categories:[6]

Table 1

Occupational Distribution of the Refugees Arriving
Between October 30, 1918 and June 15, 1924

		State	15,835
Public		Municipal, village	5,772
Employees	44,253	State railroad	19,092
		Other	3,554
		Independent craftsmen and merchants	5,347
Industry and		Workers in industry	
Commerce	35,553	and commerce	24,473
		Mine officials and workers	5,733
Professions	621	Pharmacists and doctors	280
		Lawyers	341

Agriculture (landowners and workers)	10,376
Men of independent means	8,323
Pupils and university students	86,375
Housewives and other dependents	160,371
Occupation unknown	4,128

A closer examination of these figures gives us some indication of the occupations of the additional unrecorded 75,000 refugees. It appears that the more affluent individuals and their families who did not need the Refugee Office's aid, or those who readily assimilated into the economy of Hungary went unrecorded. Many were, most likely, officials of the higher ranks whose employment was never terminated. This is reflected in the sharp increase of officials in the higher categories. The number of classified persons (*Functionnaires de classe*) of the civil service, excluding state enterprises, actually increased between 1913 and 1924. But, whereas the number of individuals in the upper grades sharply increased, the lowest grades declined.[7] An additional sizable group of people were officers, clergymen, monks, nuns, and professionals. OMH figures are especially low in this last category: 280 doctors and pharmacists; and 341 lawyers. Yet, according to the 1930 census, there were in Hungary 2352 doctors, 841 pharmacists and chemists, and 1539 lawyers in public employment alone, who were born in the lost territories.[8] It is likely that many of these were refugees.

It is also safe to assume that the actual number of refugee officials was at least 20–25 percent higher than indicated by the *OMH Report*. A comparison of the total number of state employees in 1910 in some specific categories and the reported number of refugees in 1921 falling into the same categories supports this statement and illustrates the strength of the refugee groups. (See Table 2). In short the problem was this: a state of eight million had to provide some form of livelihood to over 400,000, employment for well over 100,000, and educational opportunities for about 100,000. There were several possible solutions to the refugee problem, but none was completely satisfactory. Only revision of the terms of the Treaty of Trianon, peacefully or otherwise, would have been able to provide a solution that was totally acceptable to both the Hungarian state and the refugees. This possibility was never abandoned as an answer to the issue; it remained an axiom of Hungary's foreign policy throughout the Horthy era. But until the day of reunification of the country some, if only a temporary, alternate solution had to be found.

Table 2

State Employees in 1910 and Refugees in 1921[9]

Employment Categories	Total in 1910	Number of Refugees in 1921 from					Total
		Slovakia	Romania	Yugosl.	Austria	Fiume	
State Officials	13,063	1,926	2,843	525	155	105	5,554
County Officials	4,106	915	1,406	255	98	0	2,674
Judges and Lawyers	2,893	493	854	210	43	9	1,609
Elementary Teachers	7,687	2,121	2,795	795	90	46	5,847
Burgher School Teachers	1,177	360	418	156	35	28	997
Secondary Teachers	1,817	341	405	122	38	58	964
Kindergarten Teachers	1,276[10]	345	408	98	25	4	880

The first requirement was to limit the refugee influx and, then, possibly even to reduce the number of refugees by encouraging remigration. Bethlen, himself, for a brief period in 1919, contemplated such a move; his friend Count Miklós Bánffy actually retired to Transylvania. It was not realistic, however, to expect that the great majority of the refugees would even consider, or that the Successor States would permit, their return. Only a handful made such a move, mostly those who had politically compromised themselves in Hungary and some peasants who had fled from their homes in the first moment of panic.

If the government could not actually reduce the number of refugees, it felt compelled to tighten controls at least over entry permits. By the time effective measures were introduced, however, the refugee problem already had assumed enormous proportions. Only in the beginning of March 1921 were the screening procedures of potential refugees intensified. Entry permits were no longer issued automatically. They had to be granted only to reunite families, to students who went to Hungary to complete their education, and to those state officials whom the Hungarian government ordered to cross into Hungary. Some who were expelled by the new authorities were also allowed to enter, but entry was subject to approval of the Refugee Office. Restrictions notwithstanding, refugees continued to pour into the country: in March 1921, 3994; in April, 4498; in May 3441; in June, 3377; in July, 3814.[11] In July, therefore, the government decided to prohibit issuing entry permits, except in special cases. Only then did the number of new refugees begin to decline.

The government's motives in limiting the number of refugees was only partly economic. Fears were widespread that through large-scale emigration the Hungarian minorities would be greatly weakened, thereby exposing themselves to rapid assimilation.[12] Reduction of the number of Hungarians in the lost territories also weakened Hungary's case for the revision of the Treaty of Trianon. These fears led some officials to adopt a rather hostile attitude toward refugees. As we have seen, already in Szeged, signs of such resentment surfaced. Béla Kelemen, then minister of education in the cabinet of Gyula Károlyi, considered flight from the Successor States virtually a treasonous act.[13] The Szeged government urged all officials in the lost territories to take the oath of loyalty, if thereby they were able to retain their positions.

Resentment over the number of refugees increased as competition for offices in Hungary intensified. Even the various refugee organizations began to attack those who wished to follow them into Hungary. The Bocskay Alliance, a Transylvanian refugee organization, repeatedly called upon all Hungarians to remain in Transylvania. They warned their Székely brothers that Romania's plan was to rob Transylvania of its Hungarian character by forcing the Hungarian intelligentsia, the official class, to emigrate to Hungary, thereby depriving the remaining Hungarian population of their natural leaders. "For this reason," according to the Bocskay Alliance, "nobody may consider it desirable or permissible for Hungarians to emigrate from Transylvania. On the contrary, out of patriotic duty we must do everything possible to assure that those who were already forced by hostile circumstances to depart temporarily should return as soon as possible."[14]

Again, according to the alliance, it was an error to believe that the only patriotic act was to leave Romania; what was far more patriotic and far more admirable was to remain, suffer, and struggle. Thus the first of the "Transylvanian's Ten Commandments" was: "Do not emigrate from Transylvania! . . . And if you left . . . immediately return, because Transylvania can be lost only if the number of Hungarians diminished. The fatherland is not made up of mountains, rivers, and meadows, but by those who live in it, the members of the nation, the people. Do not forget the truth that no one can take Transylvania from us; only we can lose it through our sins and errors."[15]

Each refugee, in fact, had to justify his departure and prove that it was the only course open to him. The refugee press was constantly forced to defend compatriots by frequent, often grossly exaggerated reports of continuing terror in the lost territories against the Hungarian population. At other times, through sentimental articles, it tried to arouse public sympathy for the mental anguish of the refugees.[16]

The suggestion was also made that if all other solutions for refugee unemployment problem failed, the burden on society might be lightened through encouragement of overseas emigration. A few individuals, indeed, departed, settling mostly in Canada and the United States. A number of refugee officers and soldiers from Slovakia and Transylvania left the country to join the French Foreign Legion. Generally, the suggestion was bitterly resented; it was tantamount to admitting that Hungary no longer had a place for the gentry officials; the gentry had become superfluous. The radical right, in fact, advocated a diametrically opposite population policy. They argued that the tiny nation surrounded by enemies could not afford to lose its most valuable human material. The nation must, therefore, do everything in its power to encourage the return to Hungary of the hundreds of thousands who had emigrated during previous decades.

The only alternative remaining was either to retrain the refugees for employment in the private sector of the economy or to absorb them in an enlarged state bureaucracy. The first option enjoyed the strong support of the government, especially after Bethlen took office. As early as 1920, organizations such as MOVE made some efforts in that direction. MOVE established some purchasing and handicraft cooperatives to make available to members and to impoverished officials and refugees food and other items of necessity at a reduced cost.[17] It also organized secretarial schools for the wives and daughters of the intelligentsia. Similarly, but on a much larger scale, the National Refugee Office, too, attempted to retrain and find employment for the refugees. It even offered to support the refugees during their retraining. OMH's activities, therefore, fell into two categories. One, it established enterprises designed to provide temporary employment and aid to the refugees; two, it organized retraining courses. Initially, it was hoped that some of the refugee corporations might become permanent, thereby assuring the economic independence of its employees. The Refugee Office viewed direct economic aid as only temporary, since the "governing principle was . . . to assimilate the great masses of refugees into the population of the country and thereby end their refugee status. . . . To search for job opportunities was far more fruitful than direct aid."[18] The feeding of the refugees was handled by special refugee-owned and -operated cafeterias, where the refugees were served decent food at a reduced price or even free of charge.

Some employment was also found for a number of persons in the Refugee Industrial and Commercial Shop. Its largest division, the shoe and clothing repair shop, employed 77 workers, but the "mass production" section had only 15 and the carpenter shop 6 workers.[19] It was a rather amateurish enterprise. Not surprisingly, therefore, in August 1922, it folded because of financial problems, but, perhaps, more important, because enthusiasm for these kinds of occupations was lacking among the refugees.

OMH originally planned to organize 76 retraining courses in 23 different subject areas. For lack of interest only 16 courses were held, mostly in banking and general commerce. Courses in agronomy, wine making, bee keeping, fruit and vegetable growing, as well as in home-craft industries had to be cancelled for want of students. Only 1034 individuals signed up to take some of these courses, out of which 576 were ex-members of the officers corps, mostly reserve officers. The remainder were former officials. Of course, most of the reserve officers themselves had been members of the state bureaucracy before the war. The dropout rate in all cases was extremely high, only about half of those who began these courses actually graduated.[20] The general absence of enthusiasm among the refugees for retraining can be attributed only to their gentry mentality. Conscious of their noble background they were reluctant to accept the decline in social status by leaving state employment for industry and commerce.

Jews played a decisive role in Hungary's economic life. For example, excluding stock companies, Jews owned 40.5 percent of the large- and medium-sized industrial firms. In some other categories, the percentage of Jews was equally high: 39 percent of the white-collar workers employed in industry; 53.8 percent of the self-employed merchants; 46.5 percent of the white-collar workers in commerce and banking.[21] Thus wherever a refugee turned to find employment in commerce or industry he found himself competing, usually unsuccessfully, with Jews in enterprises owned by Jews. Not surprisingly, most refugees shied away from these occupations and gave vent to their resentments by demanding that the government take strong measures to Christianize Hungary's economic life. Helplessly, they turned again to the state, expecting a position within the state administration.

The gentry traditionally avoided the free professions, except the practice of law. It became customary among the lesser nobility to look toward the county or to the state for employment. They preferred fixed-salaried official positions which offered the security of reasonable pensions and built-in pay raises. According to Antal Balla, the gentry's "centrist political and social views found their manifestations mostly in those tendencies, which attempted to organize nearly all life functions of the collective around the state. But more significantly, [the gentry] expected even the shaping of private lives from the government. From this attitude issues that constant shoving and pushing for the so-called pensioned positions and the neglect of the free professions."[22] To this tradition, the refugee gentry remained faithful.

Bethlen, himself, realized that this was an ossified group, lacking initiative and vitality, and that, owing to their excessive dependence on the state, the gentry represented an intolerable burden on the state treasury. When he called for revitalization of the intelligentsia through retraining, he, in fact, asked them to abandon their old values and old identity as a separate privileged elite. This the gentry was incapable of doing and, therefore, opposed all efforts to remove them from state offices. In the end, the state had to yield and to absorb most of the refugee officials.

The result was that the number of state employees failed to decline in proportion to the territorial or population losses of the country. According to the 1914–15 budget, the total number of state employees had been 331,920; during the 1921–22 fiscal year it was 209,083. The reduction, however, was unevenly distributed in the various categories of employment. As can be seen in Table 3, the decline was significant only in the category of workers; in the clerk and official categories there was either no change or an actual increase.

That the increase was not greater was due largely to the wholesale dismissal of those state employees who were considered to be politically unreliable. In the eyes of the counterrevolutionary government, anyone

Table 3

Number of State Employees in 1914–15
and in 1921–22[23]

Employment category	1914–15	1921–22
State officials and clerks	65,049	69,765
Junior officers and servants	93,949	93,097
State workers and other	172,922	46,221
Total	331,920	209,083

who continued to serve under the Károlyi regime, and especially those
who served under the Hungarian Soviet Republic, were immediately
suspected of leftist sympathies. It was in the interest of the refugees that
this purge of the state bureaucracy should be as widespread as possible;
hence, they fully supported any government effort in this direction. The
persecution of the liberal- and left-leaning state employees began almost
immediately after the defeat of the Hungarian Soviet regime. In August
1919, the Friedrich government ordered the dismissal of all those who
had obtained their employment between October 31, 1918 and August
1919.[24] Almost at the same moment, the Szeged government was issuing
its instruction to Prónay and the leaders of the other officers' detachments to remove all suspicious officials and to restore to their posts the
employees of the old regime. Every public institution was carefully
combed in search of politically dangerous elements — the courts, the
prison administrations, universities, schools, state, county, and city
offices, the state railroad, the post office, even the sanitation department. Disciplinary procedures were initiated against thousands of individuals on the flimsiest of charges, and the slightest amount of compro-
mising evidence was sufficient cause for dismissal. It was sufficient to
have accepted the slightest promotion during the Soviet Republic, to
have dropped a few unguarded words, to have recognized the dictatorship of the proletariat, to have carried out an order, or to be maliciously
informed against by a personal enemy, and the life of an official was
destroyed; he was branded for decades. The state could afford to adopt
an uncompromising attitude toward the suspected officials because for
every dismissed official, judge, or teacher, several refugees were waiting
in the wings, eager to take their places.

The number of dismissals, however, was still not sufficient to provide
employment for all the refugees. The state bureaucracy, itself, had to be
expanded if accommodations for the refugees were to be found. This
forced the government to adopt a contradictory financial policy. Its
prime financial objectives were to reduce expenditures, halt run-away

inflation, stabilize the currency, open the country for foreign invest-ment; in all, to stimulate the economic recovery of the country. Only for political reasons did the state assume the refugee burden, increasing its financial obligations at the time when the country was on the verge of bankruptcy. According to the projected 1920–21 budget, for example, the state deficit was to run nearly fifty percent, 20.2-billion crowns of expenditures against 10.5 billion in revenues.[25]

It fell on Bethlen's shoulders to tackle the delicate and politically dangerous question of reduction of the number of state employees to a reasonable size. He had no other choice if Hungary was to recover economically. The reduction of the state administrative machinery was one of the prime conditions under which Hungary was allowed to float its reconstruction loan in the foreign markets under the guarantee of the League of Nations.

The first step in this direction was taken during 1922, when the so-called B-List was established. According to Ottó Szabolcs, in June 1922, 11,126 state employees were placed on the list, that is, their employment was terminated and they were either pensioned off, or received a lump sum in severance pay. Out of these, 4377 were office holders, 3616 educators, and 2918 clerks and other office employees.

Table 4

B-Listed State Employees in June 1922[26]

Ministries	Officials	Clerks	Teachers	Office Servants	Other	Total	Of these Refugees
Prime Minister	1	3	—	2	—	6	—
Foreign	11	7	—	—	—	18	—
Justice	2	10	—	1	34	47	18
Commerce	103	34	—	21	—	158	5
State R.R.	559	1,608	—	2,532	—	4,699	1,475
Postal Service	424	66	—	204	181	875	53
Postal Saving	48	6	—	8	—	62	—
State Steel Co.	78	—	—	81	—	159	89
Interior	21	19	—	7	—	47	—
Counties	227	101	—	5	—	333	333
Cities	116	54	—	4	—	174	174
Villages	278	23	—	—	—	301	301
Agriculture	97	22	—	17	—	136	58
Defense	—	25	—	1	—	26	—
Education	52	43	3,616	14	—	3,725	1,069
Welfare	14	4	—	1	—	19	—
Finance	261	60	—	20	—	341	151
Total	2,292	2,085	3,616	2,918	215	11,126	3,726

The government failed to protect the refugees adequately; consequently, in some categories, they were the only group to suffer this fate.
Numerically the hardest hit groups were refugee teachers and railroad
employees, but from the ministries of interior, defense, and foreign
affairs, no refugees were let go. Counties, municipalities, and villages
seized this opportunity to relieve themselves of a financial burden by
releasing those refugees whom they were forced to hire under government pressure. Those government bodies dismissed only the refugees.

This action was followed by additional dismissals in 1923 and in 1924.
In 1923, the government ordered a 20 percent personnel cut, that is, the
dismissal of about 40,000 employees; in the following year, a reduction
of an additional 15,000. These orders notwithstanding, the total number
of state employees was hardly reduced, especially in the administrative
categories. Table 5 clearly reflects this fact.

Table 5

Number of State Employees in 1913,
1923, and in 1924[27]

		1913 Jan. 1	1923 July 1	1924 July 1
Civil Administration		95,323	93,852	87,234
State Enterprises		104,647	53,315	51,089
Of this:	Railroads	62,778	32,774	30,968
	Postal Service	39,533	18,419	17,652
Permanent Workmen		113,816	52,302	49,689
Total		313,786	199,469	188,012

Thus, while the number of employees in the state enterprises was cut in
half, and the number of workers by more than half, the size of the civil
administration was barely below the 1913 level when the population of
the country had been well over twice as large. In some categories of the
civil administration, the numbers employed actually increased. In 1913
the civil administration had 28,543 so-called classified or graded personnel; in 1924, in spite of repeated dismissal orders, it had 33,883 in this
group.[28]

For the treasury, the expected savings from personnel cuts never
materialized. In 1924, out of a total annual budget of 351.6-million gold
crowns, 210.8 million crowns, or approximately 60 percent of the
budget, were absorbed by the salaries and pensions of state employees.
Staff reductions were often achieved by merely pensioning off some
employees; this meant only a shift of state obligations from one category
to another. Thus, while the number of employees declined, the number

of pensioners drastically increased. In 1913, the state had 63,000 pensioners; according to the 1920 census, within the reduced territory of Hungary, their numbers dipped only slightly to 60,617, but increased if the disabled war veterans are added to 64,634. By 1924, it increased even further to 98,644; by 1926, to over 102,000. According to the League of Nations' report:

> The chief reason for this is that the Successor States have made it impossible for large numbers of employees and pensioners to remain in their territories (their number is about 44,000), so that Hungary is today compelled to provide for all these persons. Reckoning the average annual pension at 1,500 gold crowns, the Hungarian State has to bear a pensions burden of about 66,000,000 gold crowns annually instead of the Succession States, and that amount is more than 50 per cent of the 129.5 million gold crowns allowed for pensions in the budget for the year 1926–1927.[29]

Generally, the refugees enjoyed a privileged position both in pensioning and in dismissals. True, they were the most affected group in the 1922 series of employee reductions; the 1923 and 1924 laws ordering cuts specifically prohibited discharging refugees by fixing overall reduction ratios. Right-wing refugees were able to marshal all their government and parliamentary allies, as well as the support of the rightist organizations and secret societies, to exempt them from dismissal. If they were, nevertheless, unsuccessful, they were often able to find new positions in another government department. In 1923, for example, the EKSz specifically called upon its members to inform the leadership immediately upon dismissal so that the decision might be reversed.

The consequences of this were twofold. First, the government was never able to achieve its projected goals for reductions. Employees discharged in one area using their connections drifted back into state employment in another. In 1923, for example, instead of the planned 40,000 reduction the actual number of permanently eliminated positions was only 14,813.[30] Second, the proportion of the refugees employed by the state steadily increased at the expense of employees born in inner Hungary. According to the Hungarian government reports submitted to the League of Nations, in 1924, the state maintained approximately 35,000 refugees, out of which there were 12,700 pensioners, and 22,700 employees on active duty.[31] By 1926, the total number of refugee state employees rose to 27,815; those of the pensioners to 15,971. According to the country of origin, these figures divide as indicated by Table 6. Refugee gains were made in spite of additional reductions between 1924 and 1926. According to the 1926–27 budget, the total number of state employees was 160,548.[32] Thus, the nearly 28,000 refugees represented approximately 17.2 percent of the total number. Szabolcs offers the following data:[33]

Table 6

Refugee State Employees and Pensioners in 1926

Refugee from	Pensioners and Widows	Active State Employees	Total
Czechoslovakia	5,280	10,072	15,352
Romania	6,603	11,048	17,651
Yugoslavia	3,295	5,103	8,398
Austria	316	789	1,105
Other	477	803	1,280
Total	15,971	27,815	43,786

Refugee strength among the state employees is even more impressive if their proportions in the various categories of employment are taken into consideration. To illustrate this fact, let us use the 1930 census figures.[34] Generally, the highest concentration of the refugees may be found in the most prestigious positions. Thus, proportionally their numbers were the greatest in the judiciary, among the government officials, especially in the various ministries, and in the field of education. Fully 43 percent of the judges and public prosecutors were born in the lost territories, and 34 percent of the state officials. These figures are truly impressive in themselves, but especially if we consider that those who were born in the lost territories comprised only 5.8 percent of the total population in 1930. The refugees were not as successful in penetrating the less prestigious county, city, and village bureaucracies. In these areas the old officials were more entrenched and less susceptible to government pressures to absorb the refugees. In the urban areas political pressure to limit the number of extreme right wing elements in the city administration was also successful, thus the number of refugees was lowest in the city bureaucracies. Even there the proportion of those born in the lost territories was three times as high as warranted by their numerical strength in the country. Among refugee judges and officials, Transylvanians were, by far, the most numerous. (See Table 8.)

Refugee strength in the various categories of education is almost as impressive. For example, from the same 5.8 percent came about a quarter of the primary school teachers and about a third of secondary-school and university faculties. This strong representation of the refugees among educators was achieved in spite of the numerous though unsuccessful attempts at personnel cuts by the government. Each order

Table 7

Refugee Strength in the State Administration[35]

Administrative Position	Total 1910	Total 1920	Total 1930	Born in Lost Areas	Percentage of Total
State officials and clerks	15,252	17,506	15,343	5,240	34.2
County officials and clerks	5,202	2,374	2,489	624	25.0
City officials and clerks	8,781	7,018	9,128	1,585	17.4
Village officials and clerks	12,207	5,524	3,832	839	21.9
Judges and public prosecutors	2,893	1,894	1,779	763	42.9
Court and prison officials and clerks	7,291	3,630	3,813	1,260	33.0

for cuts ultimately aided the refugees, since these orders were used to dismiss the politically undesirable teachers and, gradually, to replace them with trustworthy refugee educators.

Table 8

State Officials Born Outside of
Trianon Hungary in 1930[36]

Administrative Position	Total Born in Lost Areas	Born in Slovakia	Percentage of Total	Born in Romania	Percentage of Total
State officials and clerks	5,240	1,894	36.1	2,642	50.8
County officials and clerks	624	225	36.0	298	47.8
City officials and clerks	1,585	586	36.9	731	46.1
Village officials and clerks	839	306	36.4	348	41.5
Judges and prosecutors	763	282	37.0	399	52.3
Court and prison officials and clerks	1,260	400	31.7	657	52.1

Table 9

Refugee Strength in the Field of Education[37]

	Total in 1920	Total in 1930	Of these from Lost Areas	Percentage of Total
Kindergartens	1,730	1,524	439	28.8
Elementary	19,548	20,149	5,181	25.7
Burgher Schools	2,969	3,139	1,140	36.3
Secondary	2,936	3,485	1,162	33.4
University	1,016	1,482	516	34.8

Of these the breakdown according to country of origin is as follows:

Table 10

Educators Born Outside of Trianon Hungary[38]

	Total from Lost Areas	Born in Slovakia	Percentage of Total	Born in Romania	Percentage of Total
Kindergarten	439	181	41.2	195	44.4
Elementary	5,181	2,281	44.0	2,097	40.5
Burgher Schools	1,140	459	40.3	491	43.1
Secondary	1,162	518	44.6	452	38.9
University	516	180	34.8	277	53.6

The magnitude of the refugee impact on Hungarian society can be also gauged by some of the long-range cultural changes and social dislocations that were brought about by their assimilation. From the viewpoint of the governing classes, the purge of the undesirable elements from state employment and their replacement by refugees was desirable, since it brought both the civil administration and the educational system more thoroughly in line with counterrevolutionary and revisionist causes.

The most important qualitative change can be detected in the field of education. For, an entire generation was raised in a shrill, jingoistic atmosphere that suddenly became the hallmark of all Hungarian institutions of education. The ultranationalistic tone in the universities, the wholesale dismissal of some of the most progressive and brilliant professors, and the general air of intimidation inevitably led to a decline of the intellectual level in these institutions, especially in the social sciences and the humanities. Free inquiry in these fields was constantly stifled, enmeshed in politics. For example, the once thriving fields of cultural anthropology, ethnic studies, psychoanalysis, and sociology suffered major setbacks; some passed into oblivion. But the decline of quality was not limited to these fields. Practically every area of study was hindered by the demands of the state for political orthodoxy. The result was a wholesale exodus to the West, especially during the 1930s, of some of the best and most creative minds of Hungary. The emigration of the intellectuals was, however, only partly due to the intellectual climate in the country. Another cause was the extreme high rate of unemployment among college graduates in virtually every occupation.

In spite of strenuous efforts by the government to save the middle class, from the early 1920s, Hungary was constantly plagued by the problem of the unemployed intelligentsia. The causes of this condition can be traced partly to the refugee influx between 1918 and 1924. The state successfully absorbed the majority of the refugee degree holders, but this was achieved, in part, only at the expense of the moderate elements in the state bureaucracy and in the educational institutions. Many who were replaced became permanently unemployed. But the surplus created by the refugee degree holders was not entirely responsible for the problem. At least 86,000 refugees — and, as we have seen, perhaps as many as 100,000 — were students. A large percentage of these were of college age, who came singly, or with their families, to complete their studies in Hungary. We have also noted that the government specifically exempted from visa restrictions all students who wished to enter the country, even after all other groups were severely limited. A very high number of these students were children of the old social elite, who were expected to continue their education and receive some kind of university degree and gainful employment. Thus, the number of potential university graduates nearly doubled.

Bethlen's government was confronted with a difficult dilemma. On the one hand, it came under strong pressure from refugees to create more positions on university faculties for refugee professors and instructors and to make room in the universities for refugee students. On the other hand, the growing number of unemployed degree holders and the financial plight of the government dictated an opposite policy: a reduction of the number of university students well below existing levels. Previous governments were also aware of the problems a high number of unemployed university graduates could produce. But the political cost of a reduction was always judged to be too high. Just as the earlier government leaders, Bethlen, too, had to yield to political pressure. He and his minister of education, Count Kunó Klebelsberg, merely relocated the refugee universities of Pozsony and Kolozsvár to Pécs and Szeged. The sharp increase in faculty size between 1920 and 1930 can be attributed, at least in part, to the reestablishment and expansion of refugee universities. Bethlen and Klebelsberg justified relocating these universities by pointing to the great demand for their services; but, more important, by arguing that Hungary would be able to maintain its cultural superiority over the Successor States only by educating its young.

For political reasons, therefore, Bethlen and his predecessors allowed the substantial expansion of the university system. As a result, through-out the interwar years, Hungary suffered from a gross overproduction of college-educated individuals. A few figures will illustrate this point. In 1910, when the country's population was over 18 million, 15,820 students were enrolled in all of the universities. By 1920, this number declined to 11,939; but, in the following year, university enrollment began to climb. In 1921, to 16,538 students; in 1922, to 19,717; and, in 1923, to a peak of 20,815. During subsequent years as the refugee students gradually finished their education, the numbers declined slightly but never below the 1910 level.[39]

The war was partly responsible for these dramatic increases in enrollments. Many students had to postpone their entrance to university; others were forced to interrupt their studies to serve in the army. The return of these students to the universities created a temporary and unavoidable congestion. The impact of the refugees, however, was more significant. Complete statistics on the size of the refugee student population are not available. But, according to the ministry of religion and education, in the spring of 1921, out of the 12,447 students enrolled in Budapest's institutions of higher learning, representing 75.89 percent of all university students in the country, 4679 or 37.59 percent came from the lost territories. Of those 1980 or 42.32 percent came from Romania, 1589 or 33.96 percent from Czechoslovakia, and 1110 or 23.72 percent from Yugoslavia.[40] Since some of the provincial institutions of higher learning were also transplants from the lost territories, it is not likely that the ratio of refugee students in universities outside of Budapest was lower. It is, therefore, safe to assume that out of the 16,538 students in 1921 over 6,000 were refugees.

The presence of the refugee students radically altered the social composition of the student body. In 1913–14, about 16 percent of the students came from families of officials or officers. By 1921–22 their numbers represented about 27.4 percent; a few years later, 30 percent. Conversely, the numbers and proportion of students whose parents were independent professionals, such as doctors and lawyers, greatly declined. In other words, the gentry and gentroid element in the universities had dramatically increased and the bourgeois middle-class and lower-class representation decreased. This sociological change explains, in part, student right-wing radicalism during the early 1920s and the persistent middle-class support of the right during the next two decades.

The children of the gentry or those of the non-noble officials still expected to find a place for themselves in the upper strata of society, but a change is notable in their career objectives. They were less interested in following their parents into the civil service and more inclined to prepare for the free professions. The scarcity of civil service jobs and the fierce struggle that had to be waged to secure these positions brought about a disenchantment with state employment. The younger gentry realized that state employment no longer provided the economic security and comfort of the prewar era. Thus, the younger generations were searching for alternative occupations, which, nevertheless, could be still considered befitting a gentleman. Traditionally, they might have studied law in preparation for state employment. A large number of the students still pursued that field of study, but, increasingly, they showed a greater interest in the sciences, engineering, the arts, and medicine. A shift away from law was already noticeable during the last decade before the war; after the war it became dramatic. In the 1913–14 academic year, for example, 448 students graduated with law degrees, 414 completed their medical studies, and 375 received their diplomas in engineering. A decade later, when the total enrollment was the highest, 425 received degrees in law, 681 in medicine, and 478 in engineering.[41] Or another example: at the time when the country had about 4500 practicing physicians, the number of students studying medicine and pharmacy increased from about 2900 in early 1920 to about 5500 by 1922.[42] These numbers, however, do not accurately reflect the degree of shift in the attitudes of the younger middle-class generation. In the free professions the graduates' social background changed with a marked increase in the proportion of students whose parents belonged to the gentry officials. In 1918–19 23.7 percent of university students came from that stratum; by 1922–23 their proportion had increased to 43.7 percent.[43] According to the calculations of Andor Ladányi, in 1913–14 51.17 percent, that is, more than half of the students belonging to the officials' families studied law. By 1920–21, that figure was only 21.61 percent. On the other hand, on the eve of the war 19.69 percent of this group studied medicine and 13.59 percent the technical disciplines; by 1920–21, 28.68 percent and 29.87 percent were enrolled in the schools of medicine and engineering respectively. A similar shift in career objectives can be observed among children of clergymen and educators. Between 1913–14 and 1920–21, those attending law schools declined from 31.96 to 20.12 percent; those pursuing theological studies, from 23.24 percent to 6.65; for medical and technical studies these percentages increased from 19.21 percent to 30.78 percent and from 10.69 percent to 24.21 percent.[44] Once again, middle-class refugee students, the group most affected by the crisis of the gentry middle class, led the way in the shift from legal to technical and medical education. In 1921, for example, 34.24 percent of the students at the technical university and 39.79 percent of the students enrolled in the medical school of Budapest were refugees.[45] In other words, well over two-thirds of the refugee students opted for the medical and technical professions.

The gentry's growing interest in the free professions made the old differences between noble and non-noble segments of the middle class less and less pronounced. As a consequence, the political gap between the two groups also narrowed; causes championed by the gentry, including those of the refugees, received increasing middle-class support.

We may conclude that the attempted assimilation of the refugees into Hungary's political, social, and economic life was successful. A majority of the refugees, although by no means all, through their commitment to the cause of the right were able to secure, for themselves, a position within Trianon Hungary that was similar to, though not identical with, the posts they had left behind in the Successor States. To be sure, these new positions were not capable of providing the same economic comfort that these men had enjoyed before Hungary's partition, but, at least, in the eyes of the refugees, their new offices or new professions offered a comparable social status.

The domestic cost of their assimilation, however, was high. As we have seen, the refugee problem forced an expansion of the state bureaucracy and the educational system which, in turn, created a major problem in the form of an unemployed intelligentsia. The financial burden this imposed on the state treasury strained the country's economic resources to the utmost limit.

The successful assimilation of the refugees did not remove all causes of their earlier radicalism. They remained committed to the restoration of the lost territories, to a preservation of the preeminent position of their social group in Hungarian society. At the same time, with assimilation, they became willing to accept Bethlen's conservative policies and to support his contention that, under existing conditions, only through peaceful methods was there any hope of treaty revision. The refugees made certain that the issue of revision was never lost from the view of the Hungarian public. They permeated all public institutions, state and, to a lesser degree, local bureaucracies, the greatly expanded law enforcement agencies, and especially the army officers corps. Using their positions, they were able to exercise an exceptionally strong influence on the minds of the population; to exercise a virtual veto over Hungary's foreign policy.

The policy of peaceful revision, however, was doomed to failure. Throughout the interwar period, the Successor States viewed any revisionism as a threat to their security. They rigidly held onto their excessive territorial gains, refusing to correct even the most obvious injustices of the Treaty of Trianon. The resulting cool relations between Hungary and its neighbors weakened them all, increased their isolation, and prepared the way for domination of the entire region by a great power.

NOTES

Introduction

1. István Bethlen, *Bethlen István gróf beszédei és írásai* [Speeches and Writings of Count István Bethlen] (Budapest, 1933), I: 286.

Chapter 1

1. Emil Petrichevich-Horváth, ed., *Jelentés az Országos Menekültügyi Hivatal négy évi működéséről* [Report on the Four Years of Operation of the National Refugee Office] (Budapest, 1924), p. 37. Henceforth cited as *OMH Report*.

2. For functions of OMH see, Hivatalos Kiadványok, *A m. kir. ministerelnök 3240/1920 számú rendelete az Országos Menekültügyi Hivatal (O.M.H.) szervezéséről* [The Royal Hungarian Prime Minister's Edict, Numbered 3240/1920, on the Organization of the National Refugee Office (O.M.H.)] (Budapest, 1920).

3. As early as 1916, at the time of the Romanian invasion of Transylvania, a refugee organization was established which continued to function to the end of the war. In 1918, a number of political organizations also came to life to promote the defense of Transylvania and to function as refugee aid offices.

4. *OMH Report,* pp. 10–11.

5. Magyar Királyi Központi Statisztikai Hivatal, *Recensement de la population en 1920,* New Series, 93 (Budapest, 1928), pp. 8–9.

6. *OHM Report,* p. 37.

7. Hungary at the Paris Peace Conference [*Delegation Information Supplementary Document* (Budapest, 1920),] 11. The Peace Delegation statistics reflect only the strength of positive and negative internal migrations (gains and losses), county by county, but do not provide absolute figures. Those can be found only among the raw data of the 1910 census. They were, nevertheless, useful as controlling figures for the establishment of representative sample communities and districts. The results of our calculations had to be further modified, taking into consideration internal migration between 1910 and 1914, which we assumed to be similar to the rate of the 1900 and 1910 period, and especially the heavy movement of population during the war years. These figures, of course, still, do not reflect those individuals who went to inner Hungary temporarily during the war, but were prevented from returning to their homes by the establishment of new frontiers.

8. In comparing the 1910 statistics with those of the postwar period, adjustments had to be made to account for the change of population due to natural causes. Between 1910 and 1914 the birth rate, and therefore the increase of population, continued roughly at the rate of the preceding decade; it declined sharply during the war years, and during the immediate postwar years, owing to

the absence of males, malnutrition, higher infancy mortality rate, and epidemics. In addition the 661,000 military losses of Trianon Hungary had to be taken into account. See József Kovácsics, ed., *Magyarország történeti demográfiája; Magyarország népesedése a honfoglalástól 1949-ig* [Historical Demography of Hungary; The Population of Hungary from the Time of Conquest to 1949] (Budapest, 1963), pp. 229–38. Also, László Buday, *Megcsonkított Magyarország* [Dismembered Hungary] (Budapest, 1920), pp. 36–39.

9. Raw data was obtained from the following sources: books quoted in note 8; Károly Kugotowitz, *Etnographical Map of Hungary* (Budapest, 1929); *Cechoslovakische Statistic*, vol. 9, series VI: *Volkszählung in de Cechosloslovakischen Republik vom 15 Febr. 1921*, part I (Prague, 1924); László Fritz, *Az erdélyi magyarság lélekszáma és megoszlása* [The Numbers and Territorial Distribution of the Transylvanian Hungarians] (Kolozsvár, 1930); Elemér Jakabffy, *Erdély statisztikája* [Statistics of Transylvania] (Lugos, 1923).

10. In Hungary, as in most multinational states, a large number of individuals were of doubtful national origin; therefore, they easily passed for Hungarians. These individuals, such as those with mixed parentage, benefited from declaring themselves Hungarian before the war. It was only natural for them to change their nationality to Slovak, Ruthenian, Romanian, Serbian or Croatian after the change of regimes. But the largest single block of Hungarian minorities where the change of nationality adversely affected its numerical strength was the Jews. In 1910 most Jews of Hungary were recorded as Hungarians, but in the Successor States a great majority of them was carried in the statistics as a separate minority. This, alone, in the case of Czechoslovakia, accounts for the "loss" of 94,000 Hungarians; and in Transylvania, of 125,000. Iván Nagy, *A magyarság világstatisztikája* [World Statistics of Hungarians] (Budapest, 1930). pp. 12, 23. Similarly, many half-assimilated Germans, who claimed to be Hungarians in 1910, were recorded as Germans in the Successor States. Adjustments were made for several other factors, such as the natural increase of population, which was significant, however, only in the case of Romania. Further adjustments had to be made for Hungarian emigration during the postwar years. The unreliability of data on the number of individuals who migrated into the former Hungarian territories from the prewar kingdoms of Romania and Serbia created the greatest difficulty.

11. *OHM Report*, p. 37. It should be noted that figures in the report were added incorrectly.

Chapter 2

1. For details of the immediate repercussions of the dissolution of the Habsburg monarchy see Béla K. Király, Peter Pastor, and Ivan Sanders, eds., *Essays on World War I: Total War and Peace Making; A Case Study of Trianon* (Boulder, Colo., 1983). For discussion of Western war aims and approach to peacemaking see Arno J. Mayer, *Politics and Diplomacy of Peacemaking: Containment and Counterrevolution at Versailles, 1918–1919* (New York, 1967);

W. H. Rothwell, *British War Aims and Peace Diplomacy. 1914–1918* (Oxford, 1971); Wilfred Fest, *Peace or Partition: The Habsburg Monarchy and British Policy, 1914–1918* (New York, 1978); Kenneth J. Calder, *Britain and the Origins of the New Europe. 1914–1918* (Cambridge, 1976).

2. Peter Pastor, *Hungary between Wilson and Lenin: The Hungarian Revolution of 1918–1919 and the Big Three* (Boulder, Colo., 1976), p. 40.

3. U.S., Department of State, *Papers Relating to the Foreign Relations of the United States: The Paris Peace Conference, 1919* (Washington, D.C., 1942), II: 175–82. Henceforth cited as *FRUS PPC.*

4. For reasons of delay in reaching agreement see Vilmos Böhm, *Két forradalom tüzében, októberi forradalom, proletárdiktatúra, ellenforradalom* [In the Crossfire of Two Revolutions, The October Revolution, Dictatorship of the Proletariat, Counterrevolution] (Vienna, 1923), pp. 68–71. Cf. Oscar Jászi, *Revolution and Counter-Revolution in Hungary* (New York, 1969), pp. 53–54; Michael Károlyi, *Faith Without Illusion: Memoirs of Michael Károlyi* (London, 1956), pp. 130–37. See also, Pastor, *Hungary between Wilson and Lenin,* pp. 60–66; Zsuzsa L. Nagy, *A párizsi békekonferencia és Magyarország, 1918–1919* [The Paris Peace Conference and Hungary, 1918–1919] (Budapest, 1965), pp. 8–12.

5. For text of the Belgrade Military Convention see *FRUS PPC* II: 183–85.

6. Ibid., pp. 183, 185. For an interpretation of these lines see Jászi, *Revolution,* pp. 57–59; see also, D. Perman, *The Shaping of the Czechoslovak State: Diplomatic History of the Boundaries of Czechoslovakia, 1914–1920* (Leiden, 1962), p. 79.

7. László Kővágó, *A magyarországi délszlávok 1918–1919-ben* [South Slavs of Hungary during 1918–1919] (Budapest, 1964), pp. 58–59.

8. Ibid., p. 61. See also, László Kővágó, *A Magyarországi Tanácsköztársaság és a nemzeti kérdés* [The Hungarian Soviet Republic and the Nationality Question] (Budapest, 1979), p. 8.

9. According to the 1910 Hungarian and 1921 Yugoslav censuses the distribution of the population was as follows:

National Group	1910 Census		1921 Census	
Serbo-Croatian	454,625	33.4	514,121	37.2
Other Slavs	58,134	4.3	67,886	4.9
Hungarian	443,006	32.5	382,070	27.7
German	312,350	22.9	328,173	23.8
Romanian	81,790	6.0	74,099	5.4
Slovenian	48	0.0	7,949	0.6
Others	12,067	0.9	6,112	0.4
Total	1,362,020		1,380,410	

10. Kővágó, *A magyarországi délszlávok,* pp. 91–92. That interpretation of the Padua Armistice Agreement was incorrect. Hungary was no longer in a state of war. Károlyi did not reject the Padua Agreement; the Belgrade Military Convention did not supersede it. The latter agreement was merely an extension, an elaboration of the former. See Pastor, *Hungary between Wilson*

and Lenin, p. 66; L. Nagy, *A párizsi békekonferencia,* pp. 11–12; Tibor Hajdu, *Károlyi Mihály* (Budapest, 1978), p. 290.

11. József Breit, *A magyarországi 1918/19 évi forradalmi mozgalmak és a vörös háború története* I: *A Károlyi korszak főbb eseményei* [Hungarian Revolutionary Movements of 1918/19 and the History of the Red War, Vol. I: Main Events of the Károlyi Era] (Budapest, 1929), pp. 115–16. See also Leslie Charles Tihany, *The Baranya Dispute, 1918–1921: Diplomacy in the Vortex of Ideologies* (Boulder, 1978), p. 18.

12. Already, in 1915, the *k. und k.* army suffered mass desertion of peasant soldiers. The number of deserters, in 1915, was 26,251; in 1917, it rose to 81,605; during the first three months of 1918 alone, there were as many as 44,611. Tibor Hajdu, *Az őszirózsás forradalom* [Revolution of White Hollyhocks] (Budapest, 1963), pp. 48–49. Out of an estimated 400,000 deserters about 200,000 were South Slavs. József Galántai, *Magyarország az első világháborúban, 1914–1918* [Hungary in the First World War, 1914–1918] (Budapest, 1974), pp. 396–97. Deserters presented a major security problem to the Hungarian authorities and were the first troops to rally to the flags of the secessionists.

13. Jászi, *Revolution,* p. 61.

14. Tibor Hajdu, *Az 1918-as magyarországi polgári demokratikus forradalom* [The 1918 Hungarian Bourgeois Democratic Revolution] (Budapest, 1968), pp. 97–98.

15. See Royal Hungarian Ministry of Foreign Affairs, *The Hungarian Peace Delegation at Neuilly s/S, from January to March 1920* (Budapest, 1921) I: 366–67. Henceforth cited as *HPN.* See also, Kővágó, *A magyarországi délszlávok,* pp. 95–96.

16. Breit, *A magyarországi 1918/19 évi forradalmi mozgalmak,* I: 116. For the repeated but fruitless protests of the Hungarian government see Enclosures to Note IX, *HPN* I: 360, 362, 368. As a result of the occupation of the Muraköz, an estimated 5300 individuals became refugees.

17. The first group of legionnaires left Vladivostok on January 15, 1919 and arrived in Naples only on March 11. Thus, the legionnaires could not be used until late spring or early summer.

18. Zoltán Szviezsényi, *Hogyan veszett el a Felvidék?* [How was Upper Hungary Lost?] (Budapest, 1921), p. 84.

19. Ferenc Boros, *Magyar-csehszlovák kapcsolatok 1918–1919-ben* [Hungarian-Czechoslovak Relations during 1918–1919] (Budapest, 1970), p. 11.

20. Jenő Horváth, *A trianoni béke megalkotása; 1915–1920. Diplomáciai történelmi tanulmány* [The Creation of the Treaty of Trianon. A Study in Diplomatic History] (Budapest, 1924), p. 22.

21. Pastor, *Hungary between Wilson and Lenin,* p. 70; L. Nagy, *A párizsi békekonferencia,* p. 29.

22. Fest, *Peace of Partition,* p. 255.

23. Perman, *The Shaping of the Czechoslovak State,* p. 88.

24. Enclosure LXXI to Note IX, *HPN* I: 383–84.

25. For details of negotiations see Boros, *Magyar-csehszlovák kapcsolatok,*

pp. 45–48; Pastor, *Hungary betwen Wilson and Lenin,* p. 84; Hajdu, *Károlyi Mihály,* pp. 272, 300.

26. Enclosure CXXII and CXXIII to Note IX, *HPN* I: 384–85.

27. Breit, *A magyarországi 1918/19 évi forradalmi mozgalmak* I; 86, 88, 91. Also, Eduard Beneš, *My War Memoirs* (London, 1928), p. 482; R. W. Seton-Watson, ed., *Slovakia, Then and Now* (London, 1931), p. 20.

28. Gyula Lábay, *Az ellenforradalom története az októberi forradalomtól a kommün bukásáig* [History of the Counterrevolution from the October Revolution to the Collapse of the Commune (Budapest, 1922), p. 3.

29. Szmrecsányi had estimated that 10–12,000 men would be sufficient to throw back the Czechs; he intended using the rest of his forces to carry out his counterrevolutionary designs. István Friedrich, then undersecretary of war, was informed of these plans and promised Szmrecsányi weapons and officers to organize that army. Lábay, *Az ellenforradalom története,* pp. 5–6. Also, Béla Kelemen, *Adatok a szegedi ellenforradalom és a szegedi kormány történetéhez* [Documents to the History of the Counterrevolution and of the Government of Szeged] (Szeged, 1923), p. 368. Henceforth, cited as *ASzET.* Szmrecsányi also had contacts with Gyula Gömbös, leader of the rightist officers' association, MOVE. Richárd Hefty, *Adatok az ellenforradalom történetéhez* [Facts to the History of the Counterrevolution] (Budapest, 1920), p. 20.

30. Nearly all the city officials of higher ranks fled the city, leaving only a few clerks behind. László Hangel, ed., *Mit élt át a Felvidék?* [What did Upper Hungary Endure?] (Budapest, 1939), p. 460.

31. László Boros, ed., *Magyar politikai lexikon, 1914–1929* [Lexicon of Hungarian Politics, 1914–1929] (Budapest, 1929), p. 330. Henceforth cited as *MPL.* From the students of the Forestry College, a battalion of 800 men was formed, but it was disarmed by the government before it could be used in defense of the city. Nonetheless, the students fled to inner Hungary. Szviezsényi, *Hogyan veszett el a Felvidék,* p. 88.

32. *MPL,* p. 122; Hangel, *Mit élt át a Felvidék,* p. 566.

33. In late 1919, he was arrested by the Romanian military authorities and charged with inciting the Ruthenian population to armed resistance. *MPL,* pp. 252–53. For a detailed examination of the transfer of Ruthenia to Czechoslovakia see Paul R. Magocsi, *The Shaping of a National Identity: Subcarpathian Rus', 1848–1948* (Cambridge, Mass., 1978), pp. 85–102; for the activities of Kutkafalvy: ibid., pp. 203, 312. A group of pro-Hungarian Slovaks with Hungarian backing tried to prevent union of Upper Hungary with Bohemia and Moravia by declaring Slovakia's independence. This group's leader, Győző Dvorcsák, was condemned to death by Czech courts, but managed to escape to Poland, and then to Hungary, where he was elected to the National Assembly in 1920. *MPL,* p. 96.

34. Szmrecsányi, Beniczky, Pethes, Kutkafalvy, and Dvorcsák became members of the National Assembly; Fornet remained in the county administration and, later, was rewarded with a seat in the Upper House.

35. Seventeen allied divisions were concentrated around Hungary — six Ro-

manian, four Serbian, four Czech, and three French. Böhm, *Két forradalom,* p. 327. Cf. Ervin Liptai, *A Magyar Tanácsköztársaság* [The Hungarian Soviet Republic] (Budapest, 1958), p. 269.

36. Galántai, *Magyarország,* pp. 190–92, 236.

37. Ibid., pp. 351–52.

38. No ethnic, only historical differences exist between Hungarians and Székelys. Székelys are Hungarian residents of eastern Transylvania, who in the past enjoyed certain privileges. We refer to the entire area ceded to Romania as Transylvania only for the sake of convenience. Historically, that is inaccurate. In addition to Transylvania, Romania was also awarded a broad strip of the Great Hungarian Plains adjacent to Transylvania. This area always formed a part of inner Hungary. Whenever necessary, to distinguish between the two regions, we shall refer to Transylvania proper as historical Transylvania.

39. In mid–1919 the *székely akció* still had 30-million crowns in its treasury. It was used, in part, to finance the counterrevolutionary National Army of Szeged. *ASzET,* p. 300.

40. This offer may have been made, though it is not confirmed by reliable sources. Nevertheless, at the time, many Hungarians believed it.

41. *FRUS PPC* II: 183–85.

42. In the mixed Hungarian and Romanian Arad county, for example, by the end of December, out of 45 *gendarmerie* stations only seven were still manned. Hajdu, *Az 1918-as magyarországi polgári demokratikus forradalom,* p. 102.

43. Miron Constantinescu *et al, Unification of the Romanian National State: The Union of Transylvania with Old Romania* (Bucharest, 1971), p. 235.

44. Zoltán Szász, "Az erdélyi román polgárság szerepéről 1918 őszén" [On the Role of the Transylvanian Romanian Bourgeoisie during the Fall of 1918], *Századok* 106, no. 2 (1972): 328–29. Cf. Constantinescu, *Unification,* pp. 265–66.

45. Ibid., p. 244; Pastor, *Hungary between Wilson and Lenin,* pp. 72–74.

46. Róbert Braun, *Magyarország feldarabolása és a nemzetiségi kérdés* [Dismemberment of Hungary and the Nationality Question] (Budapest, 1919), p. 45. Cf. *FRUS PPC* II: 394. Also, Constantinescu, *Unification,* p. 252.

47. *FRUS PPC* II: 396.

48. This decree was published on December 26. But France, along with the other Western Powers, refused to recognize its validity. As the French ambassador to the United States wrote to the secretary of state: "This has, in the eyes of my Govt. no consequence one way or the other from the international point of view, for such an annexation cannot be consecrated by Roumania alone, but by the general Treaty of Peace." Ibid., p. 404.

49. By the end of December 1700 Székelys were serving in the division. Gradually its strength grew to 10,000. Breit, *A magyarországi 1918/19-i forradalmi mozgalmak* I: 37. Also, Endre Koréh, *Erdélyért: A székely hadosztály és dandár története, 1918–1919* [For Transylvania: History of the Székely Division and Brigade, 1918–1919] (2nd ed., Budapest, 1929) I: 36–37, 47.

50. Enclosures XLVI–L to Note IX, *HPN* I: 371–74.

51. Koréh, *A székely hadosztály* I: 154, 168.

52. Breit, *A magyarországi 1918/19-i forradalmi mozgalmak* I: Appendix 15, p. 208.

53. Enclosure LIV to Note IX, *HPN* I: 374–75.

54. Koréh, *A székely hadosztály* I: 146.

55. Ibid., p. 169.

56. Among the victims 14 were women; 32 persons, above the age of 60. Ibid. II: 48–52, 54.

57. Peace Conference Delegation, *Atrocities Committed by Roumanians and Czechs. Memorandum to the Mandatories of the Associated Powers at Budapest re. the Abuses Perpetrated by the Powers of Occupation in the Territories Subjected to Czecho-Slovak and Roumanian Administration* (N.p., n.d. [1921]); Appendix 2, p. 10.

58. Commenting on the lack of mass support for the Székely Division, on June 10, 1919, Samu Barabás, a refugee Calvinist minister from Kolozsvár, wrote in his journal: "At the beginning of recruiting the public mood was the worst possible. With the October Revolution the people felt themselves liberated from the burden of work, discipline, and duty. . . . Upon the promise of land distribution . . . the ancient hostility between noble and peasant sharpened, resulting in a social paralysis." Defense of the nation's frontiers was viewed by the peasants as a problem concerning only the nobility. Koréh, *A székely hadosztály* I: 215–17.

59. Annex 6 to Note VIII, *HPN* I: 215. Also, Breit, *A magyarországi 1918/19-i forradalmi mozgalmak* III: 84. The Székely Division's desertion came at the height of the military crisis caused by the powerfully reinforced Romanian army's renewed attack in mid-April.

60. See Koréh, *A székely hadosztály* I: 200, 211; II: 152.

Chapter 3

1. *FRUS PPC* II: 183.

2. Ştefan Pascu, "The National Unity of the Romanians and the Breakup of the Austro-Hungarian Empire," *Austrian History Yearbook* IV–V (1968–1969): 82.

3. Harold Nicolson, *Peacemaking 1919* (New York, 1965), p. 279.

4. Plans to invade Slovakia were drawn up by some of the refugee organizations and were considered in the highest Hungarian circles, even by Horthy himself. Dezső Nemes, *Iratok az ellenforradalom történetéhez 1919–1945* [Documents to the History of the Counterrevolution 1919–1945] (Budapest, 1956) I: 200–207, especially pp. 205–206. Henceforth cited as *IET*. For later invasion plans see Miklós Szinai and László Szűcs, eds., *Horthy Miklós titkos iratai* [Secret Papers of Miklós Horthy] (Budapest, 1963), pp. 74–81.

5. HPPC, *Supplementary Documents*, no. 9. This ratio was even higher in the old minority areas.

6. Peace Conference Delegation, *Atrocities*, p. 10.

7. Buday, *Megcsonkított Magyarország*, p. 260.

8. See Notes 173, 325, 345, and 400, *HPN* II: 485, 529–30, 533, 542.

9. Seton-Watson, *Slovakia*, p. 215.

10. Ibid., pp. 217, 221.

11. Peace Conference Delegation, *Atrocities*, p. 1. As the Hungarian Peace Delegation in Paris protested: "The Czecho-Slovak and Roumanian Governments compel the Hungarian officials, professors and teachers — under charge of instant dismissal and expulsion — to take the oath of allegiance to the Czecho-Slolvak and Roumanian State respectively, this being a manifest infraction of Article 45 of the Hague Convention."

12. Tivadar Battyány, *Beszámolóm* [My Report] (Budapest, 1927) I: 298–99.

13. HPPC, *Supplementary Documents*, no. 16. To be sure, a large number of state officials had a Slovak ethnic background. Most were assimilated Slovaks who, in 1910, declared themselves to be Hungarian.

14. The Czechs and Slovaks disagreed on the level of development of Slovakia. The Czechs always preferred to paint Slovakia's backwardness in the blackest colors, and their views found their way into Western historical literature. According to one assertion, in 1918, only 500 Slovaks had the requisite education to perform administrative duties. Seton-Watson, *Slovakia*, p. 219. In another work he wrote: "the number of educated and nationally conscious Slovaks in 1918 did not exceed 750 to 1000!" R. W. Seton-Watson, *History of the Czechs and Slovaks* (London, 1943), p. 323. Slovakia's backwardness served as a justification for domination of Slovakia by Czechs. At least that was the view of the Slovaks. They resented both the implications of Czech cultural superiority and Prague's paternalism. See Joseph Mikus, *Slovakia; A Political History: 1918–1950* (Milwaukee, 1963), pp. 26–37. The Czechs promised to withdraw their officials as soon as native Slovaks were trained, but even in 1938 about 121,000 Czechs lived in Slovakia, while unemployment was high among Slovak intellectuals. S. Harrison Thomson, *Czechoslovakia in European History* (Princeton, 1943), p. 292.

15. Seton-Watson, *Slovakia*, pp. 245–47. For other repressive measures against Hungarian officials see Annex 1 to Note IX, Notes LXXVIII and XCI, *HPN* I: 355–56, 387, 393; also, Note 334, II: 512.

16. Buday, *Megcsonkított Magyarország*, p. 260.

17. See Enclosures I–VIII to Note LXIV, *HPN* I: 379–81; also, Notes LXII and LXIV, pp. 378–79. The demand of loyalty oath illustrates the prevailing legal confusion. It was logical to demand such oaths if the Romanian government still considered the population of Transylvania citizens of the Hungarian state. If, on the other hand, the Royal Proclamation of Union accomplished the annexation of the region, the population, including ethnic Hungarians, should have automatically acquired Romanian citizenship. That would have made such an oath superfluous.

18. Peace Conference Delegation, *Atrocities*, p. 7. In Fogaras out of 6000 Hungarians about 1000 were forced to leave.

19. Ibid., p. 11.

20. Zsombér Szász, *Erdély Romániában. Népkisebbségi tanulmány* [Transylvania in Romania. A National Minority Study] (Budapest, 1929), p. 82.

21. Ibid., pp. 83–84.

22. HPPC, *Supplementary Documents*, no. 2.

23. Ibid., no. 16.

24. See Notes LXI and LXVIII in *HPN* I: 377, 382; note 333, II: 513. See also, Seton-Watson, *A History of Czechs and Slovaks*, p. 323.

25. The lower literacy rate among some Hungarian national minorities was viewed by the Successor States as evidence of a deliberate antiminority policy by the prewar Hungarian regime. The great divergence of literacy among the different national groups, however, contradicts that thesis. Correlation between literacy and the level of economic development of a particular region is far stronger than between literacy rate and the state's nationality policy. Thus, in the more developed Nyitra county, 80.5 percent of Slovaks could read and write, whereas in the remote Zemplén county, the rate was 41.5 percent. Similarly, in Temes county, 40.1 percent of the Romanians were literate; in Szolnok-Doboka county, only 14.7 percent. Illiteracy was also high among the Hungarian agrarian proletariat working on the large estates. This further underlines the argument that the reason for some groups' educational backwardness among the national minorities was due to economic causes, to the survival of an antiquated social system.

26. *HPN*, III/A: 264–65. At the time of compilation of these statistics, the Bánát was still claimed by both Yugoslavia and Romania. Hence, the disputed area was carried in a separate column.

27. Seton-Watson, *Slovakia*, p. 125.

28. The dismissed teachers, furthermore, were encouraged to leave Slovakia by the refusal of the state to honor its pension obligations. The dismissal notice normally ended with the statement: "As regarding your claims to a pension you are referred to the Hungarian Government, which at the same time is informed by us of your dismissal." Peace Conference Delegation, *Atrocities*, p. 9.

29. Andor Ladányi, *Az egyetemi ifjúság az ellenforradalom első éveiben (1919–1921)* [University Students during the First Years of the Counterrevolution (1919–1921)] (Budapest, 1979), p. 12.

30. Magyar Sorskérdések, *A jugoszláviai magyarság helyzete* [Conditions of Hungarians in Yugoslavia] (Budapest, 1941), p. 14.

31. A number of denominational schools were financed by the Hungarian state, which were treated by the Romanian government as state schools. In some statistics these schools appear as denominational while in others as state schools.

32. Szász, *Erdély Romániában*, p. 233.

33.

Number of Denominational Elementary Schools
in Historic Transylvania and Szatmár

Denomination	1918	1919	1920	1921	1922	1923	1924	1925
Catholic	206	213	305	277	265	256	235	318
Calvinist	195	198	504	515	494	476	423	389
Unitarian	27	27	86	53	46	43	30	30
Total	428	438	895	845	805	775	698	647

Source: Szász, *Erdély Romániában*, p. 232.

34. Romania expropriated 95.5 percent (277,645 yokes) of landed property of the Catholic Church. Protestant churches lost 45.2 percent (36,686 yokes) of their lands. Nicholas Móricz, *The Fate of the Transylvanian Soil: A Brief Account of the Rumanian Land Reform of 1921* (Budapest, 1934), p. 81.

35.   Number of Students at the University of Kolozsvár (Cluj)

Academic Year	Romanian	Hungarian and Saxon	Jewish
1918–19	332	2240	394
1921–22	1625	264	555
1923–24	1184	286	227

Source: Szász, *Erdély Romániában*, p. 252.

36. Ladányi, *Az egyetemi ifjúság*, p. 12.
37. *OHM Report*, p. 37.
38. Buday, *Megcsonkított Magyarország*, p. 260.

Chapter 4

1. HPPC, *Supplementary Documents*, no. 19. This statistic, however, fails to give the complete picture. Most landholding Slovaks and Ruthenians owned only tiny plots. The relative well-being of the various national groups may be also gauged by a comparison of the proportion of property they owned, the percentage of the national group in the total population, and their share of direct taxes:

National Group	% in Population	% of Land	Direct Taxes Paid
Hungarians	54.5	59.9	62.1
German	10.4	9.9	16.1
Slovak	10.7	7.7	6.2
Romanian	16.1	16.0	8.7
Croatian	1.1	0.5	0.9
Serbian	2.5	2.5	3.5
Ruthenian	2.5	2.3	0.8
Other	2.2	1.2	1.5

Source: Kővágó, *A magyarországi délszlávok*, p. 12.

These figures, of course, fail to reflect the distribution of wealth within each of these national groups — they fail to measure the degree of social stratification. The greatest extremes of wealth and poverty existed among the Hungarians; but among Serbs, Slovaks, Ruthenians, and Romanians, property was more evenly distributed.

2. Of the approximately 1.7–1.8 million people who permanently emigrated from Hungary after 1899, 33 percent were Hungarians, 25 percent Slovaks, 18 percent Romanians, 4.5 percent Ruthenians, and 2.6 South Slavs. Péter Hanák, ed., *Magyarország története* [History of Hungary] (Budapest, 1978) VII: 412–13.

3. Lucy E. Textor, *Land Reform in Czechoslovakia* (London, 1923), p. 25.

4. Ifor L. Evans, *The Agrarian Revolution in Roumania* (Cambridge, 1924), p. 102.

5. Textor, *Land Reform,* pp. 31–32, 95, 99.

6. Jarmila Meclová and Ferdinand Stočes, *Land Reform in Czechoslovakia* (Prague, 1963), pp. 30, 32.

7. From the total amount of expropriated land, 79.8 percent was owned by Hungarian landowners, 11.2 percent by the Catholic Church, and the remainder by Germans, Slovaks, and Ruthenians. C. A. Macartney, *Hungary and Her Successors* (Oxford, 1937), pp. 172, 123.

8. Ibid., p. 399. Another source gives a slightly different set of figures. According to this, in northern Yugoslavia, 720 estates were forced to contribute to the land pool. From these, 369 estates were owned by private individuals, 50 by corporations, 77 by the churches and monasteries, 171 by various municipalities, 44 by the state, and 9 by others. Of the 369 private owners, 310 were "foreigners," 142 Austrians, 126 Hungarians, 10 Italians, 8 Czechoslovaks, 3 Germans, and 17 others. Jozo Tomasevich, *Peasants, Politics, and Economic Change in Yugoslavia* (Stanford, 1955), p. 366.

9. Magyar Sorskérdések, *A jugoszláviai magyarság,* p. 9.

10. Ibid.

11. Maximum limits on landholdings were finally set in 1931. Limits varied with areas, depending on local conditions. Thus, for example, in Herzegovina all land holdings above 50 hectares were subject to expropriation; in the Voivodina, a landowner was allowed to retain as much as 300 hectares of agricultural and 500 hectares of land in total, if all local needs were satisfied. Tomasevich, *Peasants,* p. 364.

12. The most scholarly presentation of the Romanian side of the argument is David Mitrany's *Land and the Peasant in Rumania: The War and the Agrarian Reform, 1917–1921* (Oxford, 1930). Yet, his data should be used with care, since he generally accepts the unreliable official Romanian statistics. The best opposing view in English is Móricz, *The Fate.* It was written with the aim of challenging and correcting Mitrany's book. Another useful source is Jakabffy's *Erdély statisztikája.*

13. The distribution was as follows:

	Number of Holdings	Amount of Land Held	Percentage of Arable Land
Small holdings of less than 11.2 hectares	920,939	3,153,645	40.29
Medium sized holdings (11.2–112 hectares)	38,723	862,800	11.2
Large estates (above 112 hectares)	5,385	3,810,351	48.7

Source: Evans, *The Agrarian Revolution,* p. 76.

14. József Baróthy, *Magyar föld román kézen* [Hungarian Land in Romanian Hands] (Budapest, 1940), p. 28.

15. Ferenc Matheovits, *A magyar-román birtokper. Nemzetközi jogi tanul-*

mány [The Hungarian-Romanian Property Litigation. A Study in International Law] (Budapest, 1929), p. 19. The number of Romanian landowners in the upper categories, however, was low:

Distribution of Middle Sized and Large Estates
According to Nationality

Estate Size in Yokes	Number of Owners	Hungarian	German	Romanian	Other
100–200	1692	937 (55.4%)	151 (8.9%)	601 (35.5%)	3 (0.2%)
200–1,000	2750	1735 (63.1%)	237 (8.6%)	771 (28.0%)	7 (0.3%)
Above 1,000	221	187 (84.5%)	13 (5.9%)	19 (8.6%)	2 (1.0%)

Source: Ibid., p. 39.

16. Zoltán Tóth, *Magyarok és románok. Történelmi tanulmányok* [Hungarians and Romanians. Historical Studies] (Budapest, 1966). pp. 376–85; 394–96.

17. Between 1907 and 1912 alone, Romanian nationals bought about 166,000 yokes from Hungarian landlords, 96,000 yokes of arable and 70,000 yokes of forest land. That represented an approximate 6.6 percent decrease of Hungarian-owned property. Baróthy, *Magyar föld,* p. 45.

18. Szász, "Az erdélyi román polgárság," pp. 304–305.

19. See for example Gusztáv Beksics, *Román kérdés és a fajok harcza Európában és Magyarországon* [The Romanian Question and the Struggle of Races in Europe and in Hungary] (Budapest, 1895); esp. pp. 166–69.

20. Bethlen, *Bethlen István* I: 60–61.

21. See, for example, László Tokaji's *Új honfoglalás Erdélyben* [New Conquest in Transylvania] (Kolozsvár, 1912). For a contrasting earlier, and more optimistic, view see Gusztáv Beksics, *A magyar faj terjeszkedése és nemzeti konszolidációnk különös tekintettel a mezőgazdaságra, birtokviszonyra és a népesedésre* [The Expansion of the Hungarian Nation and Our National Consolidation, with Special Emphasis on Agriculture, Property Relations and Population] (Budapest, 1896). Also, Gusztáv Beksics, *Magyarosodás és magyarosítás. Különös tekintettel városainkra* [The Natural and Forced Process of Magyarization. With Special Emphasis on our Cities] (Budapest, 1883).

22. From the total of 2,377,928 yokes of land seized before the land reform, 150,000 were taken in 1919 and before, 830,000 in 1920, and the rest in 1921. About 87 percent of the affected land was owned by Hungarians. Baróthy, *Magyar föld,* p. 50.

23. Mitrany, *Land and the Peasant,* pp. 126, 171–72.

24. Móricz, *The Fate,* p. 176.

25. Baróthy, *Magyar föld,* p. 99. Mitrany gives high figures: he placed the number of Romanian recipients at 228,000, whereas other nationalities at 83,000, altogether receiving 785,000 yokes. Mitrany, *Land and the Peasant,*

p. 210. From the remaining land area, the state retained 900,000 yokes of pasture lands, 70,000 yokes of forests, and, finally, 57,000 yokes were designated for purposes of colonization. Baróthy, *Magyar föld*, p. 98.
26. Macartney, *Hungary and Her Successors*, p. 123.
27. Magyar Sorskérdések, *A jugoszláviai magyarság*, p. 8.
28. Kővágó, *A magyarországi délszlávok*, pp. 12–14. See also Macartney, *Hungary and Her Successors*, p. 427.

Chapter 5

1. Honoré de Balzac, *Cousin Bette* (Hammondsworth, 1965), p. 73.
2. See, for example, Eva Bene, "Anxiety and Emotional Impoverishment in Men under Stress," *British Journal of Medical Psychology* 34 (1961): 281–89.
3. As was reported by Leo Eitlinger, in "The Incidents of Mental Desease among Refugees in Norway," *Journal of Mental Science* 105 (April 1959): 326–338.
4. Ágnes Várkonyi, "A nemzet, a haza fogalma a török harcok és Habsburg-ellenes küzdelmek idején," [The Concept of Nation and Homeland during the Time of Anti-Turkish and Anti-Habsburg Struggles] *A magyar nacionalizmus kialakulása és története* [Development and History of Hungarian Nationalism] (Budapest, 1964), p. 30.
5. Ibid., p. 61. See also, Ferenc Salamon, *Magyarország a török hódítás korában* [Hungary during the Time of Turkish Occupation] (Pest, 1864), p. 136.
6. Figures vary according to sources consulted. Thus, Elek Fényes offers a figure of 537,000. *Magyarországnak s hozzákapcsolt tartományoknak mostani állapotja* [The Present Condition of Hungary and Its Appendages] (Pest, 1841), p. 43. Hóman and Szekfű give a figure of 680,000, for 1848. Bálint Hóman and Gyula Szekfű, *Magyar történet* [Hungarian History] (Budapest, 1935–36) 5: 661. See also Béla K. Király, *Hungary in the Late Eighteenth Century* (New York, 1969), p. 37, n. 50; p. 38.
7. Ibid., p. 37.
8. For example, Count Mihály Károlyi's unforgivable crime, in the eyes of his fellow aristocrats, was not his radical ideas, but his becoming a traitor to his estate. It was considered his birth right to indulge in unorthodox behavior, to embrace peculiar ideas. But, after 1919, when it became clear that he was no longer bound by the standards of aristocracy and was willing to sacrifice the interests of the nobility for his ideals, he was denounced in terms more venomous than those reserved for Béla Kun. Károlyi was repeatedly called a "worthless cretin," a mental and physical cripple and degenerate, implying that only mental deformity or disorder could have brought a Hungarian aristocrat to abandon his estate. See, for example, Miklós Surányi, *Bethlen. Történetpolitikai tanulmányok* [Bethlen. Historical and Political Studies] (Budapest, 1927), p. 90.
9. Andrew C. Janos, "Hungary: 1867–1939; A Study of Social Change and the Political Process" (Ph.D. diss., Princeton University, 1961), pp. 50–51. The

economic crisis which followed the Napoleonic wars spelled financial ruin for many nobles with small- and middle-sized estates, swelling the ranks of the already numerous group of landless nobles. See B. G. Iványi, "From Feudalism to Capitalism: The Economic Background to Széchenyi's Reform in Hungary," *Journal of Central European Affairs* XX (April 1960), pp. 270–88. In 1830, there were 180,000 nobles with less than 100 yokes of land, 120,000 peasant nobles, living as feudal tenants and 120,000 "honoratiores," or landless nobles. At the same time, 108,000 owned between 100–10000 yokes; at the top of the pyramid stood 800 magnates.

10. In 1848, the number of middle-sized estates of between 200–1000 yokes of land was 30,000. By 1910, their numbers had diminished to less than 10,000. Iván Berend and György Ránki, "Economic Factors in Nationalism: The Example of Hungary at the Beginning of the Twentieth Century," *Austrian History Yearbook* III, part 3 (1967): 167. Only the magnates possessed sufficient resources to modernize; members of the gentry were often forced to sell their lands. Béla Balázs, *A középrétegek szerepe társadalmunk fejlődésében. Egy évszázad magyar történelmének néhány sajátosságáról, 1849–1945* [The role of the Middle Strata in the Development of Our Society. A Few Characteristics of a Century of Hungarian History, 1849–1945] (Budapest, 1958), pp. 30–31.

11. In Transylvania, for example, between 1890 and 1900, the number of officials in the Hungarian counties, where most of the newly dispossessed gentry resided, was expanded by 31.4 percent; in the predominantly Hungarian towns, by 29.6 percent. At the same time in the Romanian-populated areas, the number of county officials declined by 6.7 percent; in the cities, by 13.6 percent. Ferenc Pölöskei, "Nacionalizmus a dualizmus korában" [Nationalism during the Dualist Era] *A Magyar nacionalizmus*, p. 170.

12. Péter Hanák, *Magyarország a Monarchiában. Tanulmányok* [Hungary in the Monarchy. Studies] (Budapest, 1975), p. 366. See also Iván Berend and György Ránki, *A magyar gazdaság száz éve* [Hundred Years of Hungarian Economy] (Budapest, 1972), p. 86.

13. Ottó Szabolcs, *A köztisztviselők az ellenforradalmi rendszer társadalmi bázisában, 1920–1926* [Public Officials in the Social Base of the Counterrevolutionary Regime, 1920–1926] (Budapest, 1965), n. 1, p. 150.

14. Eugene N. Anderson, *Political Institutions and Social Change in Continental Europe in the Nineteenth Century* (Berkeley, 1967), p. 183.

15. This is not to argue that the Hungarian bureaucracy was free of corruption. Misappropriations and embezzlements or careless "borrowings" from state funds were not infrequent, although they were generally hushed up. But bribery was not part of conducting routine government business and corruption was rarely systematic.

16. Gyula Kádár, *A Ludovikától Sopronkőhidáig* [From the Ludovika to Sopronkőhida] (Budapest, 1978), pp. 31–32. Also, Balázs, *A középrétegek szerepe*, p. 86.

17. Gyula Szekfű, *Három nemzedék és ami utána következik* [Three Generations and What Follows] (Budapest, 1934), p. 313.

18. For a more detailed analysis of the decline of the gentry middle class, see Hanák, *Magyarország a Monarchiában*, pp. 359–68; Endre Kovács, ed., *Magyarország története* [History of Hungary] (Budapest, 1979) VI: 1270–71 and Hanák, *Magyarország története* VII: 458–63.

19. Ibid., p. 165. The idea of an "empire of thirty million Hungarians" originated with Jenő Rákosi, who, along with Béla Grünwald, Pál Hoitsy and Gusztáv Beksics, publicized extreme-nationalist theories.

20. See, for example, Beksics's *Magyarosodás és magyarosítás*. A lower death rate among the Hungarians was also held to be responsible for the increase of the proportion of the Hungarian population, but it was more than offset by the declining birth rate, which alarmed many nationalists. See, for example, The Hungarian Eugenic Society, *The Consequences of the Division of Hungary from the Standpoint of Eugenics*, reprint from *Nemzetvédelem* I, no. 4 (1919): 1–2.

21. Bethlen, *Bethlen István* I: 52.

22. Tihany, *A Baranya Dispute*, p. 19.

23. Hungarian Eugenic Society, *The Consequences of the Division of Hungary*, pp. 3–5.

Chapter 6

1. Hajdu, *Az őszirózsás forradalom*, p. 186.

2. Károlyi, *Faith Without Illusion*, p. 127. See also, Böhm, *Két forradalom*, pp. 148–49, 193–94; Mrs. Mihály Károlyi, *Együtt a forradalomban* [Together in the Revolution] (Budapest, 1978), p. 432.

3. Of the returning prisoners of war to Hungary 94,000 were Romanians, 80,000 Croatians, 44,000 Slovaks, and 4000 Serbs. Antal Józsa, *Háború, hadifogság, forradalom: Magyar internacionalista hadifoglyok az 1917-es oroszországi forradalmakban* [War, Prisoners of War Experience, Revolution: Hungarian Internationalist Prisoners of War in the 1917 Russian Revolutions] (Budapest, 1970), pp. 101–103.

4. Breit, *A magyarországi 1918/19 évi forradalmi mozgalmak* I: 37. Ervin Liptai, *Vöröskatonák előre! A magyar Vörös Hadsereg harcai, 1919* [Forward, Red Soldiers! The Wars of the Hungarian Red Army, 1919] (Budapest, 1969), p. 12. Mrs. Rudolf Dósa, *A MOVE: egy jellegzetes magyar fasiszta szervezet, 1918–1944* [The MOVE: A Typical Hungarian Fascist Organization, 1918–1944] (Budapest, 1972), p. 34.

5. Hajdu, *Károlyi Mihály*, pp. 314–15.

6. Károlyi, *Faith Without Illusion*, pp. 126–27.

7. Jászi, *Revolution*, p. 43.

8. Rudolf Tőkés, *Béla Kun and the Hungarian Soviet Republic* (New York, 1967), p. 106, no. 23. Count Tivadar Battyány, minister of interior in Károlyi's first government, related an incident from the middle of November 1918. A village gendarme personally had to call the minister of interior for instructions, because no one remained in the entire law enforcement chain of command who could give him orders. Battyány, *Beszámolóm* I: 297–98.

9. Jászi, *Revolution*, p. 45. In his memoirs, Battyány detailed government efforts to expand the state police, *gendarmerie,* and border police, but, in spite of allocation of substantial funds, recruitment proceeded slowly. Battyány, *Beszámolóm* I: 295, 313. See also Ervin Liptai, *Vöröskatonák,* pp. 14–16. On the other hand, Gyula Kádár, who was a young recruiting officer at the time, argued that volunteers were many, but lack of funds doomed the effort. Kádár also asserted that the key mistake was rapid demobilization of the army; in early November, he argued, soldiers in many of the returning units still obeyed their officers. Kádár, *A Ludovikától Sopronkőhidáig,* pp. 68–75.

10. See for example Károlyi's appeal to President Wilson on November 16 and 25, 1918. *FRUS PPC* II: 191–92.

11. Originally, this plan was developed as a proposal for the postwar reorganization of the Habsburg monarchy. Although it seemed realistic and even generous at the time it was drafted, the situation had changed drastically by the time those who made these proposals came to power. Oscar Jászi, *Der Zusammenbruch des Dualismus und die Zukunft des Donaustaaten* (Vienna, 1918); Oscar Jászi, *A nemzeti államok kialakulása és a nemzetiségi kérdés* [Development of Nation-States and the Nationality Question] (Budapest, 1912); Béla K. Király, "The Danubian Problem in Oscar Jászi's Political Thought," *Hungarian Quarterly* V, no. 1–2 (1965): 120–34.

12. Jászi, *Revolution,* p. 37. Scholars generally agree that Károlyi clung to an illusion about Wilson. As one author put it: "he believed that the aim of Wilsonian democratic pacifism, which he held to be the dominant principle of the Western Allies, was a just peace, freely negotiated, without territorial expansion and war indemnity." Hajdu, *Károlyi Mihály,* p. 254; see also, Pastor, *Hungary between Wilson and Lenin,* p. 90.

13. *FRUS PPC* II: 204–205; see also Hajdu, *Károlyi Mihály,* p. 306.

14. *FRUS PPC* XII: 413–16. Also, Tibor Hetés, ed., *A magyarországi forradalmak krónikája, 1918–1919* [Chronicles of the Revolutions in Hungary, 1918–1919] (Budapest, 1969), pp. 143–45. For the origins and history of the controversial "Vix note" see Pastor, *Hungary between Wilson and Lenin,* pp. 130–39.

15. Károlyi, *Faith without Illusions,* p. 158.

16. Many of these individuals had never appeared in the official statistics as refugees, even though they may have considered themselves such. Thus OMH figures must be considered only as minimal. See Kovácsics, *Magyarországi történeti demográfiája,* p. 240. See also, *OMH Report,* p. 37.

17. By September 1920, the number of individuals who resided in freight cars had risen to 16,500. In subsequent months their numbers had declined, but then, once again, began to climb to 16,000 by September 1921. Even in 1923 between three and four thousand individuals lived under such conditions. *OMH Report,* p. 37.

18. Battyány, *Beszámolóm* II: 261–63.

19. Lábay, *Az ellenforradalom,* p. 99.

20. Dósa, *A MOVE,* pp. 32, 35.

21. László Deme and József Keleti, *Az ellenforradalom Vasvármegyében*

és Szombathelyen [The Counterrevolution in Vas County and at Szombathely] (Szombathely, 1920), p. 12. Also, Gyula Gömbös, *Egy magyar vezérkari tiszt bíráló feljegyzései a forradalomról és az ellenforradalomról* [A Hungarian Staff Officer's Critical Comments on the Revolution and Counterrevolution] (Budapest, 1920), p. 29.

22. Ibid. These plans were carried forward in spite of the fact that MOVE was outlawed. Ibid., pp. 30–31. Also, Deme and Keleti, *Az ellenforradalom Vasvármegyében*, pp. 11, 18; Dósa, *A MOVE*, p. 41.

23. Dósa, *A MOVE*, p. 47.

24. Ágnes Szabó and Ervin Pamlényi, eds., *A határban a Halál kaszál . . . : Fejezetek Prónay Pál feljegyzéseiből* [Death Reaps in the Countryside . . . : Chapters from the Journals of Pál Prónay] (Budapest, 1963), pp. 58–59.

25. Tőkés, *Béla Kun*, p. 107.

26. There is little doubt that Communist nationalist propaganda was greatly responsible for their successes. In fact, it seems that Béla Kun's nationalist rhetoric was viewed in the Soviet Union with some misgivings. At the same time, for a brief period, this nationalist policy assured broad support for the Communist regime. See March 26, 1919 letter from "Taylor in Belgrade to H. C. Hoover" American Relief Administration (henceforth cited as ARA) — Paris —H73, Hoover Institution, Stanford University. In another letter Taylor wrote: "The Hungarian situation assumes each day more the appearance of a well-organized communistic *coup d'etat,* but still with nationalistic character." And, commenting on the ultimatum of Colonel Vix to Károlyi, he wrote: "Those of us who have been in this country are convinced that an error was made in announcing the decision on Hungarian boundaries in advance of announcement of other disputed boundaries and in advance of the presence of the delegates from the defeated countries in Paris." March 29, 1919, Taylor from Trieste to H. C. Hoover in Paris, ARA — Paris — H73.

27. The willingness of the refugee peasants to serve in the Red Army is illustrated by the case of the refugees from Arad. On March 22, the day after the declaration of the Hungarian Soviet Republic, the French commander of Arad, General Henri Gondrecourt, ordered the expulsion of the local Hungarian military units, who were suspected of leftist sympathies. Those troops were accompanied by some 14,000 inhabitants of the city — workers, leftist intellectuals, and even a large number of peasants, who often fled with their families. Within days, most of those peasants were organized into the Red Army, and served with distinction against the Romanians. *ASzET,* pp. 216–17.

28. Tibor Szamuely, *Összegyűjtött írások és beszédek* [Collected Writings and Speeches] (András Simor and Pál Máthé, eds.) (Budapest, 1975), p. 603.

29. Ottó Korvin, *". . . a Gondolat él . . ."* [". . . The Thought Lives . . ."] (András Simor and János Márton, eds.) (Budapest, 1976), p. 152.

30. A good example of this is the makeup of the 19-men group led by István Friedrich and András Csilléry. Among them, there were seven officers, three lawyers, three police officials, two officers in the merchant marine, one dentist,

an engineer, a professor, and a state official. Six out of the nineteen were assimilated Germans. Lábay, *Az ellenforradalom,* p. 176.

31. It was headed by General István Sréter and the brother of Admiral Horthy, István Horthy. See Zsuzsa L. Nagy, *Forradalom és ellenforradalom a Dunántúlon, 1919* [Revolution and Counterrevolution in Transdanubia, 1919] (Budapest, 1961), p. 84.

32. Deme and Keleti, *Az ellenforradalom Vasvármegyében,* p. 74; cf. L. Nagy, *Forradalom,* pp. 135–36.

33. Dezső Sulyok, *A magyar tragédia* [Hungarian Tragedy] (Newark, N.J., 1954), pp. 237–42. According to the chief prosecutor of the Horthy regime, during the Soviet Republic, 238 proven cases of executions or murders took place. Györgyi Markovits, ed., *Magyar pokol. A magyarországi fehérterror betiltott és üldözött kiadványok tükrében* [Hungarian Hell. The Hungarian White Terror Mirrored in Forbidden and Persecuted Publications] (Budapest, 1964), p. 28. The total number of victims was put around five to six hundred. Vilmos Böhm, however, argues that the 587 claimed victims included everyone who died a violent death during the Hungarian Soviet Republic. It included all those who died with weapons in their hands, resisting the state. Böhm, *Két forradalom,* pp. 398–99.

34. Among the nearly dozen different right-wing groups that promised to support the planned uprising, the heaviest concentration of refugees was in the Hungarian Christian Cultural League, originally a Transylvanian refugee organization, and in the Hun Alliance.

35. Hetés, *A magyarországi forradalmak,* pp. 309–13. Cf. Tőkés, *Béla Kun,* p. 193, Böhm, *Két forradalom,* p. 371.

36. Originally, the date of the insurrection was fixed for June 12, by Count István Bethlen, who, although already in Vienna, was still the recognized leader of the planned coup. But forty-seven of the conspirators were arrested a few days earlier; this contributed to the ultimate failure of the June 24 *coup d'état.* Lábay, *Az ellenforradalom,* pp. 101–107. Also, Hetés, *A magyarországi forradalmak,* p. 311.

37. Kálmán Benkő, *Az 1919. évi juniús hó 24-iki tengerészeti forradalom* [The Sailors' Revolution of June 24, 1919] (Budapest, 1920), pp. 20–56. Cf. L. Nagy, *Forradalom,* pp. 165–67; Böhm, *Két forradalom,* pp. 371–73; Lábay, *Az ellenforradalom,* pp. 66–68.

Chapter 7

1. *ASzET,* p. 253.

2. Szinai, *Horthy Miklós titkos iratai,* p. 14, n. 3. Cf. Hefty, *Adatok,* p. 37.

3. Gömbös, *Egy magyar vezérkari tiszt,* pp. 40–41.

4. Szabó and Pamlényi, *Fejezetek,* p. 63.

5. *ASzET,* pp. 71, 120, 134.

6. Gusztáv Gratz, *A forradalmak kora: Magyarország története, 1918–1920* [The Age of the Revolutions: History of Hungary, 1918–1920] (Budapest, 1935), pp. 189–90, 195.

7. Ibid., p. 196. Count Pál Teleki had similar conversations with some American representatives. He reiterated to them the ABC's willingness to participate in a liberal coalition government-in-exile. See "Letter to Captain Gregory in Trieste from E Caskie, U.S. Food Commission, Vienna," 3 May 1919. MS, ARA-Paris, H 73, folio No. 2.

8. Lábay, *Az ellenforradalom*, p. 151.

9. Eva S. Balogh, "The Hungarian Social Democratic Centre and the Fall of Béla Kun" *Canadian Slavonic Papers* 18 (March 1976): 15–35.

10. Miklós Kozma, *Az összeomlás, 1918–1919* [The Collapse, 1918–1919] (Budapest, 1935), p. 207.

11. See Gratz, *A forradalmak kora*, p. 194. Deme and Keleti, *Az ellenforradalom Vasvármegyében*, p. 69.

12. For details of the *Bankgasse* affair, see, Hefty, *Adatok*, pp. 42–43; László Koncsek, *A rengassei összeesküvés* [The Conspiracy of Rengasse] (Budapest, 1959), pp. 78–86; *IET* I: 392–94. Not all the money, however, was used for the cause; some members of the ABC who had access to this money, especially members of the Szmrecsányi group, were later accused of squandering great sums on their own pleasures. Repeated parliamentary inquiries during the 1920s failed to uncover the truth about the disposal of these funds. Szmrecsányi and his followers, of course, denied any impropriety, and cleared their honor by fighting several duels with their accusers.

13. Hefty, *Adatok*, pp. 46–53; Gratz, *A forradalmak kora*, p. 199; Koncsek, *A rengassei összeesküvés*, pp. 142–48. What this group lacked in numbers they perhaps made up in prestige. Ten out of the 44 members were young aristocrats, among them three Count Zichys, Counts István Csáky, and József Pálffy-Duan, and Margrave György Pallavicini. Some participants in this affair, officers, such as the sadistic Count Hermann Salm, subsequently reemerged as members of the Prónay detachment.

14. Kővágó, *A magyarországi délszlávok*, p. 229, n. 170.

15. Ibid., p. 229. For a slightly different point of view see L. Nagy, *Forradalom*, p. 132.

16. In addition, Brodmann and Stürgkh delivered about 300 guns and 50 men. Kővágó, *A magyarországi délszlávok*, p. 233; see also, pp. 230–31.

17. Anton Lehár, *Erinnerungen. Gegenrevolution und Restaurationsversuche in Ungarn, 1918–1921* (Vienna, 1973), pp. 83–86.

18. Dósa, *A MOVE*, p. 65.

19. *ASzET*, p. 37.

20. Ibid., pp. 45–46; Lábay, *Az ellenforradalom*, p. 148.

21. During the interwar years, right-wing authors tried to minimize the role of these Jewish officers in ousting the Communists from Szeged. According to some liberal sources, two out of the five leaders of that countercoup, and 33 out of the 72 participants were Jewish. See *Egyenlőség évkönyve és naptára, 1921* [The Yearbook and Calendar of Equality, 1921] (Szeged, 1921), pp. 127–28 in *ASzET*, p. 118. Cf. Jób Paál, *A száz napos szegedi kormány* [The Hundred-Day Government of Szeged] (Budapest, 1919), pp. 28–32.

22. Koréh, *A székely hadosztály* II: 84.

23. *MPL*, pp. 398–99; *ASzET*, pp. 347–48. About 600 ultimately joined Horthy's National Army. Ibid., p. 348.

24. Gömbös, *Egy magyar vezérkari tiszt*, p. 44; Szabó and Pamlényi, *Fejezetek*, pp. 63–65; *ASzET*, p. 368.

25. Prónay, *Fejezetek*, p. 74.

26. According to the 1920 census figures, the population of Szeged was 118,000. Of these, 16,000 were born in the lost territories: about eight thousand in Yugoslavia, six thousand in Romania, and fewer than two thousand in Czechoslovakia. Központi Statisztikai Hivatal, *Az 1920 évi népszámlálás*, new series, 73 (Budapest, 1928), pp. 8–9. A comparison with the 1910 census figures seems to indicate that roughly six thousand of these settled in Szeged before 1910, mostly from the territories subsequently awarded to Yugoslavia; it shows that about 10,000 were refugees. In addition, however, an estimated three to four thousand refugees from the Successor States and 12–15,000 refugees from the Communist-held territories left Szeged at the time or soon after the departure of the National Army; thus, they were not included in the 1920 census figures. Szilveszter Somogyi, the mayor of Szeged, in 1919, estimated that the population of Szeged, including all the refugees, was around 150,000; an indication of a refugee population of around 35–40,000. *ASzET*, p. 303.

27. Ibid., pp. 348, 498.

28. *Délmagyarország* [South Hungary] (Szeged), June 26, 1919, abstracted in *ASzET*, p. 305. Prónay, one of the chief instigators of these street attacks, regretted only that his plans of revenge became prematurely known. He wrote: "It proved to be a great error on our part, that is on the part of the counterrevolutionaries, to trumpet our intentions of revenge so loudly and so openly. We were still too weak, we did not even organize, and already we emphasized our intention of revenge when we came to power. There is an old folk saying: 'You cannot catch a sparrow with drums,'" Szabó and Pamlényi, *Fejezetek*, p. 75.

29. *Szegedi Napló* [Journal of Szeged], July 11, 1919, abstracted in *ASzET*, p. 355. This paper argued that the refugees should depart, partly because of food shortages, but, more important, because far too many were undesirables. Its outburst was the sharpest against what the paper called the "piratic opportunism" of the refugee politicians, against those "well dressed gentlemen, who, armed with their noble patronymics," sought only to advance their own careers. *Szegedi Napló*, June 29, 1919, in *ASzET*, p. 312; also, pp. 237, 355.

30. The first anti-Communist group was formed by the liberals under the leadership of Lajos Varjassy and Lajos Pálmai. This group established contacts with the French, who suggested the formation of a countergovernment. Paál, *A száz napos szegedi kormány*, pp. 12–15. Cf. Albert Kaas and Fedor de Lazarovics, *Bolshevism in Hungary. The Béla Kun Period* (London, 1931), p. 278. Count Gyula Károlyi, a local magnate, was a moderate conservative politician — a rather modest and retiring man, who assumed the post reluctantly. The Arad liberals' first candidate was Gábor Ugron, a moderate Transylvanian politician, who was rumored to be already marching against Budapest at the head of the Székely Division. The second choice was Lajos Návay, the former president of the Lower House, who was, however, captured

as he traveled to Arad and executed by a Communist terror group. Károlyi's name came up only as an afterthought. Paál, *A száz napos szegedi kormány*, p. 19.

31. *ASzET*, pp. 257, 302, 334, 346.

32. See a confidential memorandum of the National Army, July 1919, in Tibor Hetés and Mrs. Tamás Morva, eds., *Csak szolgálati használatra! Iratok a Horthy-hadsereg történetéhez, 1919–1938* [For Service Use Only! Documents to the History of the Horthy army, 1919–1938] (Budapest, 1968), pp. 62–63. Henceforth cited as *IHHT*.

33. *ASzET*, p. 220. Also, Kaas and Lazarovics, *Bolshevism in Hungary*, p. 278.

34. The British and the Italians were promised by both the right-wing groups and by the Social Democrats to form a pro-British and pro-Italian government if their faction was helped to power. Dezső Nemes, *Az ellenforradalom története Magyarországon, 1919–1921* [History of the Counterrevolution in Hungary, 1919–1921] (Budapest, 1962), pp. 16–18. Colonel Cuninghame, head of the British mission in Vienna, maintained regular contacts with both the ABC and the moderate Socialists. He indicated that both a pro-British monarchist or a pro-British Socialist government would have been acceptable to his government. The United States also supported the idea of an all-Socialist government. Herbert Hoover's aide in Vienna, Captain Thomas Gregory, held several discussions to this effect with some of the moderate Social Democratic leaders. The Italian government even toyed with the idea of maintaining the Communists in power and supplied some arms to the Red Army. Herbert C. Hoover, *An American Epic. Famine in Forty-five Nations. The Battle on the Front Line, 1914–1923* (Chicago, 1961) II: 126.

35. For the various Serbian-Hungarian contacts see *ASzET*, pp. 286–87, 371, 394, 430, 487; *IHHT*, pp. 63, 69–73. See also Nicholas Horthy, *Memoirs* (London, 1956), p. 101; Paál, *A száz napos szegedi kormány*, pp. 56–57.

36. *ASzET*, p. 482; *IHHT*, pp. 65–66.

37. *ASzET*, pp. 145, 148, 160, 162, 207. Such a *union sacrée* was already formed in Arad even before the establishment of the Károlyi government; yet, in Szeged, where the liberal and extreme right split was much more intense, it was difficult to achieve cooperation. Paál, *A száz napos szegedi kormány*, p. 18.

38. *ASzET*, pp. 119–20, 134, 160.

39. For the text of the proclamation, see, ibid., pp. 207–208. Also in Kaas and Lazarevics, *Bolshevism in Hungary*, Appendix, nos. 24 and 26, pp. 399–401.

40. Szabó and Pamlényi, *Fejezetek*, p. 90; *ASzET*, pp. 209–210.

41. "A Solemn Memorandum of the Jewish citizens of Szeged," (in Hungarian) June 23, 1919, ibid., pp. 299–300.

42. Ibid., p. 362. Also, Kaas, *Bolshevism in Hungary*, p. 285.

43. Letter from the Székely National Council to Károlyi, see *ASzET*, p. 575. See also, pp. 574–75, 211.

44. Minutes of the Ministerial Council, June 13, 1919, ibid., p. 269; see also, p. 270.

45. Ibid., p. 243.

46. Hefty, *Adatok*, pp. 82–84.

47. Minutes of the Ministerial Council, June 29, 1919, *ASzET*, pp. 314–17; Minutes of the Ministerial Council, July 12, 1919, ibid., p. 356. For repeated French demands of changes in the composition of the government see ibid., pp. 257, 300, 327, 334, 346. See also Gömbös, *Egy magyar vezérkari tiszt*, p. 58; *ASzET*, pp. 398–99.

48. *IET* I: 120.

49. Ibid., p. 122; also *AszET*, p. 472.

50. Gömbös, *Egy magyar vezérkari tiszt*, p. 52.

51. Naively, some of the refugees assumed that once the standards of counter-revolution were raised the majority of the people, and especially the peasantry, would rally around the flag. See letter of American chargé d'affaires Dodge to Paris, April 11, 1919. ARA — Paris — H73, folio no. 2.

52. *ASzET*, p. 145.

53. Among the confiscated arms in question there were 6512 German, Austrian, and even Mexican rifles and carbines, 52 machine guns of similar variety, and 29 artillery pieces. From this, on August 8, 1919, the National Army finally received 5428 rifles, all the machine guns, and 9 artillery pieces. Ibid., p. 451.

54. From the approximately 24-million crowns collected, excluding Teleki's three million, the ministries of interior and defense spent together 21.5-million crowns. Ibid., p. 504.

55. Ibid., pp. 590–92. Cf. *IHHT*, pp. 57–61.

56. According to a contemporary police report, the workers of Szeged threatened to desert and join the Red Army if they were drafted into the National Army. *IHHT*, p. 61.

57. György Borsányi, ed., *Páter Zadravecz titkos naplója* [Secret Diary of Father Zadravecz] (Budapest, 1967), pp. 238–39.

58. *ASzET*, pp. 492–493.

59. Some estimates of the number of officers in Szeged go as high as 3500, but this figure may be an exaggeration. Lábay, *Az ellenforradalom*, p. 158. Cf. Kozma, *Az összeomlás*, p. 301.

60. *ASzET*, pp. 592–93.

61. Ibid., pp. 495–96. Szabó and Pamlényi, *Fejezetek*, p. 70. In the Ostenburg detachment, the old "k. und k. spirit," the spirit of the joint army, and the German element were stronger than in the Prónay company. A large contingent of officers in the Ostenburg detachment were refugee Transylvanian Saxons. Ibid., p. 166.

62. For a complete list of the names of the original Prónay detachment at Szeged see *ASzET*, p. 495. Hefty argues that even a higher percentage, about three-fourth came from the ranks of the gentry. Hefty, *Adatok*, p. 77. Cf. Szabó and Pamlényi, *Fejezetek*, p. 30.

63. Ibid., p. 91.

64. British Joint Labour Delegation to Hungary, *The White Terror in Hungary* (London, 1920), p. 11.

65. *ASzET*, pp. 523–24.

66. Koréh, *A székely hadosztály* II: 183–84. Also, *IHHT*, p. 75.

67. Lehár, *Erinnerungen*, pp. 93, 118.

68. For instructions of the National Army concerning the necessity of cooperation with the Romanians, see, *IHHT*, pp. 77–78.

69. Kozma, *Az összeomlás*, p. 380.

Chapter 8

1. According to some estimates, over 100,000 individuals fled from Hungary
after the victory of the right. Böhm, *Két forradalom*, p. 478. A more recent
estimate put the number of those new refugees at 140,000. Ágnes Godó, "A
Horthy-rendszer kalandor háborús tervei, 1919–1921" [The Planned Military
Adventures of the Horthy Regime, 1919–1921] *Hadtörténeti közlemények*
[Bulletins of Military History] VIII, no. 1 (1961): 140.

2. *IET* I 110–15.

3. Nemes, *Az ellenforradalom története*, p. 32.

4. Balogh, "The Hungarian Social Democratic Centre," pp. 28–35.

5. For a discussion of Romanian and Allied roles in the overthrow of the Peidl
government, see Eva S. Balogh, "Romanian and Allied Involvement in the
Hungarian Coup d'État of 1919," *East European Quarterly* IX, no. 3 (1975):
299–307.

6. *IET* I: 125.

7. Ibid., pp. 182–83, 211–12.

8. On August 22, 1919, the Zionist Organization of Hungary made a special
appeal to Friedrich in which they gratefully remembered his past efforts to help
the Jews, including his attempt at organizing the Zionist Guards immediately
after the October Revolution, and offered to use the considerable financial
resources of the Jewish community to support his government. That is, the
Jewish upper bourgeoisie lined up behind Friedrich. Ibid., pp. 123–24.

9. *IHHT*, pp. 84–85; Ladányi, *Az egyetemi ifjúság*, p. 25.

10. Ibid., pp. 81–82.

11. *IET* I: 122.

12. This party was first established in February 1919 by the Bethlen faction, but
it remained dormant during the time of the Hungarian Soviet Republic. In the
original party, the Transylvanian group was dominant; in the one established in
September 1919, that group no longer occupied a central position.

13. Horthy retained this admiration of the emperor to the end of his life. As he
wrote in his memoirs: "His Majesty had been my great teacher, to whom I knew
that I owed much. How often had I not, in performing my task as Regent, asked
myself, 'What would His Majesty Francis Joseph have done in a case like this?'
Even after his death, I continued to trust in his wisdom, and I have never
regretted that I retained so many of his arrangements, tested by centuries of use,
in dealing with Hungarian problems." Horthy, *Memoirs*, pp. 152–53.

14. See, for example, *IHHT*, pp. 14–16.

15. From Kaposvár, for example, Prónay was forced to withdraw under
pressure of the local authorities and the local nobility, who were opposed to the
terror he was instigating. Szabó and Pamlényi, *Fejezetek*, p. 125.

16. Nemes, *Az ellenforradalom története*, p. 121. The expansion of the army

continued even after November 1919, when Horthy marched into Budapest. By mid-1920 it stood around 80–90,000 men. Ibid., p. 388. For the merger of Horthy's and Lehár's forces, see *IHHT*, p. 91.

17. The report explains that except for the Székelys, most men joined the gendarmerie not from conviction, but because service was the only available livelihood for these people. Ibid., pp. 149–50.

18. *IET* I: 187–88.

19. Ibid., p. 188, n. 1. Similarly, the officers' detachments had to be also renamed. *IHHT*, pp. 106–108.

20. All draftees had to be classified according to their political reliability. *IET* I: 191. See also *IHHT*, pp. 101, 131–32.

21. *IET* I: 183–84.

22. *IHHT*, p. 14.

23. *IET* I: 194–95.

24. The most important of these were: cutting wages roughly in half; *IET* I: 129, 138; elimination of unemployment compensation in view of severe large-scale unemployment, (ibid., p. 128); and dismissal of dangerous workers. Some officers wished to minimize the political danger presented by the mass unemployment by drafting workers into the army; by using them as forced laborers on reconstruction projects, or as supplementary farm workers on the large estates. Ibid., pp. 23, 135. Tibor Eckhardt, a close associate of Horthy believed that this would be advantageous because the drafted workers "if not in name, but in fact would be interned and the problem of their political supervision would be easily solved." Ibid., p. 147.

25. For examples of this special relation see *IHHT*, pp. 151, 166.

26. Szabó and Pamlényi, *Fejezetek,* p. 103. These claims of Prónay are confirmed by the official instruction issued to the First Division by General Károly Soós on August 7, 1919. *IHHT*, pp. 80–81.

27. Edgar von Schmidt-Pauli, *Nikolaus von Horthy* (Hamburg, 1942), p. 160, quoted in Horthy, *Memoirs,* p. 106.

28. *IET* I: 155.

29. Ibid., p. 107.

30. Szabó and Pamlényi, *Fejezetek,* p. 113.

31. György Száraz, *Egy előítélet nyomában* [Tracing a Prejudice] (Budapest, 1976), p. 212.

32. *FRUS PPC* XII: 695. The British military observers similarly denied the White Terror's existence. See report of Admiral Ernest Troubridge in [British Foreign Office] *Report on the Alleged Existence of "White Terror" in Hungary* (London, 1920), pp. 3–5. A similar report was also sent by General Reginald Gorton to his military superiors. Ibid.

33. *FRUS PPC* XII: 695. Cf. *IET* I: 162.

34. Lehár, *Erinnerungen,* pp. 99–100. See also, Kádár, *A Ludovikától Sopronkőhidáig,* pp. 121, 124.

35. *FRUS PPC* XII: 708.

36. A reference to the practice of throwing bodies of murdered victims into the Danube. *IET* I: 167. See also Markovits, *Magyar pokol,* pp. 95–96.

37. Both the government and the military tried to convince Sir George Clerk that the Social Democratic Party and the liberals were most unpopular in the country, that they had no political base outside of Budapest. To underline their arguments, they instructed the provincial authorities, county officials, military commanders, to send delegations of respectable citizens as well as letters and telegrams with similar messages. *IET* I: 208–10.

Chapter 9

1. *IET* I: 230. This police report described the mood and expectations of the workers. The revolutionary mood among the workers aroused some anxiety, especially since an estimated 100,000 weapons were hidden by the workers for the time of a second revolution.

2. *FRUS PPC* XII: 724.

3. *IET* I: 215–16.

4. The Friedrich electoral law of 1919 gave the franchise to 74.6 percent of the population above age 24, the minimum age. All prewar parliaments were elected according to the 1874 law, which gave the vote to only 15.5 percent of the population of inner Hungary. In 1922, Bethlen reduced the size of the electorate to 58.4 percent. Rezső Rudai, "Adalékok a magyar képviselőház szociológiájához" [Data to the Sociology of the Hungarian Parliament], *Társadalomtudomány* [Social Science] XIII, no. 3–4 (July–December 1933): 220. See also, Antal Balla, ed., *A magyar országgyűlés története, 1867–1927* [History of the Hungarian Parliament, 1867–1927] (Budapest, 1927), p. 464.

5. Ránki, *Magyarország története* VIII: 345. Also, Pölöskei, *Horthy,* pp. 35–36.

6. The perpetrators's names also became known; some were even taken into custody, though not the leaders of the group. Héjjas with some of his key men were given sanctuary by Prónay, whose detachment they were allowed to join. All criminal procedures against the accused were subsequently halted under considerable pressure from Horthy. Eventually the suspects came under the general amnesty decreed by Horthy for all politically inspired crimes committed by the right. *IET* I: 228. See also pp. 221–28.

7. Ibid., pp. 231–32, 168–69. A similar though less extensive spy system was already organized by the government. See also pp. 143–44.

8. Gratz, *A forradalmak kora,* p. 261. For details of some of these see Markovits, *Magyar pokol,* pp. 193–243.

9. In one institution alone, which under normal circumstances housed about 1000 prisoners, by mid-December, about 2500 inmates were kept. *IET* I: 142–43.

10. For a description of conditions and maltreatment of the prisoners by the army at the Hajmáskér concentration camp, see British Labour Delegation, *The White Terror,* p. 8. Cf. Markovits, *Magyar pokol,* pp. 75–77. According to one estimate by Count Albert Apponyi, a strong opponent of White Terror, the inmate population at the various camps was as follows: Hajmáskér 9000,

Csepel 4000, Zalaegerszeg 2400, Eger 2000, Cegléd 3000, Komáromho-
mokhegy 2000. Pölöskei, *Horthy*, p. 72. Also *IET* I: 169.
11. Nemes, *Az ellenforradalom története*, pp. 216–17. The actual figures
may be higher. Another source puts their number well above 70,000. Elek
Karsai, *Számjeltávirat valamennyi magyar királyi követségnek* [Cypher
Telegram to All Hungarian Embassies] (Budapest, 1969), p. 14. Ágnes
Godó put the number of the imprisoned at 40,000; the number of refugees
who fled abroad at 140,000. Godó, "A Horthy-rendszer," p. 140.
12. *IET* I: 239–41.
13. Ibid., p. 231.
14. For details of that smear campaign and political trial see Sándor Hege-
dűs, *Egy politikai per kulisszatitkai* [Backstage Secrets of a Political Trial]
(Budapest, 1976); see also Szabó and Pemlényi, *Fejezetek*, pp. 211–14.
15. The symbolism of these names needs some explanation. Etelköz is the
Hungarian name of the place where the semilegendary blood alliance was
formed between the seven Hungarian tribes before their entry into the Carpathian basin. There, Árpád was to have been raised on a shield by the
seven chieftains, symbolizing his election as chief of chiefs. The apostolic cross
refers to the archiepiscopal cross of St. Stephen in Hungary's coat of arms. In
as much as the coat of arms, just as the Holy Crown of St. Stephen, symbolized the indivisibility of the crown-lands of Hungary, the name of the organization indicated the commitment of the members to the restoration of the
ancient unity of the lands of the Holy Crown. The "Resurrection" refers
similarly to this goal.
16. The other members were Miklós Kozma, László Magasházy, the two
Görgey brothers, Kálmán Hardy, Miklós Koós, Gyula Toókos, Béla
Márton, Antal Vetter, Lajos Keresztes-Fisher, and Géza Igmándy-
Hegyessy. Nemes, *Az ellenforradalom története*, p. 153. Their proximity to
Horthy assured, for all, excellent careers, during subsequent years. Gömbös
ultimately became prime minister, Kozma his minister of interior, others rose
to high positions within the army.
17. Borsányi, *Páter Zadravecz*, p. 133.
18. *Magyar Tudományos Fajvédő Egyesület.*
19. Even today, little is known about the operations of these societies.
Information about them must be extracted from such journals and notes as
those of Zadravecz and Prónay, who broke their oaths of silence after they
fell out with the EKSz and freely discussed its affairs. Their opinions, laced
with malice, cannot be taken at face value.
20. Borsányi, *Páter Zadravecz*, p. 129.
21. Ibid., pp. 130, 131, 134. At the same time, Zadravecz contradicted himself
when he maintained that Gömbös "for a long time terrorized Horthy and
Bethlen by warning that the Ex represented a great and frightfully powerful
force, which was completely in his hands. For this reason Bethlen frequently
conferred with Gömbös, and even authorized the use of state funds, but at
the same time worked for the . . . weakening of the Ex." Ibid., p. 141.
22. Ibid. The exact number of EKSz members in the First National Assembly,

elected in 1920, is not known, but it is safe to assume that their strength was considerable.

23. *IHHT*, p. 190. Cf. Godó, "A Horthy-rendszer," pp. 127–38.

24. *IHHT*, pp. 208–12. A small Slovak force was indeed established in Poland, but the movement soon collapsed.

25. *FRUS PPC* XII: 694, 700–701, 680–81. *HPN* II: pp. 504–505.

26. *IET* I: 268–69.

27. Ibid., pp. 270–71.

28. *OMH Report*, p. 37.

29. This estimate is based on 1920 census figures. The census does not distinguish between old and new residents of the city, merely records place of birth. Központi Statisztikai Hivatal, *Recensement de la population en 1920*, new series, (Budapest, 1928) 73: 8.

30. *IHHT*, p. 135. Subsequently, as Gömbös and Horthy drifted apart, all active officers were forced to resign from the MOVE. Ibid., p. 137. Cf. Dósa, *A MOVE*, pp. 87, 118–19.

31. Ibid., pp. 105, 149.

32. Every officer had to surrender 1/30th of his salary to the MOVE for the purposes of economic aid to destitute officers. In addition, Gömbös was given large sums of money by the government for aid and other refugee-related expenses. For alleged mishandling of these funds Gömbös was attacked several times on the floor of the National Assembly by legitimist politicians. *Nemzetgyűlési Napló, 1920–1921* IV: 507–22; V: 95–102. The charge, however, was never proven.

33. Dósa, *A MOVE*, p. 89.

34. Of the 29 leading figures of the Awakening Hungarians about whom we were able to collect sufficient biographical data, 14 were born in the lost territories, or resided there in 1918. Ten came from Transylvania, the rest from other areas.

35. *MPL*, pp. 65, 96–97, 227, 238, 244. Vilmos Prőhle and Tibor Eckhardt were born in inner Hungary, but, at the time of collapse, they were officials in Transylvania.

36. For a history of one of the main institutions for the militarization of youth, the "Levente" organization, see Ferenc Gergely and György Kiss, *Horthy leventéi* [The Leventes of Horthy] (Budapest, 1976).

37. Pölöskei, *Horthy*, p. 17.

38. *IET* I: 256.

39. Nemes, *Az ellenforradalom története*, p. 166.

40. Twenty-two of the uncontested seats went to KNEP members, mostly to party leaders, such as Károly Huszár, Ödön Beniczky, István Haller, Jakab Bleyer, György Szmrecsányi, Lajos Hegyeshalmi, Sándor Ernszt, Gyula Pekár, and Bishop Ottokár Prohászka. Seventeen of the Smallholders ran unopposed, among them Gyula Rubinek, István Nagyatádi Szabó, Baron Frigyes Korányi, Gaszton Gaál, and István Sokorópátkai Szabó. Similarly, two independent legitimists, Counts Albert Apponyi and Gyula Andrássy, Jr., were unopposed. Ibid., p. 187.

41. *IET* I: 244.

42. Balla, *A magyar országgyűlés*, p. 433.

43. *Pesti Hírlap,* February 12, and March 14, 1920, cited in Pölöskei, *Horthy,* pp. 34, 130.

44. Magyar királyi külügyminisztérium, *Papers and Documents Relating to the Foreign Relations of Hungary* (Budapest, 1939) I: 139–40. Also, *IET* I: 257–58.

45. For the highly complicated legal arguments for and against this theory see Dezső Polónyi, *A magyar királykérdés* [The Question of the Royal Succession] (Budapest, 1928), specifically pp. 114–18, 162–72.

46. *IET* I: 256–57.

47. Nemes, *Az ellenforradalom története,* p. 205.

48. *IET* I: 394–409; II: 230–45.

49. Surányi, *Bethlen,* pp. 50–52. Bethlen, according to Surányi, considered himself a follower of Epicurus, and his favorite philosopher was Montaigne.

50. Bethlen, *Bethlen István,* I: 158.

51. Surányi, *Bethlen,* p. 110; *IET* I: 245–54.

52. The total number of deputies after the June elections was only 207. But, subsequently, othr elections were held in Baranya, which until 1921 was under Yugoslav occupation. Other vacancies, due to deaths, resignations, or appointments to high government posts, were filled through special elections. In all, we have collected biographical information on 464 individuals who served in the First and Second National Assemblies or in the 1926 parliament. Of these 150 individuals or 32.3 percent were born in the territories awarded to the Successor States. Data were collected in the following categories: place and date of birth, education, occupation, political party affiliation, membership in various organizations, military service during the war, participation in the revolutionary and counterrevolutionary movements, and property losses in the Successor States. In our statistics, those indivduals who were born in the lost areas but moved to inner Hungary before the war were, nevertheless, grouped with the refugees. Those, however, who were born in areas retained by Hungary but moved to the lost territories before 1914 and returned to inner Hungary after the war were not counted with the refugees. Nor did we include in that group those individuals who suffered the loss of their estates in the Successor States but were born elsewhere, even if they closely identified with the refugees. Statistics, unless otherwise indicated, were based on my own calculations.

Chapter 10

1. The vast literature on this subject attest to this fact. It is possible only to sample some of the pamphlets and books that were written since the turn of the century. See, for example: Albert Berzeviczy, *A gentryről* [About the Gentry] 2 vols. (Budapest, 1905); Miklós Szemere, *Gentry* (Budapest, 1912); János Makkai, *Urambátyám országa* [The Country of Gentry] (2nd ed., Budapest, 1941); József Szücsi (Bajza), *A gentry* [The Gentry] (Budapest, 1910); Szekfű, *Három nemzedék*; László Tóth, *A gentry társadalom történetéhez* [To the History of Gentry Society] (Budapest, 1939); Zoltán Szabó, *Cifra nyomorúság* [Gaudy Misery] (Budapest, 1938); János Árfa Nagy,

"Az értelmiségi foglalkozású keresők száma Magyarországon 1890 óta" [The Numbers of Intellectual Wage Earners in Hungary since 1890] *Statisztikai Szemle* [Statistical Review] 6 (1935): 501–15; Gyula Kornis, *Mi a középosztály?* [What is the Middle Class?] (Budapest, 1926); Alajos Kovács, *Értelmiségünk nemzeti jellegének biztosítása* [Preservation of the National Character of Our Intelligentsia] (N.p., n.d.); Lajos Sávoly, *Miért jutott koldusbotra a magyar középosztály?* [Why did the Hungarian Middle Class Become Impoverished?] (Budapest, n.d.).

2. Bethlen, *Bethlen István* II: 157.

3. Ibid., p. 162.

4. The most exhaustive study on the official class of the post-World War I period is Ottó Szabolcs's *Köztisztviselők.* See also, by the same author, *Munkanélküli diplomások a Horthy-rendszerben, 1919–1944* [Unemployed University Graduates during the Horthy Regime, 1919–1944] (Budapest, 1964). For a general treatment of the history of the middle classes, see Balázs, *A középrétegek szerepe.* For an older but still useful analysis of Hungarian society during the late 1920s, see István Weis, *A mai magyar társadalom,* and Dezső Laky, *Az értelmiség válságának gazdasági és társadalmi háttere* [Economic and Social Background of the Crisis of the Intelligentsia] (Budapest, 1931).

5. Balázs, *A középrétegek szerepe,* p. 94.

6. *OMH Report,* p. 37.

7. League of Nations, *Financial Reconstruction of Hungary. 25 Reports of the Commissioner-General of the League of Nations for Hungary (May 1924 to June 1926. Third Report, July 1–21, 1924.* (Geneva, 1927), p. 6.

8. Központi Statisztikai Hivatal, *Recensement général de la population en 1930,* new series (Budapest, 1936) 96: 138, 147, 148. Of course, many of those recorded in 1930 received their degrees between 1920 and 1930, thus, in the refugee statistics, they were still registered as students.

9. *HPPC, Supplementary Documents,* no. 2. Also, Buday, *Megcsonkított Magyarország,* pp. 259–60. It should be kept in mind that, during the last two decades before the war, the number of Hungarian teachers in the minority areas had sharply increased. Many teachers migrated to those areas from inner Hungary.

10. These are 1913 figures.

11. *OMH Report,* p. 17.

12. See, for example, the pamphlet of the Hungarian Eugenic Society, "The Consequences of the Division of Hungary from the Standpoint of Eugenics," reprint from *Nemzetvédelem* [Defense of the Nation] I (1919), no. 4.

13. *ASzET,* p. 243.

14. Bocskay Szövetség, *A magyar-román békeszerződés magyarázata; az új állampolgárság; a magyar és székely kisebbség védelme a béke-szerződésben* [Explanation of the Hungarian-Romanian Peace Treaty; the New Citizenship, the Protection of the Hungarian and Székely Minorities under the Terms of the Peace Treaty] (Budapest, 1921), p. 7.

15. Ibid., p. 21.

16. See, for example, the *Magyar Irredenta,* October 21, 1920, October 31, 1920, and March 13, 1921 issues, or any issue of *Szózat.*
17. MOVE, *A MOVE budapesti főosztályának 1920. évi jelentése* [Report of the MOVE, Budapest Division, for the Year 1920] (Budapest, 1920), pp. 7, 12.
18. *OMH Report,* pp. 24, 25, 38.
19. Ibid., pp. 13, 25–26. The enterprise's eight divisions were clothing (77 employees), mass production, manufacturing toys and rattan goods (15 employees), arts and crafts (16 workers), janitorial service (25), carpenters (6), tinware (1), machinists (3), and moving. Some smaller shops were also established in other towns.
20. Ibid., pp. 30–32.
21. Ernő László, "Hungary's Jewry: A Demographic Overview, 1918–1945," in Randolph L. Braham, ed., *Hungarian Jewish Studies* II (1958): 147.
22. Balla, *A magyar országgyűlés,* p. 483.
23. Szabolcs, *Köztisztviselők,* p. 28.
24. Szabolcs, *Munkanélküli diplomások,* pp. 22–23.
25. Nemes, *Az ellenforradalom története,* p. 387.
26. Szabolcs, *Köztisztviselők,* p. 85.
27. League of Nations, *Financial Reconstruction of Hungary. Third Report,* Annex IV, p. 11.
28. Ibid., p. 6.
29. League of Nations, *The Financial Reconstruction of Hungary. General Survey and Principal Documents* (Geneva, 1926), p. 123.
30. Szabolcs, *Köztisztviselők,* p. 87.
31. Ibid., p. 30.
32. League of Nations, *Financial Reconstruction of Hungary. General Survey,* p. 122.
33. Szabolcs, *Köztisztviselők,* p. 32.
34. The 1930 census figures reflect only the number of those who were born in the lost territories, without differentiating between the refugees and those who arrived before 1918. Between 1920 and 1930, the total number of those born in the lost territories dropped by about ten percent, but the proportion of the refugees in the group increased from an estimated 76 percent in 1920 to 82 percent in 1930.

Number of Individuals Born Outside the
Territory of Trianon Hungary

Born in Territories Ceded to	1920 Census	1930 Census
Czechoslovakia	265,145	224,740
Romania	197,181	192,933
Yugoslavia (excluding Croatia)	74,412	74,242
Austria	21,416	12,768
Total	558,154	504,683

Source: Központi Statisztikai Hivatal, *Recensement de la Population en 1920,* 73: 8–9; *Recensement général de la Population en 1930,* 96: 190–91.

The total decline is only partly attributable to natural causes. After the settlement of the Burgenland question, some remigration to Austria took place. Also, in the case of Czechoslovakia, some families of Slovak national origin eventually resettled there. These figures, however, do not reflect those who though were born in inner Hungary at the time of the country's partition, resided in the lost areas. Their number was most significant in the case of Transylvania. In using these census figures, therefore, to illustrate the strength of the refugees from the various lost parts of the country, we may consider the number of those from Romania as the minimum; those from Czechoslovakia as the upper limit of the refugee strength. At the same time, it is safe to assume that, regardless of their place of residence at the moment of collapse, the loss of their homeland was psychologically important for all these individuals and, therefore, even those who moved to Hungary before 1918 identified with the refugees to a greater degree than those born in inner Hungary.

35. Központi Statisztikai Hivatal, *Recensement de la population en 1920*, 72: 478–91; *Recensement général de la population en 1930*, 96: 132–53; 124–29. Also, HPPC, *Supplementary Documents*, no. 2. Clerks generally represented only a sixth to a quarter of the totals.

36. Központi Statisztikai Hivatal, *Recensement général de la population en 1930*, 96: 132–53.

37. Ibid.

38. Ibid.

39. Szabolcs, *Munkanélküli diplomások*, pp. 60–61. For 1921, Ladányi gives a slightly lower figure of 16,401. Ladányi, *Az egyetemi ifjúság*, p. 14.

40. Ibid., p. 41.

41. Szabolcs, *Munkanélküli diplomások*, pp. 51–52.

42. Ladányi, *Az egyetemi ifjúság*, p. 15.

43. Szabolcs, *Munkanélküli diplomások*, p. 51.

44. Ladányi, *Az egyetemi ifjúság*, p. 48.

45. Ibid., p. 41.

Hungarian Mass Organizations and Political Parties

Hungarian Names	English Translations	Abbreviations
Antibolsevista Comité	Antibolshevik Committee	ABC
Az Apostoli Kettőskereszt Vérszövetség	Blood Alliance of the Apostolic Cross	KKV
Attila Szövetség	Attila Alliance	
Bocskay Szövetség	Bocskay Alliance	
Délvidéki Liga	Southlands League	
Disszidens-Csoport	Dissident Group	
Ébredő Magyarok Egyesülete	Association of Awakening Hungarians	ÉME
Egyesült Keresztény Nemzeti Liga	United Christian National League	
Egységes Párt (Keresztyén Kisgazda-Földmíves-és Polgári Párt	United Party (Christian Smallholder-Agricultural-Worker-and Bourgeois Party)	
Erdélyi Magyar-Székely Szövetség	Transylvanian Hungarian-Székely Alliance	
Etelközi Szövetség	Alliance of Etelköz	EKSz, Ex, or X
Fajvédő Párt	Race Protector Party	
Feltámadás	Resurrection	
Felvidéki Liga	Upland League	
Honszeretet Egyesület	Association for Patriotism	
Keresztény Magyar Kulturliga	Hungarian Christian Cultural League	
Keresztény Nemzeti Egyesülés Pártja	Christian National Unity Party	KNEP
Kisgazda-Földműves-és Polgári Párt	Smallholder-Agricultural Worker-and Bourgeois Party	
Kommunisták Magyarországi Pártja	Hungarian Communist Party	KMP
Külügyi Társulat	Foreign Affairs Association	
Magyar Országos Véderő Egyesülét	Hungarian National Defense Association	MOVE
Menekülteket Védő Szövetség	Alliance for Refugee Defense	
Nemzeti Középpárt	National Center Party	
Nemzeti Polgári Demokrata Párt	National Bourgeois Democratic Party	

Nemzeti Polgári Párt	National Bourgeois Party	
Országos Magyar Gazda-sági Egyesület	Hungarian National Agrarian Association	OMGE
Országos Menekültügyi Hivatal	National Refugee Office	OMH
Székely Akció	Székely Action	
Székely Nemzeti Tanács	Székely National Council	
Szepesi Szövetség	Szepes Alliance	
Szociáldemokrata Párt	Social Democratic Party	SzPD
Társadalmi Egyesületek Szövetsége	Alliance of Social Associa-tions	TESz
Területvédő Liga (Magyar-ország Területi Épségé-nek Védelmi Ligája)	League for the Defense of Hungary's Territorial Integrity	TEVÉL
Tizenkét Kapitány	Twelve Captains	
Magyarországi Cionista Szer-vezet	Zionist Organization of Hun-gary	

Gazetteer

Listed below are names of places or geographical areas used in this volume. Whenever the name was changed owing to the transfer of locale or region to another state, the current Czechoslovak, Romanian, Yugoslav, or Russian form is given to the right of the original Hungarian name. In parenthesis the present country location of the region or place is provided, using the following abbreviations: Austria (A), Czechoslovakia (CS), Hungary (H), Romania (R), the Soviet Union (SU), and Yugoslavia (Y). When an area was split both states are designated.

Apátfalva	(H)
Arad	Arad (R)
Arad, county	(R)
Bács-Bodrog, county	(Y, H)
Bácska	Bačka (Y)
Baja	(H)
Balassagyarmat	(H)
Balaton, lake	(H)
Bánát	Banat (Y, R)
Baranya, county	(H, Y)
Bars, county	(CS)
Belgrade	(Y)
Bereg, county	(CS, H)
Brassó	Braşov (R)
Bucharest	(R)
Budapest	(H)
Burgenland	(A)
Cece	(H)
Cegléd	(H)
Csallóköz (Schütt), island	Žitný ostrov (CS)
Csepel, island	(H)
Csík, county	(R)
Csót	(H)
Danube, river	
Debrecen	(H)
Déva	Deva (R)
Dráva, river	(H, Y)
Eger	(H)
Eperjes	Prešov (CS)
Érsekújvár	Nové Zámky (CS)

Esztergom	(H)
Esztergom, county	(CS, H)
Feldbach	(A)
Fogaras	Făgăraş (R)
Gömör, county	(CS, H)
Graz	(A)
Győr	(H)
Gyulafehérvár	Alba Iulia (R)
Hajmáskér	(H)
Háromszék, county	(R)
Hódmezővásárhely	(H)
Hont, county	(CS, H)
Iaşi	(R)
Ipoly, river	Ipel (CS, H)
Kalocsa	(H)
Kaposvár	(H)
Kassa	Košice (CS)
Kecskemét	(H)
Kolozsvár	Cluj-Napoca (R)
Komárom	(H)
Komárom, county	(H, CS)
Kőszeg	(H)
Lajta, river	(A, H)
Losonc	Lučenec (CS)
Máramaros, county	(R)
Máramarossziget	Sighetul Marmaţiei (R)
Mareşeşti	(R)
Maros, river	Mureş (R, H)
Maros-Torda, county	(R)
Marosvásárhely	Tîrgu-Mureş (R)
Miskolc	(H)
Munkács	Mukachevo (SU)
Mura, river	Mur (A, Y, H)
Muraköz, region	(Y)
Nagybánya	Baia Mare (R)
Nagyvárad	Oradea (R)
Négerfalu	Negru (R)
Nyitra	Nitra (CS)
Nyitra, county	(CS)
Orgovány	(H)
Pécs	(H)
Pest, county	(H)
Pozsony	Bratislava (CS)

Pozsony, county	(CS)
Rába, river	Raab (H, A)
Rimaszombat	Rimavská Sobota (CS)
Ruthenia	(SU)
Salgótarján	(H)
Siófok	(H)
Somogy, county	(H)
Sopron	(H)
Szabadka	Subotica (Y)
Szabolcs, county	(H, R)
Szamos, river	Someşul (R, H)
Szatmár, county	(R, H)
Szatymáz	(H)
Szeged	(H)
Székesfehérvár	(H)
Szolnok-Doboka, county	(R)
Szombathely	(H)
Tata	(H)
Temes, county	Timiş (R)
Temesvár	Timişoara (R)
Tisza, river	(SU, H, Y)
Torda-Aranyos, county	(R)
Torontál, county	(Y, R)
Transdanubia	(H)
Túróczszentmárton	Turčiansky Svätý Martin (CS)
Udvarhely, county	(R)
Ung, river	Uzh (SU)
Ungvár	(SU)
Veszprém	(H)
Voivodina	(Y)
Zagreb	(Y)
Zala, county	(H)
Zalaegerszeg	(H)
Zemplén, county	(CS)
Zilah	Zalău (R)
Zombor	Sombor (Y)

Biographical Index

The present country location of birthplaces is indicated by using the following abbreviations: Austria (A); Czechoslovakia (CS); France (F); Great Britain (GB); Hungary (H); Italy (I); Poland (P); Romania (R); the Soviet Union (SU); and Yugoslavia (Y).

Ábrahám, Dezső (Debrecen, H; 1875–1973)
Prime minister of the second Szeged government, 1919.
Allizé, Henri
French representative to Vienna.
Aleksander (1888–1934)
Regent of Serbia, 1914–18; Regent of the Kingdom of Serbs, Croats and Slovenes, 1918–21; King of Yugoslavia, 1921–34.
Andrássy, Gyula, Jr., Count (Tőketerebes, CS; 1860–1929)
Magnate from Northern Hungary; last foreign minister of the Austro-Hungarian monarchy.
Apáthy, István (Pest, H; 1863–1922)
Professor at the University of Kolozsvár; Hungarian High Commissioner for Transylvania, 1918–19.
Apponyi, Albert, Count (Vienna, A; 1846–1933)
Magnate from Northern Hungary; head of the Hungarian Peace Delegation to Paris, 1920.
Bacsó, Béla (Kassa, CS; 1891–1920)
Journalist for the socialist *Népszava*; murdered by members of the Ostenburg detachment.
Bánffy, Miklós, Count (Kolozsvár, R; 1874–1950)
Transylvanian magnate; foreign minister of Hungary, 1921–22.
Bánffy, Zoltán, Baron (Beresztelke, R; 1886–?)
Transylvanian magnate; member of the Hungarian Peace Delegation to Paris, 1920.
Bárdoss, Béla
Captain; member of the Prónay detachment.
Bartos, János (Besztercebánya, CS; 1885–?)
High commissioner for Esztergom, Győr, Fejér, Komárom, and Veszprém counties, 1919.
Battyány, Tivadar, Count (Zalaszentgrót, H; 1859–1931)
Minister of interior, 1918.
Bédy-Schwimmer, Róza (Budapest, H; 1877–1948)
Hungarian ambassador to Switzerland, 1919.

Beneš, Edvard (1884–1948)
Foreign minister of Czechoslovakia, 1918–35; prime minister of Czechoslovakia, 1921–22; president of Czechoslovakia, 1935–38; 1946–48.

Beniczky, Ödön (Zólyom, CS; 1878–1931)
High-sheriff of Bars and Esztergom counties; minister of interior, 1919–20; legitimist politician.

Berthelot, Henri (1861–1931)
French general, commander of the French forces in Romania, 1918–19.

Bethlen, István, Count (Gernyeszeg, R; 1874–1947)
Prime minister of Hungary, 1921–31.

Bleyer, Jakab (Dunacséb, Y; 1874–1933)
From a Transylvanian Saxon family; professor at the University of Kolozsvár; minister of national minorities, 1919–20.

Böhm, Vilmos (Budapest, H; 1880–1949)
Minister of defense in the Berinkey government and during the Hungarian Soviet Republic, 1919.

Bónis, Arkangyal
Franciscan priest, attached to the officers' detachments; member of the EKSz.

Borghese, Livio Giuseppe, Prince (1874–1939)
Special emissary of Italy to Vienna, 1919.

Bornemissza, Gyula, Baron (Kolozsvár, R; 1873–?)
Foreign minister of the Szeged government, 1919.

Brodmann, Willibald (1883–1922?)
Leader of the Austrian *Bauernkommando Straden,* 1919.

Budaváry, László (Magyarkomjáth, R; 1889–?)
Member of the National Assembly; vice-president of ÉME.

Buday, László (Pécs, H; 1873–1925)
President of the Magyar Statisztikai Társaság [Hungarian Statistical Association].

Clerk, George, Sir (1876–1943)
British diplomat; special emissary of the Allies to Hungary, 1919.

Csáky, Imre, Count (Szepesmindszent, CS; 1882–1961)
Hungarian foreign minister, 1920.

Csernoch, János, Cardinal (Szakalca, CS; 1852–1927)
Prince Primate of Hungary, 1913–27.

Cserny, József (?; 1892–1919)
Commander of a terror group during the Hungarian Soviet Republic; executed in 1919.

Csilléry, András (Budapest, 1883–?)
Minister of health and public welfare, 1919.

Cuninghame, Thomas, Sir (1877–1945)
British colonel, head of the British Military Mission in Vienna, 1919.
d'Esperey, Franchet (1856–1942)
French general; commander-in-chief of the Allied Armies of the Orient.
Diaz, Armando (1861–1928)
Commander-in-chief of the Allied forces in Italy.
Dvorcsák, Győző (Felsővízköz, CS; 1878–?)
Member of the National Assembly.
Eckhardt, Tibor (Makó, H; 1888–1972)
County official in Tordaaranyos; director of the press bureau of Prime Minister Teleki; member of the National Assembly; president of the ÉME; member of the EKSz.
Ernszt, Sándor (Galgóc, CS; 1870–1938)
Papal prelate; a leader of KNEP.
Feilitzsch, Berchtold, Baron (1867–?)
Prewar high-sheriff of Szabolcs county; president of EKSz; vice-president of the Arrow Cross Upper House, 1944–45.
Ferdinand I
King of Romania, 1914–27.
Foch, Ferdinand (1851–1929)
Marshal of France; commander-in-chief of the Allied armies after April 1918.
Fornet, Gyula (Rimaszombat, CS; 1869–?)
Last deputy-sheriff (*alispán*) of Gömör county.
Franz Joseph (1830–1916)
Emperor of Austria, 1848–1916; King of Hungary, 1867–1916.
Friedrich, István (Malacka, CS; 1883–1958)
Prime minister of Hungary, 1919.
Gaál, Gaszton (Székesfehérvár, H; 1868–1932)
Member of the National Assembly; president of the Smallholders Party, 1921.
Gömbös, Gyula (Murga, H; 1886–1936)
Captain in the General Staff of the Imperial and Royal Army; prime minister of Hungary, 1932–36; president of MOVE; a founder of EKSz; one of the Twelve Captains.
Gondrecourt, Count, Henri de (1867–?)
Commander of the French forces in Szeged.
Görgey, György
Captain, aide-de-camp to Horthy; colonel, 1927, commander of the Royal Palace Guards; member of EKSz; one of the Twelve Captains.

Görgey, József (Debrecen, H; 1886–?)
Cavalry captain; member of parliament; member of EKSz; one of the Twelve Captains.

Gorton, Reginald (1866–1944)
General; British member of the Allied Military Mission to Hungary, 1919–22.

Gratz, Gusztáv (Gölnicbánya, CS; 1875–1946)
Member of the Vienna ABC; legitimist politician; foreign minister of Hungary, 1920–21.

Gregory, Thomas
Captain (U.S.); aide to Herbert C. Hoover, American Relief Administration.

Grünwald, Béla (Szentantal, H; 1839–1891)
Historian; member of Parliament.

Haller, István (Mezőpetrény, R; 1880–1964)
Minister of propaganda, 1919; minister of religion and education, 1919–20.

Hardy, Kálmán
Captain; aide-de-camp to Horthy; member of EKSz; one of the Twelve Captains.

Haubrich, József (Detta, R; 1883–1939)
Commissar of defense during the Hungarian Soviet Republic; minister of defense in the Peidl government; executed during Stalin's purges, 1939.

Hegyeshalmi, Lajos (Budapest, H; 1862–1925)
Minister of commerce, 1919; 1920–22.

Héjjas, Iván (Kecskemét, H; 1891–?)
Leader of a terror group, 1919–20; member of parliament; member of ÉME.

Hír, György (Pákozd, H; 1880–1926)
Leader of an officers' detachment; member of National Assembly; member of ÉME and EKSz; murdered by antilegitimists, 1926).

Hodža, Milan (1878–1944)
Prime minister of Czechoslovakia, 1935–38.

Hoover, Herbert C. (1874–1964)
Director general of the European Relief and Reconstruction Commission and chairman of the Interallied Food Council; president of the United States, 1929–33.

Horowitz, Nathan
Colonel, U.S. Army.

Horthy, István (Kenderes, H; 1858–1937)
General.

Horthy, Miklós (Kenderes, H; 1868–1957)
Admiral; Regent of Hungary, 1920–1944.
Huszár, Elemér (Ipolybalog, CS; 1883–?)
Legitimist politician; member of the National Assembly.
Huszár, Károly (Nussdorf, A; 1882–1941)
Prime minister of Hungary, 1919–20.
Igmándy-Hegyessy, Géza
Captain; one of the Twelve Captains.
Jancsó, Benedek (Gelence, R; 1854–1930)
Historian, expert on Hungary's nationality questions.
Jankovich-Besán, Endre, Count (Terezovac, CS; 1884–?)
Landowner; leader of an officers' detachment, 1919; member of the National Assembly; member of EKSz.
Jászi, Oszkár (Nagykároly, R; 1875–1957)
Sociologist; minister of national minorities, 1918–19.
Habsburg, József (Joseph), Archduke (Alcsut, H; 1872–1962)
Governor of Hungary, 1919.
Joseph II
Emperor of Austria, 1780–90.
Károly IV (Emperor Karl) (1887–1922)
King of Hungary, 1916–18.
Károlyi, Gyula, Count (Nyírbakta, R; 1871–1947)
Landowner; prime minister of the governments of Arad and Szeged, 1919; prime minister of Hungary, 1931–32.
Károlyi, Imre, Count (Mácsa, R; 1873–1943)
Landowner, economist; president of the Magyar-Angol Bank; member of EKSz.
Károlyi, Mihály, Count (Budapest, H; 1875–1955)
Magnate; prime minister of Hungary, 1918–19; president of Hungary, 1919.
Kelemen, Béla (Szeged, H; 1863–?)
Minister of interior in the Szeged government, 1919.
Keresztes-Fisher, Lajos
Captain in the General Staff of the Imperial and Royal Army; one of the Twelve Captains; Chief of Staff of the Hungarian army, 1938.
Kiss, Menyhért (Nyáradkőszvényes, R; 1880–?)
Member of the National Assembly; vice-president of ÉME.
Klebelsberg, Kunó, Count (Magyarpécska, R; 1875–1932)
Minister of interior, 1921–22; minister of religion and education, 1922–30.
Koós, Miklós
Captain; aide to Horthy; one of the Twelve Captains; member of EKSz; later lieutenant general.

Korányi, Frigyes, Baron (Pest, H; 1869–1935)
Minister of finance, 1919–20; 1931–32.

Koródi Katona, János (Nagybánya, R; 1890–?)
County official in Transylvania; member of the National Assembly; member of ÉME.

Korvin, Ottó (Nagybocskó, R; 1894–1919)
Bank official; head of the political division of the commissariat of interior during the Soviet Republic, 1919; executed in 1919.

Kosciuszko, Tadeusz (1746–1817)
Polish general; leader of the national resistance during 1792–95.

Kossuth, Lajos (Monok, H; 1802–1894)
Leader of the 1848–49 Hungarian Revolution.

Kozma, Miklós (Nagyvárad, R; 1884–1941)
Cavalry captain; minister of interior, 1935–37; member of EKSz; one of the Twelve Captains.

Kramař, Karel (1860–1937)
Prime minister of Czechoslovakia, 1918–19.

Kratochwill, Károly (Kőszeg, H; 1869–?)
Colonel; commander of the Székely Division, 1918–19.

Kun, Béla (Szilágycsehi, R; 1886–1939)
Leader of the Hungarian Soviet Republic, 1919. Executed during Stalin's purges, 1939.

Kutkafalvy, Miklós (Nagyruszka, SU; 1882–?)
Leader of national resistance in Ruthenia, 1918; member of the National Assembly.

Lehár, Antal, Baron (Sopron, H; 1867–1962)
Colonel; commander of the Feldbach group; commander of the Szombathely or "Lehár" Division.

Lovászy, Márton (Zenta, Y; 1864–1927)
Liberal politician; minister of religion and education, 1918; foreign minister, 1919.

Mackensen, August von (1849–1945)
Field marshal; commander of the combined Austro-Hungarian and German armies in Romania, 1916–18.

Madary, Antal
Captain; commander of an officers' detachment, 1919.

Magasházy, László (Sárkeresztúr, H; 1879–1959)
Captain in 1919; aide-de-camp to Horthy, 1920–29; general, 1937; member of EKSz; one of the Twelve Captains.

Márton, Béla (Budapest, 1896–?)
Landowner; member of MOVE; one of the Twelve Captains; member of parliament.

Návay, Lajos (1870–1919)
President of Parliament, 1911–12; executed by the Cserny group, 1919.

Odescalchy, Károly, Prince
Landowner, legitimist politician; member of EKSz.

Ostenburg-Moravek, Gyula (Marosvásárhely, R; 1884–1944?)
Captain in 1919; commander of an officers' detachment, 1919–20; a military leader of the second legitimist putsch, 1921.

Pallavicini, György, Margrave (Budapest, 1881–1946)
Landowner, legitimist politician; member of the Vienna ABC; member of the National Assembly.

Pállfy-Duan, József, Count (Stübing, A; 1892–1945?)
Landowner; staff captain in the National Army.

Pálmai, Lajos (Arad, R; 1866–?)
Liberal politician; minister of food supplies in the Arad and Second Szeged governments; minister of justice in the Gyula Károlyi government, 1919.

Pašić, Nikola (1845?–1926)
Prime minister of Serbia, 1903–21; prime minister of Yugoslavia for most of the 1921–26 period.

Peidl, Gyula (Ravazd, H; 1873–1943)
Moderate Socialist politician; prime minister of Hungary, August, 1919.

Pekár, Gyula (Debrecen, H; 1867–1937)
Writer; member of the White House group; minister without portfolio, 1919; member of the National Assembly.

Perényi, Zsigmond, Baron (Pest, H; 1870–1946)
Minister of interior, 1919.

Pethes, László (Selmecbánya?, CS; 1885–?)
High commissioner in Selmecbánya, 1918; member of the Szeged ABC; served in the National Army; member of the National Assembly.

Petrichevich-Horváth, Emil, Baron (Dés, R; 1881–1945)
High-sheriff of Nagyküküllő county, R, 1917–18; member of the National Assembly; head of the National Refugee Office.

Pogány, József (Budapest, H; 1886–1939)
Commissar of defense and foreign affairs during the Hungarian Soviet Republic, 1919; executed during Stalin's purges, 1939.

Polnay, Jenő
Minister of food supplies, 1919.

Prohászka, Ottokár (Nyitra, CS; 1858–1927)
Bishop of Székesfehérvár, H, 1905–27; president of KNEP; member of the National Assembly.

Prőhle, Vilmos (Fülek, CS; 1871–1946)
Professor at the University of Kolozsvár until 1919; member of the National Assembly; a founder of EKSz and ÉME.

Prónay, Pál, Baron (Romhány, H; 1875–1944 or 1945)
Landowner; commander of an officers' detachment, 1919–20; member of EKSz, ÉME, and MOVE.

Ráday, Gedeon, Count (Budapest, H; 1872–1937)
Landowner; member of the Vienna ABC; member of the National Assembly; minister of interior 1921.

Raffay, Sándor (Cegléd, H; 1866–1947)
Lutheran bishop, 1918–47.

Rákosi, Jenő (Acsád, H; 1842–1929)
Editor of *Budapesti Hírlap*.

Rakovszky, István (Vienna, A; 1858–1931)
Landowner; legitimist politician; president of the National Assembly.

Ravasz, László (Bánffyhunyad, R; 1882–?)
Bishop of the Reformed Church from 1921.

Rubinek, Gyula (Ohaj, CS; 1865–1922)
President of OMGE; minister of agriculture, 1919–20.

Somssich, József, Count (Graz, A; 1864–1941)
Landowner; minister of foreign affairs, 1919–20.

Soós, Károly (Nagyszeben, R; 1869–1953)
General; chief of staff of the National Army, 1919; minister of defense, 1920; member of EKSz.

Sréter, István (Cserhátsurány, H; 1867–1942)
General; minister of defense, 1920; member of the National Assembly; member of EKSz.

Szabó, István (Nagyatádi) (Erdőcsokonya, H; 1863–1924)
Leader of the Smallholders Party; minister of economy, 1919; minister of agriculture, 1919, 1922–24; minister of food supplies, 1920–21.

Szabó, István (Sokorópátkai) (Sokorópátka, H; 1878–1938)
A leader of the Smallholders Party; minister of Smallholders affairs, 1919–21.

Szálasi, Ferenc (Kassa, CS; 1897–1946)
Officer; leader of the Arrow Cross Party; dictator of Hungary, 1944–45. Executed for war crimes, 1946.

Szamuely, Tibor (Nyíregyháza, H; 1890–1919)
Deputy commissar of defense during the Hungarian Soviet Republic, 1919; president of the Court of Summary Justice; shot while trying to escape to Austria, 1919.

Szapáry, László, Count (Perkáta, H; 1864–1939)
Wealthy landowner in west Hungary; Hungarian minister to London, 1922–24.

Szász, Zoltán (Kolozsvár, R; 1877–1944)
Journalist for *Az Újság* and *Pesti Napló*.

Széchenyi, István, Count (Vienna, 1791–1860)
Leading moderate reformer of the pre-1848 period.

Szmrecsányi, György (Felsőkubin, CS; 1876–1932)
Legitimist politician; member of the Viennese ABC; a founder of KNEP; vice-president of the National Assembly; president of ÉME.

Szörtsey, József (Szörtcse, R; 1888–?)
A leading revisionist; president of Attila Szövetség; co-president of the Hungarian Revisionist League; president of TESz; member of MOVE.

Tánczos, Gábor (Budapest, H; 1872–1953)
General; minister of foreign affairs, 1919.

Teleki, Pál, Count (Budapest, H; 1879–1941)
Transylvanian magnate; geographer; a leader of the Viennese ABC; prime minister of Hungary, 1920–21, 1939–41; president of TEVÉL and other revisionist organizations.

Tisza, István, Count (Geszt, H; 1861–1918)
Prime minister of Hungary, 1903–1905; 1913–17.

Tisza, Kálmán (Geszt, H; 1830–1902)
Prime minister of Hungary, 1875–1890.

Tkalecz, Vilmos
Slovene nationalist leader of the Mura Republic, 1919.

Toókos, Gyula
Cavalry captain; attached to the high command of the National Army, 1919; a leader of EKSz.

Troubridge, Sir Ernest (1862–1926)
Admiral (GB); president of the International Danube Commission, 1919–24.

Ugron, Gábor (Marosvásárhely, R; 1880–1960)
Minister of interior, 1917–18; founder of the Székely National Council; president of the National Bourgeois Democratic Party.

Ulain, Ferenc (Nagyszeben, R; 1881–?)
Editor of the radical nationalist paper, Szózat; member of the National Assembly; co-founder of the Race Protector Party.

Ullmann, Adolf, Baron (Pest, 1857–1925)
Member of the Viennese ABC; president of the Hungarian General Credit Bank.

Urmánczy, Nándor (Maroshévíz, R; 1868–1940)
Transylvanian landowner; member of prewar parliament; a leader of some revisionist organizations.

Varjassy, Lajos
Mayor of Arad; liberal member of the counterrevolutionary governments of Arad and Szeged; minister of commerce, 1919.

Vetter, Antal
Captain; aide-de-camp to Horthy; one of the Twelve Captains.
Vix, Fernand
Lt. colonel (F); head of the Allied Military Mission to Hungary, 1918–19.
Wild, József (Budapest, 1881–?)
Member of the Viennese ABC; member of the National Assembly.
Wilson, Woodrow (1856–1924)
President of the United States, 1913–21.
Windischgrätz, Lajos, Prince (Cracow, P; 1882–1967)
Landowner; minister of food supplies, 1918; member of the National Assembly; member of EKSz and other secret organizations.
Wolff, Károly (Érsekújvár, CS; 1874–1936)
Member of the National Assembly; leader of the United Christian National League; a leader of ÉME and TESz.
Zadravecz, István (Csáktornya, Y; 1884–1965)
Bishop of the army; a leading revisionist; a leader of EKSz and other secret societies.
Zichy, Aladár, Count (Nagyláng, CS; 1864–1937)
Magnate; leader of the prewar Catholic People's Party; member of the Viennese ABC; active in the Szeged counterrevolution.
Zichy, Géza, Count (1882–?)
Member of the Viennese ABC; deputy high commissioner of Transdanubia, 1919.
Zichy, János, Count (Nagyláng, CS; 1868–1944)
Magnate, minister of religion and education, 1918; member of the Viennese ABC; member of the National Assembly.

BROOKLYN COLLEGE STUDIES ON SOCIETY IN CHANGE
Distributed by Columbia University Press (except No. 5)
Editor-in-Chief: Béla K. Király

No. 1
Tolerance and Movements of Religious Dissent in Eastern Europe.
Edited by B. K. Király, 1975. Second Printing, 1977.

No. 2
The Habsburg Empire in World War I. Edited by R. A. Kann, B. K.
Király, P. S. Fichtner, 1976. Second Printing, 1978.

No. 3
*The Mutual Effects of the Islamic and Judeo-Christian Worlds: The East
European Pattern.* Edited by A. Ascher, T. Halasi-Kun, B. K. Király,
1979.

No. 4
Before Watergate: Problems of Corruption in American Society. Edited
by A. S. Eisenstadt, A. Hoogenboom, H. L. Trefousse, 1978.

No. 5
East Central European Perceptions of Early America. Edited by B. K.
Király and G. Barany. Lisse, The Netherlands: Peter de Ridder Press,
1977. Distributed by Humanities Press, Atlantic Highlands, N.J.

No. 6
The Hungarian Revolution of 1956 in Retrospect. Edited by B. K.
Király and P. Jónás, 1978. Second Printing, 1980.

No. 7
Brooklyn U.S.A.: Fourth Largest City in America. Edited by R. S.
Miller, 1979.

No. 8
János Decsy. *Prime Minister Gyula Andrássy's Influence on Habsburg Foreign Policy during the Franco-German War of 1870–1871,*
1979.

No. 9
Robert F. Horowitz. *The Great Impeacher: A Political Biography of
James M. Ashley,* 1979.

* * *

Nos. 10–19
Subseries: War and Society in East Central Europe (see also Nos.
30–40)

No. 10 — Vol. I
Special Topics and Generalizations on the Eighteenth and Nineteenth Centuries. Edited by B. K. Király and G. E. Rothenberg, 1979.

No. 11 — Vol. II
East Central European Society and War in the Pre-Revolutionary Eighteenth Century. Edited by G. E. Rothenberg, B. K. Király, and P. Sugar, 1982.

No. 12 — Vol. III
From Hunyadi to Rákóczi: War and Society in Late Medieval and Early Modern Hungary. Edited by J. M. Bak and B. K. Király, 1982.

No. 13 — Vol. IV
East Central European Society and War in the Era of Revolutions, 1775–1856, edited by B. K. Király, forthcoming.

No. 14 — Vol. V
Essays on World War I: Origins and Prisoners of War. Edited by S. R. Williamson, Jr., and P. Pastor, 1982.

No. 15 — Vol. VI
Essays on World War I: Total War and Peacemaking, A Case Study on Trianon, Edited by B. K. Király, P. Pastor, and I. Sanders, 1983.

No. 16 — Vol. VII
Thomas M. Barker. *Army, Aristocracy, Monarchy: Essays on War, Society, and Government in Austria, 1618–1780,* 1982.

No. 17 — Vol. VIII
The First Serbian Uprising, 1804–1813. Edited by Wayne S. Vucinich, 1982.

No. 18 — Vol. IX
Kálmán Janics. *Czechoslovak Policy and the Hungarian Minority, 1945–1948,* 1982.

No. 19 — Vol. X
At the Brink of War and Peace: The Tito–Stalin Split in Historic Perspective. Edited by Wayne S. Vucinich, 1983.

* * *

No. 20
Inflation Through the Ages: Economic, Social, Psychological, and Historical Aspects. Edited by N. Schmukler and E. Marcus, 1983.

No. 21
Germany and America: Essays on Problems of International Relations and Immigration. Edited by H. L. Trefousse, 1980.

No. 22
Murray M. Horowitz. *Brooklyn College: The First Half Century*, 1982.

No. 23
Jason Berger. *A New Deal for the World: Eleanor Roosevelt and American Foreign Policy*, 1981.

No. 24
The Legacy of Jewish Migration: 1881 and Its Impact. Edited by D. Berger, 1983.

No. 25
Pierre Oberling. *The Road to Bellapais: Cypriot Exodus to Northern Cyprus*, 1982.

No. 26
New Hungarian Peasants: An East Central European Experiment with Collectivization. Edited by Marida Hollós and Béla Maday, 1983.

No. 27
Germans in America: Aspects of German-American Relations in the 19th Century. Edited by E. Allen McCormick, 1983.

No. 28
Linda and Marsha Frey. *A Question of Empire: Leopold I and the War of the Spanish Succession, 1701–1705*, 1983.

No. 29
Szczepan K. Zimmer. *The Beginning of Cyrillic Printing—Cracow, 1491. From the Orthodox Past in Poland*. Edited by Ludwik Krzyzanowski and Irene Nagurski, 1983.

* * *

Nos. 30–40
Subseries: War and Society in East Central Europe (continued; see also Nos. 10–19)

No. 30 — Vol. XI
The First War Between Socialist States: The Hungarian Revolution of 1956 and Its Impact. Edited by Béla K. Király, Barbara Lotze, and Nándor Dreisziger, 1983.

No. 31 — Vol. XII
István I. Mócsy. *The Effects of World War I: The Uprooted: Hungarian Refugees and Their Impact on Hungarian Domestic Politics: 1918–1921*, 1983.

No. 32 — Vol. XIII
The Effects of World War I: The Class War after the Great War: The Rise of Communist Parties in East Central Europe, 1918–1921. Edited by Ivo Banac, 1983.

No. 33 — Vol. XIV
The Crucial Decade: East Central European Society and National Defense: 1859–1870. Edited by Béla K. Király, 1984.

No. 34 — Vol. XV
The Political Dimensions of War in Romanian History. Edited by Ilie Ceausescu, 1983.

Index

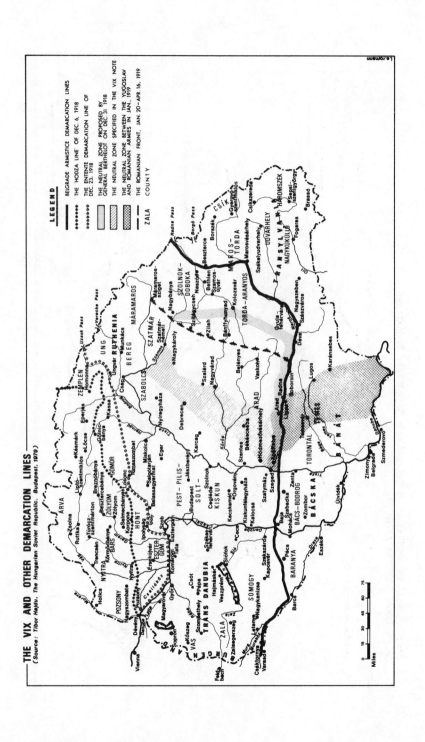

THE VIX AND OTHER DEMARCATION LINES

(Source: Tibor Hajdu, The Hungarian Soviet Republic, Budapest, 1979)

LEGEND

BELGRADE ARMISTICE DEMARCATION LINES

THE 'HODŽA LINE OF DEC. 6, 1918

THE ENTENTE DEMARCATION LINE OF
DEC. 23, 1918

THE NEUTRAL ZONE PROPOSED BY
GENERAL BERTHELOT ON DEC. 31 1918

THE NEUTRAL ZONE SPECIFIED IN THE VIX NOTE

THE NEUTRAL ZONE BETWEEN THE YUGOSLAV
AND ROMANIAN ARMIES IN JAN., 1919

THE ROMANIAN FRONT, JAN. 20–APR. 16, 1919

ZALA   COUNTY

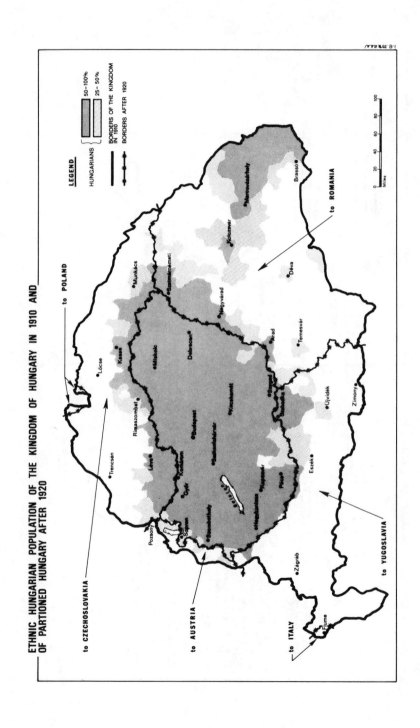

ETHNIC HUNGARIAN POPULATION OF THE KINGDOM OF HUNGARY IN 1910 AND OF PARTITIONED HUNGARY AFTER 1920